Christmas 2002
Darling Ann Happy Christmas
With Love Troy X

THE EARL OF CRANBROOK

PARNASSIAN MOLEHILL

An Anthology of
SUFFOLK VERSE

TO

FIDELITY

THE EARL OF CRANBROOK

PARNASSIAN MOLEHILL

An Anthology of
SUFFOLK VERSE
written between 1327 and 1864, with some account
of the authors and with numerous drawings by
JOHN NASH
with a new Preface by
RONALD BLYTHE

ALDEBURGH
THE ALDEBURGH BOOKSHOP

Parnassian Molehill was first published in 1953 by
W. S. Cowell, Ipswich in an edition of 500 copies.
The book was designed by John Lewis and was
printed and bound at Cowell's Buttermarket Press.

The present edition is a facsimile reprint of the original
to which has been added a new Preface by Ronald Blythe.
It is published in September 2001 by
THE ALDEBURGH BOOKSHOP
42 High Street
Aldeburgh, Suffolk
IP15 5AB

Anthology and text © Estate of the Earl of Cranbrook
Preface © 2001 Ronald Blythe

ISBN: 0-9531004-1-3

British Library Cataloguing in Publication Data
A catalogue record for this book is available from
The British Library

Printed and bound by
Smith Settle, Otley, West Yorkshire, LS21 3JP

CONTENTS

PREFACE	*page* XI
INTRODUCTION	XVI
BOOK I: THE POEMS	3
BOOK II: THE BIOGRAPHICAL NOTES	149
APPENDIX	249
INDEX OF SUFFOLK PLACE NAMES	256
INDEX OF AUTHORS	259

ILLUSTRATIONS

Decoration	page 8
Decoration	9
With snowe balles provoked me to playe	12
Poppie	14
The Silkworms	16
Come, come! the bells do cry	22
Decoration	27
My child and scholar, take good heed	29
Decoration	36
Baccanalia	37
Decoration	39
The Lover at the Door	42
The frog and the mouse fight	50
The Lonely Bird	54
And linen-horse by dog thrown down	56

Decoration	58
Decoration	60
Decoration	61
He mends the broken hedge with icy thorn	65
And lo! . . . a struggling perch is dragg'd to light!	66
Atropa belladonna	73
Decoration	74
Neptuna Coboldiae	78
And freely push about the mantling ale	82
Fill the goblet, fill it high!	84
The Lovers	86
They rush again, each on his steadfast foe	88
Decoration	90
Stay, thoughtless urchin	91
Orwell, delightful stream	96
Forsaken withered leaf, where goest thou?	102
Decoration	103
Flowers, simple flowers from blooming hedgerows wild	105
The Dying Child	106
Decoration	108
The Bathers	109
Decoration	115
Decoration	117
The nameless grave	120
Lo the golden Girasolé	124
A cloud of glory veiled th' ascending pomp	127
My lady walks as I have watched a swan	133
Suffolk! one bumper to thy Horse	141
The Red Poppy	143
In my garden bees are swarming	145

PREFACE

First a note on the three friends who created this unusual and delightful book. Jock Cranbrook its editor and inspirer was born in Kent on Easter Day 1900. He was in his early teens when he first saw Suffolk, the county which in so many admirable ways he was to make his own when he and his wife Fidelity settled in it after their marriage in 1932. He helped to administer it at all levels, and with an intelligence and kindness which are remembered to this day. He was a wonderful naturalist and a founder-member, as it were, of the conservationist movement in East Anglia. Immediately before making his home in Suffolk he had accompanied the great plant hunter F. Kingdon-Ward on his travels in Upper Burma and from then on he became an endless explorer of his own countryside. A teacher too of its local lessons. Coming to Great Glemham, one of George Crabbe's parishes, made him one of the poet-naturalist's pupils and those who came to see him in this village, and who loved plants and creatures, were themselves aware of a double influence, Jock's and the severe writer's. John Nash, the "artist-plantsman", as he liked to describe himself, and his wife Christine, were frequently at Great Glemham, and were close friends of Jock and Fidelity Cranbrook. John Nash was also one of the finest book illustrators of the period, as his work here demonstrates. John Lewis and his wife Griselda were distinguished book designers, and this anthology, both in contents and production, reveals a happy collaboration.

George Crabbe's son remembered Great Glemham as 'the Alhambra of my imagination... A small well-wooded park occupied the whole mouth of the glen whence, doubtless the name of the village was derived... The whole parish and neighbourhood resembled a combination of groves with fields cultivated like gardens.... The summer evenings in this place... dwell in my memory like a delightful dream ... We generally took a family walk through the green lanes around Glemham...my father reading aloud. I caught moths and other insects to add to his collection.' Lord Cranbrook, famously, caught bats. But it was here when he too was a boy that he captured a vision of his county as expressed by its poets. Who were they? Well, they were not all Crabbes. Nor were they, like this master, all locals. A good half of them had drifted into Suffolk from elsewhere to fill its rectories, schools and trades, though once settled here their verse took on East Anglian reflections and outlook, and reading them we are able to respect their acquired nativity.

It is nearly fifty years since *Parnassian Molehill* was published and this new edition is going to surprise and please those who have only previously heard of this book. It is both scholarship and serendipity'to perfection. It reveals the different layers of literary taste in this part over the generations, and from the best to the worst. Doggerel must always have its place for it serves a purpose. Aspiration has to be honoured. Genius – there is quite a lot of it – has to be recognised. Not the least pleasure of this anthology is its pithy list of brief biographies. All the poets, great and small, are presented to the reader in such a way that he is made to feel what it was like to write poetry at various times in a rustic or provincial world. They arrive in chronological order. First John Lydgate the 'Monk of

PREFACE

Bury' whose verses would be painted on the ceilings of chantries; and then an enchanting clutch of Tudor poets, including poor Henry Howard, who though beheaded at thirty, formed the literary link between the Italian and English renaissance. In this section we have one of the few poems on what it was like to witness a Catholic church stripped for Protestantism – in Ipswich maybe. It contains some of the most accomplished work in the anthology but also a tender farewell in the parish register of Wilby by Joseph Fletcher as he enters his wife's death, 'O we to eche were dear'. Later we have Samuel Crossman's great hymn based on a line by George Herbert, 'My Song is Love Unknown', written in his twenties at Little Henny and now sung everywhere. But the editor's real gift is for the rescuing of Suffolk rarities from obscurity, and some of the most valuable of these come from this period.

Georgian Suffolk provides classic views of the county, eventually running into the down-to-earth realities of George Crabbe. The nerve was that this clergyman- doctor- botanist- storyteller used the same conventional couplet technique as those who liked to show their classical education, but with daunting effect. No one had dared – or could – see Suffolk life as Crabbe reported it. Lord Cranbrook's choice of *The Village* challenges so much that has been written about the countryside generally.

> *Yes, thus the Muses sing of happy swains,*
> *Because the Muses never knew their pains:*
> *They boast their peasant pipes, but peasants now*
> *Resign their pipes and plod behind the plough;*
> *And few amid the rural tribe have time*
> *To number syllables and play with rhyme.*

Robert Bloomfield, Crabbe's near contemporary, had worked on his uncle's farm at Sapiston in childhood and although the toil overcame his strength, from the dark and crowded little shoemaker's shop in London such an existence remained idyllic. His poem *A Farmer's Boy* is a homage to rural contentment. It was a bestseller: 26,000 copies in 1800. Capel Lofft, the squire who helped to get it published, was more controversial as his *Inscription for a Column at Reeny Mede* reveals. It reminds us that the barons took their oath to force the king to sign Magna Carta at Bury Abbey, and that in Lofft's day the author of *the Rights of Man* was born just up the road. A streak of East Anglian radicalism runs through many of these poems, its 'do different'.

The early nineteenth century was the heyday of poetic sentiment. The young Charles Dickens satirized it, Virginia Woolf warned against it. Annuals known as pocket-books encouraged it. The funniest account of it is in *The Pickwick Papers* when Mrs Leo Hunter throws a party at Eatanswill (Sudbury) and reads her immortal *Ode to an Expiring Frog*. Sudbury then had a poet-mayor, George Fulcher, and he edited Suffolk's popular pocket-book in which appeared alongside Lord Byron, Shakespeare, *etc.*, effusions by lesser talents. Some of the most interesting have made their way into *Parnassian Molehill* – including Fulcher himself. He was a good step up from those he published and encouraged, a powerful critic of the workhouse and other social horrors. These included infant mortality. We smile at these death-bed verses but we would not have done so then. Poetic sensibility was among the few ways in which to deal with sometimes yearly loss. Here we have Mary Sewell's *Mother's Last Words*, which they say sold over a million. She was the mother of the author of *Black Beauty* and came from Sutton.

Virginia Woolf once looked back on the early eighteen-hundreds' poetry-dominated women with concern for their futures. In *The*

PREFACE

Common Reader (1925) she takes the circle of Jane and Ann Taylor – 'Twinkle, twinkle, little star'– as an example. These moralising sisters had moved from Lavenham to Colchester.

> Colchester, about the year 1800, was for the young Taylors, as Kensington had been for their mother, 'a very Elysium'. There were the Strutts, the Hills, the Stapletons; there was poetry, philosophy, engraving... Already they had won prizes in Darton and Harvey's pocket-book... The Stapletons were poetic, too. Moira and Bithi would wander over the old town wall at Balkerne Hill reading poetry by moonlight. Perhaps there was a little too much poetry in Colchester in 1800.

For some of the girls came to marital grief.

At every period *Parnassian Molehill* becomes quite an eminence from which the reader can take stock of a certain time, a certain attitude and an altering language. It is a wonderful way to learn about Suffolk. We could hardly come closer to the deeper feelings of our forebears or to their reading. A lot of them adopted the county and brought something exotic to it, FitzGerald the Irishman, for example, with his Persian view of existence. Although he and some of the other poets brought together here could claim to be on a higher level than a molehill, they would have delighted in the idea of this anthology. It was to teach and give pleasure.

RONALD BLYTHE
Wormingford
June 2001

INTRODUCTION

Today it is probably not untrue to say that the County of Suffolk is better known for its trinity of breeds, the Suffolk horse, the Red Poll cow and the Suffolk sheep, than famous for the literary attainments of its inhabitants. Indeed it is not to be expected that its maximum elevation of some 400 feet, served by Liverpool Street Station and swept by the winds for which East Anglia is famous, would be as congenial to the Muses as the heights of Parnassus, bathed in Mediterranean sunshine. The times too are not propitious: in these austere and egalitarian days a majority would doubtless rather see the magnificent crops of wheat, barley and sugar-beet which spring behind the wheel-marks of our tractors or the footprints of our Suffolk horses, than encourage genius to drink at the fountain of Hippocrene. Nevertheless, speaking as they do that tongue which above all living tongues the Muses most delight to honour, many of the inhabitants of the county have been inspired to rhyme—some even to poetry—and it has seemed to me that even the least is worth rescuing from that oblivion to which time and neglect have consigned some of the greater. Some I have felt are worth rescuing for their own intrinsic merits: others as examples of that superb egotism which seems to have affected our ancestors at all social levels, and led them to inflict on a small but long-suffering public effusions which even the most indulgent reader may think should have been left in the decent obscurity in which I found them. Be that as it may, I have tried to find all those inhabitants of the county who have drunk at the fountain which sprang from the foot-prints of the winged horse and to print a representative selection from their works.

It is curious how the literary output of the county seems to follow a well defined curve. The seventeenth century is relatively productive, the first half of the eighteenth, in spite of the increase in population and wealth which took place over that period, relatively barren, after which the example of the cultivated squires and clergy of the late eighteenth century leads on to the spate of Dying Children and Mothers' Graves in the first half of the nineteenth. It is to that last period which our truly endemic poetry mainly belongs and it is, I think, difficult to exaggerate the influence which such men as Capel Lofft must have had on the literary climate of the county. It is easy to understand how that influence caused the larger, more wealthy and self-satisfied middle and upper middle classes of the period to produce more, quantitatively, than their predecessors of the two previous centuries, but I find it difficult to explain the relatively low output of the late seventeenth and early eighteenth centuries. It may be that interest in literature was at a low ebb, though it may be that I have failed to find it, being drawn to the bibliographical curiosities of the earlier period, and the more readily available literary curiosities of the later.

I have confined myself to published works by Suffolk authors: that is, those who by birth or residence would have

INTRODUCTION

been eligible for consideration for the County side under the rules of the Football Association. I have made no selections from the ballads of earlier centuries nor from the fascinating and anonymous poetry which is found in the Newspapers, Pocket Books and Diaries of the late eighteenth and early nineteenth centuries. The former were many of them reprinted by Forde and Glyde in their 'Suffolk Garlands', the latter remains virgin territory to be tenderly explored by some future lover of the period.

In the first part are printed the poems, set out as nearly as possible by the date of the author's birth: in the second, short biographical notes alphabetically arranged, together with a list of the author's poetical works and in some cases of such other works as shed some light on the author's character. I have not considered any work published after 1870, the year of my father's birth, from sheer cowardice. Though for one reason or another the poems herein reprinted have pleased me, I cannot expect that others will agree with my choice; I would not add to the inevitable criticisms of the general reader the wrath of living authors or their near relations.

Looking back over the fields which I have surveyed, choked with weeds though some may be, it is difficult not to regret the passing of a more leisured and cultivated age, even if that loss has brought with it many welcome and necessary improvements. Boswell said of Lofft that 'though a most zealous Whig, he has a mind full of learning and knowledge': today, tied to the sink or the committee room and overwhelmed with agricultural returns, it is doubtful if even a Tory squire has the leisure or in middle age retains the capacity to translate into English verse the Georgics of Virgil, though he may many times have copied

PARNASSIAN MOLEHILL

them in his youth as a punishment. Nor do we seem to have gained on the roundabouts. Bloomfield educated himself and fought his way to fame at a time when the odds against a working man were long: today, in spite of the free education and other social improvements which have meant the passing of the leisured squire, we have no Tractor-driver Poet. There remains though a small grain of leaven which may yet lighten the whole lump and the only modern poem which I print is a rendering into Latin verse by two young scholars of the old Suffolk Ballad 'Foggy, Foggy Dew', a ballad which has helped Mr Britten and Mr Pears to rear for themselves monuments more lasting than bronze.

The material upon which this book is based has been gathered over many years and I am indebted for help, advice and information to many people, too numerous to mention by name. I am grateful to A.G.H. and G.A.S. for permission to print the poem on page 146, H.G. for that on p. 172, but to Mrs. D. E. Jervis I owe my especial thanks, without her help I could never have finished.

In conclusion I can only quote from James Carr, the shoemaker of Ipswich: 'doubtless many defects will present themselves to the practised eye of the severe critic, who I will but ask to remember that this work is no more than the oozings through the crevices of daily care and toil which I now submit to the perusal of a general public, with merely adding the beautiful adage,

"To err is human, to forgive divine."'

GREAT GLEMHAM C.

PARNASSIAN MOLEHILL

An Anthology of Suffolk Verse

by the Earl of Cranbrook

PARNASSIAN MOLEHILL

THE POEMS

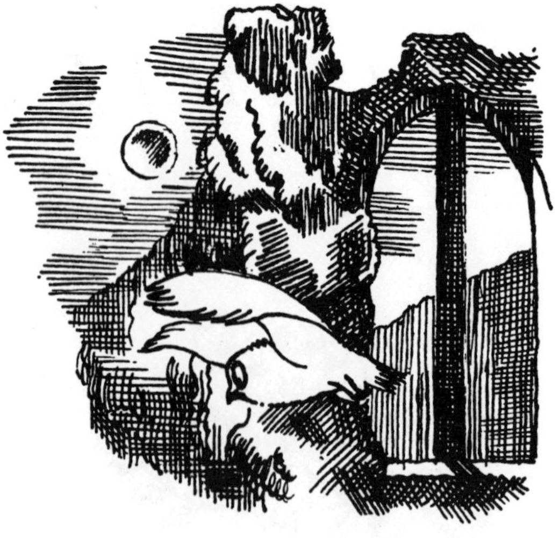

THE HOUSE OF SLEEP

JOHN GOWER 1327-1408

Under an hill there is a cave
Which of the sonne may nought have,
So that no man may knowe aright
The point betwene the day and night.
There is no fire, there is no sparke,
There is no dore which may charke,
Whereof an eye shulde unshet,
So that inward there is no let.
And for to speke of that withoute,
There stant no great tre nigh aboute,
Wheron there mighte crowe or pie
Alighte for to clepe or crie.
There is no cock to crowe day,
Ne beste none which noise may
The hille, but all aboute round
There is growend upon the ground
Poppy, which bereth the sede of slepe,
With other herbes suche an hepe.
A stille water for the nones
Rennend upon the smalle stones,
Which hight of Lethes the river,
Under that hille in such maner
There is, which giveth great appetite
To slepe. And thus ful of delite
Slepe hath his hous.

A VALENTINE TO HER THAT EXCELLETH ALL

JOHN LIDEGATE 1370–1451 (?)

Men here choose valentines in Cupids calender

Saynt valentyne, of custume yeere by yeere,
Men haue an vsavnce in this Regyoun
To looke and serche Cupydes Kalundere,
And choose theyre choys by gret affeccioun;
Suche as beon pricked by Cupydes mocion,
Taking theyre choyse, as theyre soort dothe falle

but I love one above all

But I loue oon whiche excellithe alle.

They choose for various reasons

Some choose for fayrenesse and for hye beaute,
Some for estate, and some eke for rychchesse,
Some for fredame, and some for bountee,
Some for theyre poorte and theyr gentylesse,
Some for theyre plesaunce and some for theyre goodnesse,
Lyche as the chaunce of theyre soorte doth falle,
But I love oone whiche excellethe alle.

I chose mine long ago

I chose that floure sithen goon ful yoore,
And euery yeere my choyse I shall renuwe,
Vpon this day conferme it euermore,
She is in loue so stedfast and so truwe;
Who louethe hir best, hit shal him neuer ruwe,
Yif such a grace vn-to his soort may falle,
Whome I have chose for she excellethe alle.

Mine excells Lucrece Marcia

Dido

Men speke of Lucresse that was of Roome tovne,
ffor wyvely trouth founded on clennesse,
Some wryte als of Marcea Catoun
With laude and prys for hir stedfastnesse;
And some of Dydo for hir kyndenesse,
(ffortune suche happe leet vpon hem falle)
But I loue oone that excellethe alle.

Rachel　　　　　Rachel was feyre, Lia was eke secounde,
Candace　　　　And ryche also was the qweene Candace,
Rosamund　　　 So in hir tyme Right fayre was Roosamounde,
　　　　　　　　　And Bersabee hade a goodely face,
　　　　　　　　　Of Kyng Dauid she stoode so in the grace,
　　　　　　　　　ffirst whane his look he leet vpon hir falle,
　　　　　　　　　But I loue oone whiche excellethe alle.

　　　　　　　　　The noble kyng, the mightly Assuere,
Esther　　　　　Cherisshed Hester for hir gret meeknesse,
　　　　　　　　　ffor wommanhed, and for hir humble chere,
　　　　　　　　　Made hir a qweene, and a gret Pryncesse;
　　　　　　　　　To the Juwes lawe she was defenseresse,
　　　　　　　　　In sodein mescheef that did vpon hem falle,
　　　　　　　　　But I loue oon whiche excellethe alle.

Sheba　　　　　Saba came fer for kyng Salamon
　　　　　　　　　To seen his richchesse and his sapience,
　　　　　　　　　His staately housholde, and his hye Renoun,
　　　　　　　　　Gaf him presence of gret excellence,
　　　　　　　　　Herde his proverbes and his gret prudence,
　　　　　　　　　Where as he seet in his royal stalle,
　　　　　　　　　But I loue oone, that excellethe alle.

and others　　　Gresylde whylome hade gret pacyence,
　　　　　　　　　As hit was preued fer vp in Itayle,
　　　　　　　　　Pallas Mynerua haden eloquence,
　　　　　　　　　And Pantasilia faught in plate and mayle,
　　　　　　　　　And Senobya lyouns wolde assayle,
　　　　　　　　　To make hem taame as Oxe is in a stalle,
　　　　　　　　　But I loue oone, that excellethe alle.

　　　　　　　　　And if I shal hir name specyfye,
　　　　　　　　　That folk may wit whiche shee sholde be,
She is Mary　　 This goodely fresshe called is Marye,
　　　　　　　　　A braunche of kynges, that sprange out of Iesse,
　　　　　　　　　That made the lord thorughe hir humylyte
　　　　　　　　　To let his golddewe in-to hir brest dovne falle,
　　　　　　　　　To bere the fruyt which should saue vs alle.

but I shall   From yeere to yeer for necglygence or rape,
choose   Voyde of al chaunge and nufanglenesse,
her year by year   Saint Valentyne hit shal me not escape
       Vpon thy day, in token of stedfastnesse,
       But that I shal conferme in sikurnesse
       My choys of nuwe, so as it is befalle,
       To love hir best, whiche that excellethe alle.

OSBERN BOKENHAM 1393–1447 (?)

WHERE fore Lord to thee alone I crye,
Whych welle art of mercy and of pyte,
And neythyr to Clyo ner to Melpomone,
Ner to noon othir of the musys nyne,
Ner to Pallas Mynerve ner Lucyne,
Ner to Appollo wych as old poetys seye
Of wysdam beryth both lok and Keye,
Of gay speche eek and of elequencye
But alle them wyttyrly I denye,
As evere crystene man owyth to do,
And thee oonly Lord I fle on to.

CHRIST'S TEMPTATION

JOHN BALE 1495-1563

Lo, how saye ye now? is not here a pleasaunt sight?
If ye wyll, ye maye here have all the worldes delyght.
Here is to be seane the kyngedome of Arabye,
With all the regyons of Affryck, Europe and Asye,
And their whole delyghtes, their pompe, their magnifycence,
Their ryches, their honour, their welth, their concupyscence.
Here is golde and sylver in wonderfull habundaunce,
Sylkes, velvetes, tyssues, with wynes and spyces of plesaunce:
Here are fayre women, of countenaunce ameable,
With all kyndes of meates to the body dylectable:
Here are camels, stoute horses, and mules that never wyll tyre,
With so many pleasures as your hart can desyre.

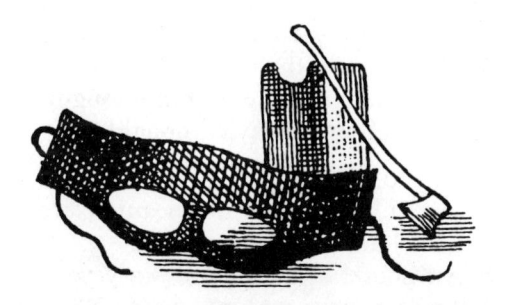

EPITAPH ON KATHERINE HOWARD

GEORGE CAVENDISH 1500-1561

By prove of me, non can denye
That beautie and lust, ennemyes to chastitie,
Hath been the tweyn that hathe dekayed me,
And hathe broughte me to this end untoward
Some tyme a queen, and now hedless Howard

THE COURTSHIP AND MARRIAGE OF GRAUNDE AMOURE AND LA BELL PUCELL

STEPHEN HAWES *d.* 1523

She Commaunded her mynstrelles ryght anone to play
Mamours the swete and the gentyll daunce
With la bell pucell that was fayre and gaye
She me recommaunded with all pleasaunce
To daunce true mesures without varyaunce
Oh lorde god how glad than was I
So for to daunce with my swete lady.

By her propre hande soft as ony sylke
With due obeyaunce I dyde her than take
Her skynne was whyte as whalles bone or mylke
My thoughtes was rauysshed I myght not aslake
My brennynge hert she the fyre dyde make
These daunces truely musyke hath me tought
To lute or daunce but it avayled nought.

For the fyre kyndled and waxed more and more
The dauncynge blewe it with her beaute clere
My hert sekened and began waxe sore
A mynute .vi. houres and .vi. houres a yere
I thought it was so hevy was my chere
But yet for to cover my grete love aryght
The outwarde countenaunce I made gladde and lyght.

And after that the gay and gloryous
La bell pucell to the chapell was ledde
In a whyte vesture fayre and precyous
With a golden chaplet on her yalowe hede
And lex ecclesie did me to her wedde
After which weddynge there was a grete fest
Nothynge we lacked but had of the best.

What sholde I tary by long continuaunce
Of the feeste for of my joye and pleasure
Wisdom can juge withouten varyaunce
That naught I lacked as ye may be sure
Payenge the swete due det of nature
Thus with my lady that was so fayre
In joye I lyved ryght many a yere.

O lusty youth and yonge tender herte
The trewe companyon of my lady bryght
God let us never from other asterte
But all in Joye to lyve bothe day and nyght
Thus after sorow Joye aryveth aryght
After my payne I had sporte and playe
Full lytell thought I that it sholde dekaye.

SUMMER

HENRY HOWARD, EARL OF SURREY 1517–1546

The soote Season that bud and bloom forth brings
   With green hath clad the hill and eke the vale:
The Nightingall with fethers new she sings:
   The Turtle to her mate hath told her tale.
Summer is come: for every spray now springs.
   The Hart hath hung his old head on the pale;
The Buck in brake his winter coat he flings;
   The Fishes fleete with new repayred scale:
The Adder all her slough away she flinges;
   The swift Swallow pursueth the flies smalle.
The busy Bee her honey how she minges!
   Winter is worne that was the floures bale.
And thus I see among these pleasant things
   Eche care decays; and yet my sorrow springs.

OF A SNOW BALLE

NICHOLAS BACON 1509–1579

A WANTON wenche uppon a colde daye
With Snowe balles provoked me to playe:
But theis snowe balles soe hette my desyer
That I maye calle them balles of wylde fyer.
Whoe woulde have thoughte in this colde snowe
Cupyde woulde hide his fonde fyrye towe,
Or that from water shoulde breede brandes fyrye,
Or colde and moyste shoulde cause hotte and drye?
What place is free from Loves slye workeinge
If under snowe his fyer lye lurkeinge?
Noe snowe nor thinge this fyer can quenche
But the like fyer of this like wenche.

THOMAS TUSSER 1534?–1580

A holy Catholike Church on earth I graunt there is
and those which frame their lives by that shall never speed amiss,
the head whereof is Christ, his word the chiefest post,
Preserver of this Temple great, is God the Holy Ghost.

I do not doubt there is, a multitude of Saints:
more good is done by resembling them, than showing them our plaints.
Their faith and works in Christ, that glory them did give,
which glory we shall likewise have if likewise we do live.

A God of heaven there is, forgiveness of our sinnes
through Christes death, through faith in it, and through none other ginnes,
If we repentant here, his mercy dayly crave
through steadfast hope and faith in Christ, forgivenes we have.

I hope and trust upon the rising of the flesh
this corpse of mine (that first must die) shall rise again afresh.
The body and soul even then, in one shall joined be,
as Christ did rise, from death to life; even so, through Christ shall me.

This is that Lord of hostes, the father of us all,
the maker of what ere was made, my God on whom I call;
Which for the love of man, sent down his onelie sonne,
begot of him before the Worldes were any whit begonne.

This is that God of Gods, whom everie soule should love,
whom all mens hearts should quake for feare, his wrath on them to move:
That this same might God, above all others chiefe,
shall save my soule from dolefull Hell, is all my whole beliefe.

THOMAS NUCE 1540?–1617

SWIFT winged love, mens fancy fond, in vayne
A mercy wanting God to bee doth fayne:
And armes his handes with wounding weapons keen
And bowes with burning brandes for lovers greene
Of Venus to be sprung they al accorde,
And blyndly forged of thunders limping lorde.
Bland love the myndes great torment sore appeares,
And buddeth first in frolicke youthful yeares
Who while we drinke of Fortunes pleasaunt cuppe,
With laysie pampring ryot, is nestled up:
Whom if to foster up you leave at length
It fleeting falles away with broken strength.
This is in all our life (as I suppose)
The greatest cause how pleasure first arose,
Which sith mankind by broodyng hydeth aye
Through gladsom love that fierce wild beastes doth sway
It never can from manly breast depart.
This selfe same God I wish withall my hart
The wedlocke lightes to beare before our grace,
And fasten Poppie sure in our bed place.

PETER MOON c. 1548

A GRET colour of holiness in y Popes church hath been bred
The which is playne wickedness, as goddes word proveth ryghte
To mainteyn the old customes, of most men now refuted
The verite clean banished, and truth put to flight
If God had not bene mercyfull, all men had lost the light
Blynde was the cerimony for all the sanctification
But now it is evident to every christen wight
How Goddes word is flourished, the light of our salvation.

In y stedde of Goddes word we had holy bread and water
Holy palmes, holy ashes, holy candles, holy fyre
Holy bones, holy stones, holy crewittes at the aulter
Holy censars, holy bannars, holy crosses, holy atyer
Holy war, holy par, holy smoke, holy smyer
Holy oyle, holy creame, holy wyne for veneration
Holy coope, holy canepy, holy reliques in y quier
Thus gods word could not florish y light of our Salvation.

THE SILKWORMS

THOMAS MOUFET 1553–1604

SILK flies I meane, which not one breast alone
But all throughout, on head, wings, sides, and feete,
Besides pure white, else colour carry none,
For creatures pure, a colour though most meete,
Martial'd the first of all in glorious throne,
Whereon shall sit the Lord and Saviour sweete,
Who with tenne thousand Angels all in white,
Shal one day judge the world with doom upright.

No spotte on them, as els on ev'ry flye,
Because in them no follies ever grew,
No crimson redde doth for revengement crye,
No wavering whatchet, where al harts be true:

No yellow, where there is not Jealousie:
No labour lost, and therefore voide of blue:
No peachy marke to signify disdaine,
No greene to show a wanton mind and vaine.

They choose not (like to other birds and beasts)
This yeare one wife, another wife the next,
Their choyse is certaine, and still certaine rests,
With former loves their mindes are not perplext,
Hee yields to her, she yields to his requests,
Neither with feare or jelosie is vext:
She clippeth him, hee clippeth her againe,
Equall their ioy, and equall is their paine.

No man so poore, but he may Mulb'ries plant,
No man so smal but wil a silke worme feede,
No worme so little (unlesse care do want)
But from it selfe wil make a clew of threede,
Ech clew weighs down, rather with more than scant,
A penny weight, from out whose hidden seede,
(After winged wormes conception)
A hundred spinsters issue forth of one.

Tis likewise sport to heare how man and maide,
Whilst winding, twisting, and in weaving, thay
Now laugh, now chide, now scan what others saide,
Now sing a Carrol, now a lovers lay,
Now make the trembling beames to cry for aide,
On clattring treddles whilst they roughly play:
Resembling in their rising and their falls,
A musicke strange of new found Claricalls.

The smel likewise of silken wool that's new,
To heart and head what comfort doth it bring,
Whilst we it wind and tooze from oval clew?
Resembling much in prime of fragrant spring,
When wild-rose buds in greene and pleasant hue,
Perfume the ayre, and upward sents to fling,
Well pleasing sents, neither to sowre nor sweete,
But rightly mixt, and of a temper meete.

As for the hand, looke how a lover wise
Delighteth more to touch Astarte slick
Then Hecuba, whose eye-browes hide her eies,
Whose wrinckled lippes in kissing seeme to prick,
Upon whose palmes such warts and hurtells rise
As may in poulder grate a nutmegge thick:
So ioy our hands in silke, and seeme ful loth
To handle ought but silke and silken cloth.

Such are the pleasures, and farre more then these,
Which head, and hart, eies, eares, and nose, and hands
Take or may take, in learning at their ease
The dieting of these my spinning bands,
Whose silken threede shal more than counterpeise
Paine, cost, and charge, what ever it us stands
So that if gaine or pleasure can perswade,
Go we, let us learne the silken staplers trade.

CELESTIAL ELEGIES

THOMAS ROGERS *c.* 1555–1616

FLORA

Crowned with wreathes of Odoriferous flowrs,
Whose sent perfumes the Empire of the Ayre,
Among the rest of the immortall powers,
Unto the land of Albion I repaire.
Where I with garlands will her Toombe adorne,
And make death proud with ceremonious rites,
That for this Ladies sake I doe not scorne delights;
To deake her Grave, with th'earths faire flowers
For sith the world was sweetned by her breath,
That breath'd rare vertues forth, as then alive,
Ile beautifie her Sepulcher, since death
Of her sweete sowle her body did deprive,
   For this brave dame was a sweet springing flower,
   Bedewde with heavenly grace till her last howre.

DIANA

Ay me; my vestall flame is now extinct,
My flowre of Chastitie doth fade away
In Lethes flouds true noblenes doth sinke,
My Empyre runnes to ruinous decay;
Pittie, Almes-deeds and charitie is fled,
Fidelitie beyond the seas is gone,
True friendship now and faithfull love is dead,
And Priapus usurpeth Cupids throne:
She that did seeke my kingdome to maintaine,
By sanctitie, religion, faith, and zeale,
Through enuie of the Destinies is slaine,
Death robs th'Eschequer of my common weale,
   For all those rites which I was wont to have,
   Are fled to heaven or buried in her grave.

THOMAS BLUNDEVILLE *c.* 1560

Like as the mightie Oke, whose rootes,
In th'earth are fixed fast,
Is able to withstand each winde,
That blowes with blustering blast:

Even so each froward Fortunes hap,
That ever maie betide,
The constant mind with vertue fraught
Is able to abide.

THOMAS TYMME 1560?–1620

The merchant man that often sayles
   Upon the rockie seas
Hath oftentimes for recompence
   The gain that doth him please.
The fisher man that castes his net
   And lays his baited ginne,
Doth trust at length by happie hap
   His pray of fishe to winne.
The plowman eke that sowes his seede
   On soyle, with toyle, for gaine,
The winters travaile being past,
   Doth reap the riped graine.
If plowman then, and fisher too,
   Have stedfast hope for gaines,
As recompence for their sore toyle
   And daily pinching paines:
Why should not I as well as they,
   By paine some profite have,
Since that my Muse as recompence
   Most truly doth it crave:
The which good reader thou shalt graunt,
   If that thou take in woorth:
This simple pamphlet at hir hande
   Which she hath nowe let foorth.

THE ROMAN CHURCH
JOHN DAY 1566–1627

If to a Woman's head, an Horses maine
A Painter would annexe: and then again
Decke every Limbe with Feathers to and fro,
And lowest parts like Fish themselves should show,
    My Friends, were you admitted to this sight,
    Could you refraine? Would you not laugh outright.

A PREFACE TO THE INCARNATION
WILLIAM ALABASTER 1567–1604

I sing of Christ: O endless argument
Profaner thoughts and cares begone, begone,
Lest thunder push down your presumption.
I sing of Christ: let many words be lent
To enrobe my thoughts with all their ornament,
And tongues of men and angels join in one
To shew the riches of invention
Before the eyes of all the firmament.
The Temple where I sing is Heaven: the quire
Are my soul's powers: the book's a living story:
Each take his time, but with a bow retire
That modesty may after reach his glory:
And let the humble base beneath begin
To show when he descended for our sin.

INCARNATIO EST MAXIMUM DEI DONUM

Like as the fountain of all light created
Doth pour out streams of brightness undefin'd
Through all the conduits of transparent kind,
That heaven and air are both illuminated,

And yet his light is not thereby abated,
So God's eternal bounty ever shin'd
The beams of being, moving, life, sense, mind,
And to all things himself communicated
But for the violent diffusive pleasure
Of goodness that left not till God had spent
Himself by giving us himself his treasure
In making man a God omnipotent.
How might this goodness draw ourselves above
Which drew down God with such attractive love.

IN TIME OF PESTILENCE

THOMAS NASH 1567–1601

Adieu, farewell earth's bliss:
This world uncertain is:
Fond are life's lustful joys,
Death proves them all but toys.
None from his darts can fly;
I am sick, I must die
      Lord, have mercy on me!

Rich men, trust not in wealth,
Gold cannot buy you health;
Physic himself must fade;
All things to end are made;
The plague full swift goes by;
I am sick, I must die
      Lord, have mercy on us!

Beauty is but a flower
Which wrinkles will devour;
Brightness falls from the air;
Queens have died young and fair;
Dust hath closed Helen's eye;
I am sick, I must die
      Lord, have mercy on us!

Strength stoops unto the grave,
Worms feed on Hector brave;
Swords may not fight with fate;
Earth still holds ope her gate;
Come, come! the bells do cry;
I am sick, I must die
      Lord, have mercy on us!

Wit with his wantonness
Tasteth death's bitterness;
Hell's executioner
Hath no ears for to hear
What vain art can reply;
I am sick, I must die
      Lord, have mercy on us!

Haste therefore each degree
To welcome destiny;
Heaven is our heritage,
Earth but a player's stage.
Mount we unto the sky;
I am sick, I must die
      Lord, have mercy on us!

ON MODERN POETRY

JOSEPH HALL 1574–1656

Whilom the sisters nine were vestal maides,
And held their temple in the secret shades
Of fair Parnassus, the two-headed hill,
Whose ancient fame the southern world did fill;
And in the stead of their eternal fame,
Was the cool stream that took his endless name,
From out the fertile hoof of winged steed:
There did they sit and do their holy deed,
That pleas'd both Heaven and Earth—till that of late
Whom should I fault? or the most righteous fate,
Or Heavn's, or men, or fiends, or ought beside,
That ever made that foul mischance betide?
Some of the sisters in securer shades
Defloured were . . . .
And ever since, disdaining sacred shame,
Done ought that might their heav'nly stock defame.
Now is Parnassus turned to a stewes,
And on bay stocks the wanton myrtle grewes;
Cytheron hill's become a brothrel-bed,
And Pyrene sweet turn'd to a poison'd head
Of coal-black puddle, whose infectious stain
Corrupteth all the lowly fruitful plain.
Their modest stole, to garnish looser weed,
Deck'd with love-favours, their late whoredoms' meed:
And where they wont sip of the simple flood,
Now toss they bowls of Bacchus' boiling blood.
I marvell'd much, with doubtful jealousie,
Whence came such litters of new poetrie:
Methought I fear'd, lest the horse-hoofed well
His native banks did proudly over-swell
In some late discontent, thence to ensue
Such wondrous rabblements of rhymesters new:

But since I saw it painted on Fame's wings,
The Muses to be woxen wantonings,
Each bush, each bank, and each base apple-squire
Can serve to sate their beastly lewd desire.
Ye bastard poets, see your pedigree,
From common trulls and loathsome brothelry.

ELEGY
WRITTEN IN THE PARISH REGISTER AT WILBY
JOSEPH FLETCHER 1577–1637

"Dear-loving, & dear-loved wife (O we to eche were dear:
The God of Love by marriage-life, in love had match't us near).
A Spotless life thou livd'st a Maid & to thy
    husband chaste:
Thy sacred vowes to God th' hast payd, & duly
    serv'd him hast.
In Musicks skill thou didst excell, & so in
    Medcine's art;
Modest, milde, merciful, kinde, coomly in
    every part.
Upon thy sixt conception, thy death being att
    the birth
Brought forth to mee heart-grief and mone,
    but to thee endless mirth.
For being freed from griping stings of
    wives-child-bearing throes,
Forthwith thy soule with Angels wings mounts
    up to heavenly joyes.
This happy lot thy name foretould should unto
    thee befall,
That being Grace in Baptism call'd, shouldst
    now be Glory all.
Wherefore since many of thy sex in vertue thou
    didst passe
The after times succeeding next shall speak
    of thy due praise.

And now sweet lovely Love farewell!
      go! sweetly rest in peace:
In that same peace I hope to dwell
      with thee when life shal cease
Our mingled corps in earthen trunk
      one stone shal them fast keep,
Till the last Judgement-sounding Trump
      raise us from our last sleep.
         [1]At this let no man grudge, or
            say its waist:
         For this halfe-leafe, twice twoo
            in yet end there's place't."

A MOST ELEGANT AND RELIGIOUS RAPTURE

SAMUEL WARD 1577–1640

Lovely Loadstone, grant to Me,
Wholely, solely, Thine to be;
Make my heart for thee to breathe
That it may itself bequeath.
      With all fervour unto thee.

Me, a base, a barking Hound,
Bleating Sheep, stray'd from my Bound;
Me, a panting, chased Deer,
Servant slack, and slow, most neer,
      Strongly draw to follow thee.

Give me such a heart as Thine,
Give my Heart to Thee to joyn;
Give Me my hard-Heart pierc'd quite,
Give't, though iron-hard, contrite
      By thy piercing Wound of Love.

---

[1] These last two lines are an apology for devoting space in the register-book to his own private grief.

Spread, Thou Rose of Sharon, fairly,
Whose sweet Savour sents, most rarely;
Fill my Nostrils with Thy sent,
Drawing from Thee more Content,
      Than from Earth's sweets, when at Fairest.

Show Thy self to Me propitious
Shun me not, though I be vitious;
Fully draw my Heart to Thee,
Fully fill Its Longs for Thee
      That, from Thee, I never stray.

A GLASSE FOR AMOROUSE MAYDENS

JAMES YATES c. 1582

Fy, maiden, fy, that Cupid's flames
  Within you so abounde,
To truste the tatling tales of same,
  Whose wordes prove oft unsounde!

Should every knave entice you so,
  To talk with you at will;
What be your wittes so simple now,
  And of such little skill.

As you can not discerne in minde
  Who leads you on the bit?
Fy, Fy, for shame! Now leave it off;
  It is a thing unfit.

You will not warned be, I see
  Until you have a nippe;
You knowe the horse which draws in cart
  Is ever nye the whippe.

But when too late you do repent,
    Repentance will not serve;
Wherefore foresee—in time I warne
    From follie fond to swerve.

Take heed, I say, in time therefore,
    So shall your state be blest,
And I shall cease to write so much
    My pen shall take its rest.

TO HIS WIFE

ZACHARY CATLIN *b. circa* 1585

The Clarian Poet nere so Lyde loved,
Nor yet Philetis Battu so approved
As thou deare wife art fixed in my brest,
Worthy with happier husband to be blest.
Had'st thou a Homer to proclaime thy name
Penelope had come behind thy fame,
Woe's me my verses have too slender force,
Thy worth trancendeth farre my weake discourse.
Yet had I still some of that former vigour,
Which is extinct and quencht by Caesars rigour,
Thou shouldst be first amongst the Noble dames
And with the best shouldst rank thy vertuous name.
And yet so far as my report can raise thee,
Thou in my verse shalt live, and all shall praise thee.

GILES FLETCHER 1588–1623

He is a path, if any be misled;
He is a robe, if any naked be;
If any chance to hunger, he is bread;
If any be a bondman, he is free;
If any be but weak, how strong is he?
    To dead men life he is, to sick men health;
    To blinde men sight, and to the needie wealth;
A pleasure without losse, a treasure without stealth.

Who can forget, never to be forgot,
The time, that all the world in slumber lies:
When, like the starres, the singing Angels shot
To earth, and heav'n awaked all his eyes,
To see another Sunne at midnight rise
    On earth? was never sight of pareil fame:
    For God before man like himself did frame,
But God himself now like a mortall man became.

A Childe he was, and had not learn't to speak,
That with his word the world before did make:
His Mothers arms him bore, he was so weak,
That with one hand the vaults of heav'n could shake.
See how small room my infant Lord doth take,
    Whom all the world is not enough to hold.
    Who of his yeares, or of his age hath told?
Never such age so young, never a Childe so old.

The Angels caroll'd loud their song of peace,
The cursed Oracles were strucken dumbe,
To see their Shepherd, the poore Shepherds presse,
To see their King, the Kingly Sophies come;
And them to guide unto his Masters home,
    A Starre comes dauncing up the orient,
    That springs for joy over the strawy tent,
Where gold, to make their Prince a crown, they all present.

THE SCHOOL-MASTER TO HIS SCHOLAR

EDMUND COOTE *c.* 1600

My Child and Scholar, take good heed
  unto the Words that here are set;
And see thou do accordingly,
  or else besure thou shalt be beat.

First, I command thee, God to serve;
  then to thy Parents Duty yield:
Unto all Men be courteous
  and mannerly in Town and Field.

Your Cloaths unbutton'd do not use,
  let not your Hose ungarter'd be,
Have Handkerchief in readiness,
  wash Hands and Face, or see not me.

Lose not your Books, Ink horn, or Pens,
  nor Girdle, Garters, Hat or Band;
Let shoes be ty'd pin shirt band close,
  keep well your Hands at any hand.

If broken-hos'd or shoo'd you go,
   or slovenly in your Array,
Without a Girdle or untruss'd
   then you and I must have a Fray.

If that you cry, or talk aloud,
   Or Book do rend, or strike with Knife,
Or laugh, or play unlawfully,
   then you and I must be at Strife.

If that you Curse, Miscall, or Swear,
   if that you Pick, File, Steal, or Lye,
If you forget a Scholar's part,
   then must you sure your Points untie.

If that to School you do not go,
   When Time doth call you to the same,
Or if you Loiter in the Streets,
   when we do meet, then look for blame.

Wherefore, my Child, behave thy self
   so decently in all Assays,
That thou may'st purchase Parents Love,
   and eke obtain thy Master's Praise.

THE SYMPATHY

OWEN FELLTHAM 1602–1688

Soul of my soul! it cannot be,
That you should weep, and I from tears be free.
All the vast room between both poles,
Can never dull the sense of souls,
   Knit in so fast a knot.
Oh! can you grieve, and think that I
Can feel no smart, because not nigh,
   Or that I know it not?

Th'are heretic thoughts. Two lutes are strung,
And on a table tun'd alike for song;
Strike one, and that which none did touch,
Shall sympathising sound as much,
   As that which touch'd you see.
Think then this world (which heaven enrolls)
Is but a table round, and souls
   More apprehensive be.

Know they that in their grossest parts,
Mix by their hallowed loves entwined hearts,
This privilege boast, that no remove
Can e'er infringe their sense of love.
   Judge hence then our estate,
Since when we lov'd there was not put
Two earthen hearts in one breast, but
     Two souls co-animate.

OF LOGIC

A THING born blind, a child, and foolish too,
Shall be made man, if it to Oxford go.

LUCESCIT

WILLIAM HAWKINS 1602?–1637

Now 'gins the faire dew-dabling blushing morne
To open to the earth heavens Easterne gate,
Displaying by degrees the new borne light.
The stars have trac'd their dance, and unto night
Now bid good night.
The young daies Centinell the morning starre
Now drives before him all his glittering flocke,
And bids them rest within the fold unseene
Till with his whistle Hesper call them forth.

Now Titan up and ready cals aloud,
And bids the rowling houres bestirre them quicke
And harnesse up his prauncing foaming steeds
To hurry out the sunnes bright Charriot.
O now I heare their trampling feet approach:
Now now I see that glorious lampe to dart
His nearer beames, and all bepaint with gold
The over-peeping tops of highest hills.

WHY SO PALE AND WAN?

JOHN SUCKLING 1608–1642

WHY so pale and wan, fond lover?
   Prethee, why so pale?
Will, when looking well can't move her,
   Looking ill prevail?
   Prethee, why so pale?

Why so dull and mute, young sinner?
   Prethee, why so mute,
Will, when speaking well can't win her,
   Saying nothing doe't,
   Prethee, why so mute!

Quit, quit for shame! This will not move;
   This cannot take her.
If of herself she will not love,
   Nothing can make her:
   The divil take her.

WILLIAM SPRING 1613–1654

So slept our former Patriots (when they
Had serv'd their country) in a bed of clay;
Flesh may incinerate, when Man doth dye,
The body in the grave may sleeping lye;
But there's a spark remaines, which shal return,
And re-inform those ashes in their turn,
Which when the last days morning shal draw nigh,
Shal raise its flame by heav'nly Chymistry:
So springs the Phoenix, from which Rise
She's ever cal'd the Bird of Paradise.

TOMORROW

THOMAS STEPHENS c. 1610–1677

What fury did create
This eager Love in mortalls, to make known
Things yet to come? Was't heav'ns gift? or their own
Ambitious thoughts, content with no estate?
We search the birth and end of time; what fate
The highest Pow'r, and hard'ned destinies
Determine for us. Hence we cast our eyes
On entrails, list'ning to the birds discourse;
We trace the stars, and reckon Phoebe's course;
And use Thessalian arts. The Golden Age
Of our forefathers never durst presage
Thus boldly: They were borne of stumps of rocks,
And only labour'd to encrease their flocks
In woods or tillage. Mortals may not strive
To know tomorrow's doome: And yet we dive,
(Poore Vulgars) in Heav'ns secrets: hence our Lies,
Feares, Anger, Craft, immodest hopes arise.

WHITENESS, OR CHASTITY

JOSEPH BEAUMONT 1615–1699

Tell me, where doth whiteness grow?
Not on Beds of Scythian Snow;
Nor on Alabaster Hills;
Nor in Canaan's milky Rills;
Nor the dainty living Land
Of a young Queen's Breast or Hand;
Nor on Cygnets lovely Necks;
Nor in Lap of Virgin Wax;
Nor upon the soft and sleek
Pillows of the Lilly's Cheek;
Nor the precious smiling Heirs
Of the Morning's pearly Tears;
Nor the Silver-shaming Grace
Of the Moon's unclouded Face:
    No; all these Candours
    Are but the handsome Slanders
Cast on the Name of genuine Whiteness, which
Doth Thee alone, fair Chastity, enrich.

THOMAS HARCOURT 1618–1679

Th'art welcom Death, for though thou art a Thief,
Instead of Robbing, I expect Relief
From thy kind hand. 'Tis long since I have found
Thou steal'st upon me, and dost still get ground.
Then welcom Death: by thee I hope t'obtain
A better Being, and secure remain
From Sin, That greatest, foulest, blackest Devil,
The Subtlest Foe, the only dreadfull Evil.
Welcom sweet Death, I chuse without Reply,
Rather to Die to Live, than Live to Die.

SYLVIA BETRAYED

SAMUEL HARDING 1618?–

Me thinkes each thing
I meete withall upbraids my fond credulity;
The soaring larke hovers aloft i'th aire,
At distance from th'inchanting glasse, that Courts
Her to her ruine! the feareful Quaile
Suspects and shuns the musicke of the pipe
That sings her into fetters.
Onely poore I am sillier than these;
Witnesse th'untimely swelling of this wombe
Pregnant to my disgrace—As I lay hid
In yonder thicket, the brambles gently swell'd
And hid my shame, which yet each triviall winde
But dallying with, persuaded from my covert!
And left me naked to heaven's eye; the boughs
Of the next willow clung about my head
As if they'd knit themselves into a garland,
Which I would weare for my forsaken lover!

THOMAS LYE 1621–1684

Truth is in Wine: but who can find it there?
For sure in Taverns men will lie and swear.

SAMUEL CROSSMAN 1624–1684

My song is love unknown;
My Saviour's love to me,
Love to the loveless shown,
That they might lovely be.
      Oh who am I,
      That for my sake
      My Lord should take
      Frail flesh and die.

Who came from his bless'd throne,
Salvation to bestow:
But men made strange, and none
The long'd for Christ would know.
    But oh! my Friend;
    My Friend indeed,
    Who at my need
    His life did spend.

In life no house, no home,
My Lord on earth might have:
In death no friendly tombe,
But what a stranger gave.
    What may I say?
    Heav'n was his home
    But mine the tombe,
    Wherein he lay.

EVE

SAMUEL SLATER 1627?–1704

My Lord, he did persuade, and did prevail.
I saw, I took, I eat. What wilt't avail
Now to deny the fact; neither despise
Me for what's done, much clearer are mine eyes,
Scales off did fall, my mind is more sublime,
Than e're I found it was before this time.
My spirits are dilated, my thoughts flie
Hither and thither with full libertie,
All my affections are rais'd, I do
Conclude myself a kind of Goddess too.

BACCANALIA

CHARLES DARBY 1635(?)–1709

So slept they sound: but while they slept
Nature which all this while, had kept
    Her last reserve of strength,
In Stomachs mouth, where, Helmot saith
The Soul its chiefest Mansion hath
    Began at length
To kick and frisk and stoutly strove
To throw the Liquid Rider off.
For now her Case, like Mariners, was grown,
In leaky Ship, She must or pump, or drown.
Or whether that the Wine, which, till this time,
Was wont to dwell in Cellar's cooler Clime,
    Now put in Stomach's boiling Pot,
Found its new Habitation too hot?
    What e're it was, the Floods gusht out
        From every spout.
Nor was that all. The surly Element,
    With Oral Channels not content,
Reverberates and downwards finds a Vent,
    Which my nice Muse to tell forbears,
And begs, for what is past, the pardon of your Ears.

FROM HORACE

JOHN LANGSTON 1639–1704

We hate and envy worthy men
    So long as they alive remain;
But when away they're taken, then
    We wish to have them here again.

       *   *   *

Smile you? a louder laughter shakes him: weep?
He his friend company in tears will keep,
But grieves not; if you say the winter's cold,
And call for fire, he'll in a rug be roll'd;
Cry but 'tis hot, he sweats; the Parasite
Dissembles thus, and plays the hypocrite.

OUR KING TURMOYLING

EDWARD CALVER c. 1640

Oh heavie, heavie what a weight I beare!
Are Royall Septers swaid with so much care?
Are these the Glories and delights that waite
Upon a Septer, priz'd at such a height?
    I am by sacred providence a head,
But here lies that which now doth presse like lead;
Those tender members which from me take life,
Are with themselves now, and with me at strife.
    My subjects who are so my members deare,
They some seduce me, others domineere;
And almost all my members goe about
To let each others dearest blood run out.
Think you a head can then be free from aking,
Whose members, heart, vaines, are thus bleeding breaking.

HENRY NORTH c. 1650

Say not to me thou art in love
While fancy, and not reason, doth thee guide:
   He that will tell me, he must dye,
        And knowest not why,
He may in torment ever more abide:
   My heart he cannot move.

   If 't be the lustre of mine eye,
Or beauty, which with love his heart doth fill:
   I doe but please his sense, and fitt
        His appetitt:
If this be all, farewell! I will be still
        Diana's votary.

TO HIS DEAD SON

JOHN RANDALL 1666–1722

Farewell, my joy, my comfort. Oh! that I,
Since I can't with you live, might with you die.
Thee, too, among my tender flock I taught,
Whilst with the rudiments of learning fraught:
I thought no pains too great, no task too hard
My labour seemed to be its own reward.
Now with reluctance I to school repair,
Which but reminds me that you once were there.
Live! I would say—and on that sweet wish dwell
But fate will only let me say—farewell.

TO IDERA

CHARLES GOODALL 1671–1689

Your Name on fallen Snow I seal'd;
The melting drops to Ice congealed;
In Crystal Prints the Letters shine,
And their material white refine.
Here daily, hourly as I pass
By this heavenly Looking-glass,
I see the picture of my Face,
And the reflecting Name embrace.
But as by Images of Wax
The Witch a real Body racks;
So as my Heart within consumes
Ice Snow-water reassumes.
My Flames to all your Cold withdraw,
Till we resolve on better Law,
That you shall never freeze to thaw.
With your Temptations, millions strong
To do me right you do me wrong.
Nay—ev'n with Chymical Experiments entice:
Your very name can make a Burning-glass of Ice.

THE NAMES CUT IN THE BARK OF A TREE

SAMUEL SAY 1675–1743

Fair Beach, that bear'st our interwoven Names
Here grav'd, the Token of our mingled Flames,
Preserve the Mark; and as thy Head shall rise,
Our Loves shall heighten till they reach the Skies:
The Wounds in Us, as These in Thee shall spread,
Larger by Time, and Fairer to be read.

Stand, Sacred Tree, here still inviolate stand,
By no rude Axe profan'd, by no unhallowed Hand.
Be Thou the Tree of Love, and here declare,
That once a Nymph was found as true as she was fair.

ARTHUR DUCK 1680?–

Belinda is reduced 'tis said,
To prostitute herself for bread:
And if they're sure to hit the white,
That mingle Profit with Delight,
Belinda's greatly in the Right.

MATHEW COPPINGER *c.* 1682

I love a Lass that will not wed,
Yet values not her Maiden-head,
That is not peevish, proud, nor poor,
That scorns the title of a Whore,
That can both Dance, and Sing, and Quaff,
And, in what ever humour, laugh;
Who swears by Fate, she'll not abuse
What Nature gives her leave to use,
Yet to a Friend, will not be coy,
But give him leave for to enjoy
What he desires, so he'll conceal
Those hidden Pleasures which they steal.

RICHARDSON PACK 1682–1728

Militat omnis amans, et habet sua castra Cupido:
Attice, crede mihi; militat omnis amans.

Cupid and mars are Generals Wise and Bold:
Trust me, Dear Friend, the Parallel will hold.
In Both their Camps alike succeed the Young:
Love Courts the Gay, and Vict'ry Crowns the Strong.

The Old in vain their useless Weapons weild,
Fumblers in Bed, and Cripples in the Field.
Recruits for Each are Chose with equal Care,
And None should dare to Woo, who cannot War.
With Frequent Duty, and with Watching spent,
(The Lover at the Door, the Soldier at the Tent)
On their cold posts Both lie whole Nights Awake;
And often, long and toilsome Marches make.
O'er Hills, through Floods, in Cruel Frost and Snow,
They seek a Mistress, or Pursue a Foe.
No distance tires, no Hazard can Affright;
The Danger serves but to Provoke the Fight.
In hostile Camps the Chiefs employ their Spies:
And Lovers watch their Rival Lovers Eyes.
Forts are Approached by Mine, or Took by Storm:
Ladies Won—Sword in Hand, or else in Form.
Your active Partisans, in Ambush laid,
Surpriz'd in Sleep their Enemies invade:

(As by finesse the Greeks did once Destroy
The Troops that Rhesus brought to Succour Troy).
Th' Alert Gallant does thus with kinder Rage,
While the dull Husband snores, the Wife engage.
Yet sometimes Both Defeated of their Aim,
Repuls'd by Guards, Retire with Loss, and Shame.
Doubtful alike's the Fate of Arms and Love:
The Vanquish'd oft, at last, the Victors prove.
Disgrace befalls as well the Great and Small;
And Those scarce Rise, you'd swear could never Fall.
Let none then Think that Love's a Sport for Boys,
He must Drudge hard, Who gains its utmost Joys.

THE OAK AND THE DUNGHILL

WILLIAM BROOME 1689–1745

On a fair Mead a Dunghill lay,
That rotting smoakt, and stunk away;
To an excessive Bigness grown,
By Night-men's Labours on him thrown.
Ten thousand Nettles from him sprung;
Who ever came but near, was stung.
Nor ever fail'd He, to produce
The baneful Hemlock's deadly Juice:
Such as of old at Athens grew,
When Patriots thought it Phocion's Due;
And for the Man its Poison prest,
Whose Merit shone above the rest.
Not far from hence, strong-rooted stood
A sturdy Oak; it self a Wood!
With friendly Height, o'ertopt the Grove,
And Look'd the Fav'rite Tree of Jove.
Beneath his hospitable Shade,
The Shepherds all, at Leisure, plaid;
They fear'd no Storms of Hail, or Rain;
His Boughs protected all the Plain:

Gave Verdure to the Grass around,
And beautify'd the neighb'ring Ground.
The Gracious Landlord joy'd to see
The prosp'rous Vigour of his Tree;
And often sought, when in Distress,
This Oak's oracular Redress:
Sprung from the old Dodonian Grove,
Which told to Men the Will of Jove.
His Boughs He oft with Chaplets crown'd,
With Azure Ribbons bound them round;
And there, in Golden Letters wrought,
Ill to the Man, who Evil thought.

With envious Rage, the Dunghill view'd
Merit, with Honour, thus pursued.
Th'Injustice of the Times, he moan'd
With inward Jealousy, he groan'd.
A Voice at length, pierc'd thro' the Smoke,
And, thus, the Patriot Dunghill spoke.

If a proud Look forerun a Fall,
And Insolence for Vengeance call;
Dost Thou not fear, insulting Oak!
The just, th'impending Hatchet's Stroke?
When all the Farmers of the Town,
Shall come with Joy, to pull Thee down;
And wear thy Leaves, all blythe, and gay,
Some happy RESTORATION DAY.
For 'tis reserv'd to those good Times,
To punish all thy matchless Crimes.

Th'astonish'd Farmers all around
Stood gaping, at th'impetuous Sound;
The Dunghill in high Triumph lay,
And swore the Oak had nought to say.
His Work was done;——the Farmers All
Might gather round, and see him fall.
Not so th'Event.——the Oak was seen

To flourish more, in fresher green,
By Scandal unprovok'd He stood;
And answer'd thus, the Heap of Mudd.

When Folly, Noise, and Slander rage,
And Calumny reforms the Age;
They, in the Wise no Passions raise;
Their Clamours turn to real Praise.
Yet sure, hard-fated is the Tree,
Reduc'd to spatter Dirt, with Thee,
Soon should a Branch, from off my Side,
Chastise thine Insolence, and Pride,
Did not the Wise obtain their Ends,
As well from Enemies, as Friends.
Thus, some Increase thy Heap receives,
Ev'n from the falling of my Leaves:
Which, like false Friends, when dropt from Me,
Assimilate, and turn to Thee.
But be they thine.——New Seasons spread
New Honours, o'er my rising Head.

ESTHER

JOHN HENLEY 1692–1756

Her Person heightened with a Nobler Air,
Which breath'd from Conscious Merit living there;
Superior twin Harmony of Form,
All over one entire distinguish'd Charm:
Her Body, fragrant as the Rising Day;
Was made some Nameless, some Uncommon Way,
Of Something finer than the finest Clay:
Such as Descending Cherubs seem to wear,
When with a Saint in Visions they confer.
      Yet these embelishments were but design'd
Foils to the Lustre of a Fairer Mind:

So Golden Fruits in Silver Pictures lye,
And glow with Bolder Life upon the Eye
She all the turns of Varying Fortune prov'd,
To no Extreams irregularly mov'd;
She all the Arts of Speech completely knew
And, what was more, the Arts of Silence too.

TO CYNTHIA WITH A PRESENT OF CROW QUILLS

ROBERT POTTER 1721–1809

These wings, with art Daedalean taught to bear
Safely a new inhabitant of air;
Those silver plumes, whose imitated pride
For Loeda's love the king of heav'n belied,
The gayly-burnish'd pinions of each dove
Yok'd to the chariot of the queen of love,
In honour yield to these, that form the line
Where glows that strong, that piercing wit of thine;
Or wake the joyful strings, when touch'd by thee,
To all the pow'r of melting melody:
With these the wanton archer of the sky
Arms all his golden shafts, and gives them wings to fly.

OF ENGLISH HUSBANDS

HUMPHREY SMYTHIES 1724–1806

Learn the advantages of age and clime.
Ladies immur'd in Homer's blinder days,
Till wedded, ne'er partook the banquet's cheer;
They spun and wove, and washed the regal robes.
After coarse feeding on the ram he stabb'd
And dress'd; each Prince took to his foul embrace
A captive maid, his share of spoil of war.

The brutish Turk, unnumbered damsels please.
The Spaniards and Italians, hold your sex
In dismal durance—Germans never melt
In love's soft flame, unconscious of your sex
Their wives but moving chattels—Ancient Rome,
The world subdu'd, was slav'd by beastly lusts,
Taught by the letter'd Greeks; their Ladies wept,
Husbands estranged by Asiatic boys.

  When warlike Caesar sought our untried shore,
The British Fair, in hutts begirt with woods,
Pass'd the dull day in drudgery and dirt;
As elegant the natives of the Cape,
Or Huron's North, or Afric's sooty wives,
Boughs in their hands, and nestling at their backs
A flat-nosed brat, whilst under downright rays
Of blazing suns, they tramp on parched sands.
Look round the habitable world, how few
Know woman's worth! Britons alone rejoice
In the fair partners of their bed and pow'r,
Gaze on their eyes, and tolerate their tongues.

A CHARACTER

CLARA REEVE 1729–1807

A QUAKER's stiffness, with a tradesman's grin;
A jesuit's conscience, with an open mien;
A tailor's breeding, with a courtier's art;
A zealot's fury, with an atheist's heart;
These are thy honours!—Not thy wild expense,
Fed and supported by the public pence,
Poured forth in awkward, splendid, motley treats,
Where dirt with cleanness, want with fullness meets.
Devoured by hungry parsons, sots and fools,
All well-picked, servile, suppliant, fawning tools:
Who with dull flatt'ry, and admiring eyes,
Applaud thy bawdy, blasphemy and lies.

CAPTAIN CUPID

JAMES MARRIOTT 1730–1803

Erst, in Cynthera's sacred shade,
When Venus clasp'd the God of War,
The laughing loves around them play'd
One bore the shield, and one the spear.

The little warriors Cupid led;
The gorget glitter'd on his breast;
The mighty helmet o'er his head
Nodded its formidable crest.

Oft since to win some stubborn maid,
Still does the wanton God assume
The martial air, the gay cockade,
The sword, the shoulder-knot and plume.

Phyllis had long his power defy'd,
Resolv'd her conquests to maintain;
His fruitless art each poet try'd:
Each Shepherd tun'd his pipe in vain.

Till Cupid came, a captain bold:
Of trenches and of palisades
He talk'd; and many a tale he told
Of battles, and of ambuscades.

How oft his godship had been drunk;
What melting maids he had undone;
How oft by night had storm'd a punk,
Or bravely beat a saucy dun;

He swore, drank, whor'd, sung, danc'd with spirit,
And o'er each pleasing topic ran;
Till Phyllis sigh's and own'd his merit,
The Captain's sure a charming man!

Ye bards, on verse let Phoebus doat,
Ye Shepherds, leave your pipes to Pan;
Nor verse, nor pipe will Phyllis note,
The Captain is the charming man.

from AUSONIUS

WILLIAM SMITH 1730–1819

Nature, we grieve that thou giv'st flowers so gay,
Then snatchest Gifts thou shew'st so swift away.
A Day's a Rose's Life—How quickly meet,
Sweet Flower, thy Blossom and thy Winding Sheet!

THE FROG AND MOUSE FIGHT

EDWARD THURLOW 1731–1806

As with a Whirlwind all together come
Into one Spot. Two Heralds also come,
Carrying the Signal for the Fight: The Gnats,
Holding great Trumpets, sound the dread Alarm
Of Battle; while Saturnian Jove on high
Thunders the Signal of disastrous War.

High-Croak first wounded Lap-well with his Spear;
Amongst the foremost, through the Belly pierc'd
In the mid-Liver, down He tumbled prone,
And soil'd his soft Down: Next him Creep-Hole spear'd
The Son of Mud-born, and his stubborn Lance
Fix'd in his Breast; Him falling sable Death
Surpriz'd, and from the Body fled the Soul.

Then Marsh-Love slew Scoop-Cheese upon the Bank;
At Sight of Scrape-Ham, Calamint took Fright:
Flying, he plung'd into the Lake, and threw
His Shield away. Water-Love slew the King
Gnaw-Gammon: with a Stone in Hand he struck
The fore-Part of his Head, and through His Nose
The Brain rill'd; and the Earth was splash'd with Blood.
Lick-Table slew good Mud-Bed with his Spear,
Assailing Him, and Darkness veil'd his Eyes.
Weed-Biter spying Hunt-Stream, by the Feet
Dragg'd Him, and strangled in the Marsh, his Neck
Clasp'd in his Hand. Crumb-Catch his dying Friend
Reveng'd, and wounded Mud-Robe in the Paunch,
To the Mid-Liver; prone He fell; His Soul
To Pluto went.

There was among the Mice a stripling Boy,
Above the rest tall, fighting close, the Son
Of blameless Snare-Loaf; He resembled Mars
Himself, bold Scrap-Catch: singly He excell'd
In Battle all the Mice. He stood alone,
Aloof from others, by the Lake, elate
Threat'ning to end the Race of Warlike Frogs:

And he had done it, for his Might was great,
But that from Heaven the Son of Saturn saw
The Frogs with Pity, and strait sent Them Aid.
Sudden, with Anvil-Back, and crooked Claws,
Marching awry, They came, in Track oblique,
Pincer-mouth'd, Shell-skinn'd Bodies all of Bone,
Broad-back'd, their Shoulders shining forth, Bow-legg'd,
Their Joints well-knitted, in the Breast their Eyes,
Eight-footed, double-headed, many-claw'd,
They are call'd Crabs. Their Mouths snapp'd Tails of Mice,
And Feet, and Hands; and back their Spears were bent;
Whom the poor Mice shrunk under, nor bore up;
But turn'd to Flight. The Sun was setting now,
And of this One-Day War an End was made.

THE SPORTSMAN

RICHARD SHEPHERD 1732–1809

There are, who count it bliss supreme, to steep
Their humid temples in the midnight bowl:
But may he share the Virgin's just disdain,
That to bright beauty's roseate glow prefers
His minion glass, base rival of her charms.
Nor in the boisterous sportsman hope to find
The lover bland, who for the headlong chase
Quits the soft raptures of the nuptial bed,
Where joy remorseless reigns: and with display
Of reason little higher than the Brute
That bears his tyrant weight o'er hill and dale,
Speeds o'er the furrow'd glebe his wild career
While Echo glads his raptured Heart
With shout of men, and cry of opening hounds,
Concord discordant to a tasteful ear.
Mean time at home the solitary fair,
Lavinia, pity! poor Lavinia's fate,
Mourns that so slow the leaden-footed Hours

Pass o'er her widowed head, not thus designed:
Hours that should nimbly post on silken wings
Shedding the honey Balm of genial love.
But now the waning Day, the lagging dogs,
And the tired steed urged on with slackened reins,
Small earnest give of longer sport, while hope
Of converse conjugal unbends the brow
Of the fond fair. Yet o'er the evening's cheer
What other theme knows he to quicken time,
Than the stale praises of his favourite hounds,
This famed for fleetness, that for nicer nose,
And panegyricks on the feats of roan?
Or on the table, mark'd with gleevy Ale,
October-brewed, the Sportsman's beveridge,
He shows the various fortunes of the day.
Than Parleys these not the papaverous rod
Of Morpheus apter to promote repose,
To bed they hie; and morn's returning light
Recalls the British Nimrod to the field.

JOHNSON

CUTHBERT SHAW 1739–1771

Here Johnson comes, unblest with outward grace,
His rigid morals stamp'd upon his face.
While strong conceptions struggle in his brain;
(For even Wit is brought to bed with pain):
To view him, porters with their loads would rest,
And babes cling frighted to the nurse's breast.
With looks convuls'd, he roars in pompous strain,
And, like an angry lion, shakes his mane.
The Nine, with terror struck, who ne'er had seen,
Aught human with so horrible a mien,
Debating whether they should stay or run,
Virtue steps forth, and claims him for her son.

With gentle speech she warns him now to yield,
Nor stain his glories in the doubtful field;
But wrapt in conscious worth, content sit down,
Since Fame, resolv'd his various pleas to crown,
Though forc'd his present claim to disavow,
Had long reserv'd a chaplet for his brow.
He bows, obeys; for Time shall first expire,
Ere Johnson stay, when Virtue bids retire.

FROM THE WORKHOUSE

ANN CANDLER 1740–1814

Within these dreary walls confin'd
    A lone recluse, I live,
And, with the dregs of human kind
    A niggard alms receive.

No sympathising friend I find,
    Unknown is friendship here;
Not one to soothe, or calm the mind,
    When overwhelm'd with care.

The tales these eastern writers feign
    Like facts to me appear,
The fabled suff'rings they contain,
    I find no fictions here.

And since, in those romantic lays,
    My miseries combine
To bless my lengthen'd wane of days,
    Their bright reverse be mine.

Look down, O God! in me behold
    How helpless mortals are,
Nor leave me friendless, poor, and old,
    But guide me with thy care.

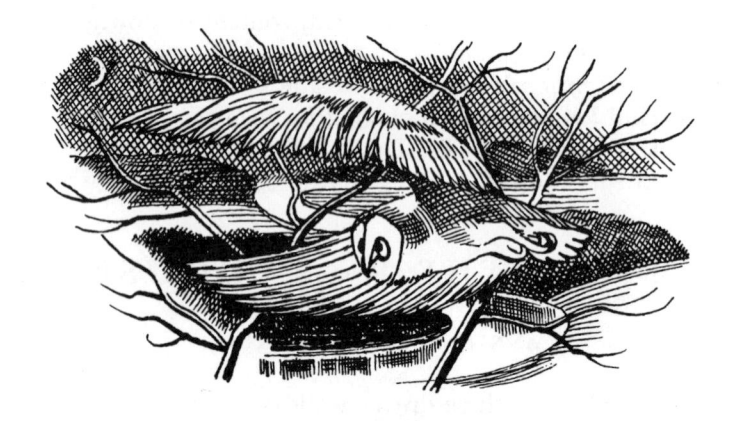

NIGHT ON THE ORWELL

W. PAGET c. 1741

The setting Sun was sunk beneath the Main,
And Cynthia shines with borrow'd Beams again,
The lonely Bird to his own Echo hoots,
And thro' the Gloom a doleful Accent shoots;
Sweet, afar off, the pensive Nightingale
To vocal Woods tells her lamenting Tale.
O blissful Bird! to live secure alone,
And to the Moon and Stars repeat thy Moan,
Wisest and sweetest of the tuneful Throng,
Nature attends in silence to thy Song,
What others shun is thy continu'd Choice,
Nor Noise nor Envy interrupt thy Voice.
As this I said, and upwards cast my Eye,
Behold the dark'ning Towers in the Sky,
Faintly inform me, wished for Ipswich nigh.

from TIBULLUS

SAMUEL HENLEY 1740–1815

No fame I seek, my Delia: if with thee
    I may but live, in glory I'd be poor:
Thee may I gaze on, till I cease to see;
    Thee clasp till, dying, I can hold no more.

Now let us while we may our loves unite;
    Death veil'd in gloom, will come with stealthy tread:
Surreptive age will numb each dear delight;
    Nor suits gay dalliance with a hoary head.

Venus, all-frolick, now may be enjoy'd,
    While a forc'd door and romp no shame bewray:
Here, a bold soldier, I the storm can guide;
    Standard and trumpets, hence ye, far away!

To those who glory covet, bear your wounds;
    And bear your wealth; I envy not the prize;
Secure, my wants I stint to narrow bounds,
    Despise the rich, and penury despise.

WASHING-DAY

ANNA LAETITIA BARBAULD 1743–1825

The Muses are turned gossips; they have lost
The buskined step, and clear high-sounding phrase,
Language of gods. Come then, domestic Muse,
In slipshod measure loosely prattling on
Of farm or orchard, pleasant curds and cream,
Or drowning flies, or shoe lost in the mire
By little whimpering boy, with rueful face;
Come, Muse, and sing the dreaded Washing-Day.

Ye who beneath the yoke of wedlock bend,
With bowed soul, full well ye ken the day
Which week, smooth sliding after week, brings on
Too soon; for to that day nor peace belongs
Nor comfort; ere the first gray streak of dawn,
The red-armed washers come and chase repose.
Nor pleasant smile, nor quaint device of mirth,
E'er visited that day: the very cat,
From the wet kitchen scared and reeking hearth,
Visits the parlour, an unwonted quest.
The silent breakfast-meal is soon dispatched,
Uninterrupted, save by anxious looks
Cast at the lowering sky, if sky should lower.
From that last evil, O preserve us, heavens!
For should the skies pour down, adieu to all
Remains of quiet: then expect to hear
Of sad disasters, dirt and gravel stains
Hard to efface, and loaded lines at once
Snapped short, and linen-horse by dog thrown down,
And all the petty miseries of life.
Saints have been calm while stretched upon the rack,
And Guatimozin smiled on burning coals;
But never yet did housewife notable
Greet with a smile a rainy washing-day.

from the French

WILLIAM CLUBBE 1745-1814

I THINK, cries Peter, (wond'rous witty)
If all the Cuckolds in our City
Collected on the shore could be,
And duck'd together in the sea,
The scene would make a deal of fun,
With little or no damage done.
Right, quoth his wife, who chance was standing near
It wou'd be fun—but can you swim, my dear?

CONSCIENCE

FITZ-JOHN BRAND 1746-1808

Two principles impell the human soul,
PASSION to urge, and CONSCIENCE to controul:
In nicest equipoize united still,
These balanced forces guide the human will:
As wheels some planet its perennial course,
Urged by attraction, and impulsive force;
With swift celerity this wings his way,
While that with gentle, secret, constant sway,
Makes man by force unseen, yet unwithstood,
Respect the central point of general good;
And more obedient to the sacred plan,
In that fixt orbit heaven prescribes to man:
Relax the golden chain, with mad career
And headlong fury, starting from his sphere
Like some red comet blazing through the skies,
Now here, now there, with maddening speed he flies,
Flames thro' the waste of life with lawless force,
And Plagues, and Death and Ruin mark his course.

[57]

ACROSTIC ON THE AUTHOR'S NAME

JAMES CHAMBERS 1748–1827

J ames Chambers is my name,
A nd I am scorn'd by rich and poor,
M any a weary step I came,
E nduring hardships very sore;
S o I design to take a wife,
C an I but have one to my mind,
H ence forth to live a better life,
A nd then we may true solace find;
M ay I but have the lass I love,
B oth to each other constant prove,
E ndeavour thus to live in peace,
R enewing love in every case,
S o to remain till life does cease.

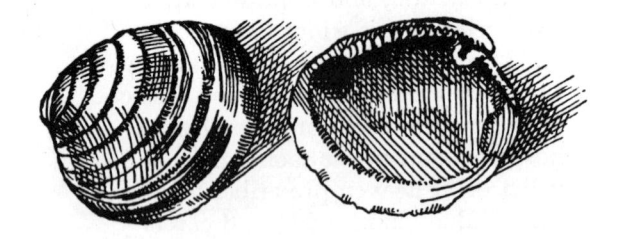

INSCRIPTION FOR A COLUMN AT RENNY MEDE

CAPEL LOFFT 1751–1824

Whoe'er thou art, if love of human kind
Dwell in thy bosom, pause; nor let the pomp
Of stately Windsor tempt thy foot from hence;
Nor pleasure, or the busy calls of life,
Urge thee to quit this Mead, ere thou revere
Beneath the open sky the Power unseen,
The guardian *Power of Freedom!*—Here arose
The *Majesty of England*; here was fix'd
The sacred law of Life and Liberty.
Hence the free *Judgment* of their *Equals* stood
Protective of the Peasant as the Prince;
And, save her own, Freedom heard no decree.
And hence the *Commons* to their Right restor'd
Became indeed a *People*; chang'd the yoke
Of kings and Barons for the equal rule
Of full consent: while Commerce, Science, Arts,
Glory and Virtue, hail'd th'immortal deed.
If captive France, within the neighbouring walls
Of yon proud palace, strike thy soul, confess
The source of triumph here; indulge her joy
Conscious of nobler victory, whose fruit
Hath been the bliss of ages.—Thus inspir'd,
How shall thy heart disdain the selfish pride
Of arbitrary rule by Kings assum'd,
Or Nations! with what transport shalt thou own
Those men thy brethren, wheresoe'er on earth,
Who know the value, and assert the cause,
Of self-dominion; nor will tamely quit,
Or impiously invade, the Rights of Men.

JAMES BLAND BURGES 1752–1824

Of Love I sing—not of that treacherous Boy
To whom the impure Venus erst gave birth,
Whose venomed shafts empoison mortal joy,
Confounding Honour, Virtue, Rank and Worth;
Whose midnight orgies stamp on lawless mirth
The forged image of celestial pleasure,
Drawing from heaven the soul of man to earth,
With foul alloy debasing purest treasure
That Boy, and that Boy's deeds shall not pollute my measure.

But Thee I sing, thou first great work of Heaven!
Pure Emanation of th'Eternal Mind!
Who, ere an impulse to our orb was given,
To guide th'unerring fabric wast designed.
Thee in each age and every clime we find,
From Zembla's frost to Afric's burning zone,
With Nature's laws and Nature's works combined;
Thy power in all created things is shewn,
And in the virtuous heart is fixed thy lasting throne.

I ask no Muse's aid thy deeds to sing,
Nor court in idle strain the tuneful Nine:
He little needs the Heliconian Spring,
Who owns the influence of Thy power divine.
Oh with thy sacred touch my heart refine!
Oh warm my soul with thy celestial ray!
Let Judgement, Fancy, Truth and Wit combine,
To tune my lyre and modulate my lay,
And grace the Tribute which to Virtuous Love I pay.

Oh Cherub! born the Universe to bless,
To guide it's laws, and harmonize its course,
Revolving ages shall thy power confess,
Bow to thy sway supreme, and own the force
Of thee, the cause of joy and pleasure's source.
Millions of willing slaves thy court shall throng,
Unchecked by guilty fear or foul remorse,
Midst new delights to boast thy influence strong,
And to Eternal Love to raise the grateful song.

THOUGHTS

SUSANNA HARRISON 1752–1784

How active, O how num'rous are my thoughts!
How hastily they fly from theme to theme!
Sometimes to heaven they take their airy flight,
Then down to hell as swiftly they descend,
Then round this habitable globe they rove,
Through seas, and fertile fields, and deserts rude;
Sometimes I roll in affluence and pride,
Then to the depths of poverty go down,
Where I must beg my bread, or starve and die;
Sometimes I reach a monarch's stately throne,
Then to the meanest cottage I retire;
Through various scenes I'm hurried to and fro;
From health to sickness, and from life to death;
Yet, in the midst of these unnumber'd thoughts,
Thy comforts, O my God! delight my soul.

Thee, thou eternal Spirit, I adore,
Who taught me to aspire to things divine;
Through whose free agency I can arise
And bid adieu to all created things!
Yea, I can tread the world beneath my feet,
And looking down, pronounce it vanity;
When wing'd with love to Jesus I can fly,
And towering far above the azure skies,
Can unmolested triumph in his smile,
There I survey the wonders of his cross,
And count the blessings purchas'd by his blood.
With his unerring word I there converse,
And rest secure upon his faithfulness.
His wisdom, justice, holiness, and love,
Uniting in redemption's work I view,
Till meditation kindles into praise;
Whilst, in the multitude of pleasing thoughts
Thy comforts, O my God! delight my soul.

R. C. DALLAS 1754–1824

An Ass, says Esop, died betwixt
    Two ricks of hay;
On neither could his choice be fixt,
    So down he lay.

A twelvemonth full young Damon stood
    By Love suspended;
Now smiled on Chloe, now on Jude,
    And both commended.

But one at length, the chosen lass,
    He made his bride:
Was Damon now the greater Ass,
    Or he that died?

THE VILLAGE

GEORGE CRABBE 1754–1832

The Village life, and every care that reigns
O'er youthful peasants and declining swains;
What labour yields, and what, that labour past,
Age, in its hour of languor, finds at last;
What forms the real picture of the poor,
Demands a song—The Muse can give no more.
Fled are those times, if e'er such times were seen,
When rustic poets prais'd their native green;
No shepherds now in smooth alternate verse,
Their country's beauty or their nymphs' rehearse;
Yet still for these we frame the tender strain,
Still in our lays fond Corydons complain,
And shepherds' boys their amorous pains reveal,
The only pains, alas! they never feel.

Yes, thus the Muses sing of happy swains,
Because the Muses never knew their pains:
They boast their peasants' pipes, but peasants now
Resign their pipes and plod behind the plough;
And few amid the rural tribe have time
To number syllables and play with rhyme.

Ye gentle souls who dream of rural ease,
Whom the smooth stream and smoother sonnet please;
Go! if the peaceful cot your praises share,
Go look within, and ask if peace be there:
If peace be his—that drooping weary sire,
Or their's, that offspring round their feeble fire,
Or her's, that matron pale, whose trembling hand
Turns on the wretched hearth th'expiring brand.
Nor yet can time itself obtain for these
Life's latest comforts, due respect and ease;

For yonder see that hoary swain, whose age
Can with no cares except its own engage;
Who, propt on that rude staff, looks up to see
The bare arms broken from the withering tree;
On which a boy, he climb'd the loftiest bough,
Then his first joy, but his sad emblem now.

He once was chief in all the rustic trade,
His steady hand the straitest furrow made;
Full many a prize he won, and still is proud
To find the triumphs of his youth allow'd;

A transient pleasure sparkles in his eyes,
He hears and smiles, then thinks again and sighs;
For now he journeys to his grave in pain;
The rich disdain him; nay, the poor disdain;
Alternate masters now their slave command,
And urge the efforts of his feeble hand;
Who, when his age attempts its task in vain,
With ruthless taunts of lazy poor complain.

Oft may you see him when he tends the sheep,
His winter charge, beneath the hillock weep;
Oft hear him murmur to the winds that blow
O'er his white locks, and bury them in snow;
When rouz'd by rage and muttering in the morn,
He mends the broken hedge with icy thorn.

"Why do I live, when I desire to be
At once from life and life's long labour free?
Like leaves in spring, the young are blown away,
Without the sorrows of a slow decay;
I, like yon wither'd leaf, remain behind,
Nipt by the frost and shivering in the wind;
There it abides till younger buds come on,
As I, now all my fellow swains are gone;
Then, from the rising generation thrust,
It falls, like me, unnotic'd to the dust.

"These fruitful fields, these numerous flocks I see,
Are others' gain, but killing cares to me;
To me the children of my youth are lords,
Slow in their gifts but hasty in their words;
Wants of their own demand their care, and who
Feels his own want and succours others too?
A lonely, wretched man, in pain I go,
None need my help and none relieve my woe;
Then let my bones beneath the turf be laid,
And men forget the wretch they would not aid."

Thus groan the old, till by disease opprest,
They taste a final woe, and then they rest.

WILLIAM HURN 1754-1829

Tapering above the polished rod he holds,
And the long line of glossy silk unfolds;
With scarlet tipt the dancing feather flies
To mark the entangled prey, and future prize.
Now, sinking deep, it leaves his gladdening sight;
And, lo! . . . . . . a struggling perch is dragg'd to light!
The beauteous victim mourns his native sand;
In agony the golden fins expand
And strike the unwelcome grass and fatal land.

Some, where the pebbled current gurgles by,
Whirl on its surface the insiduous fly:
The lively dace behold the floating freight,
Rush at the lure, and seize the barbed bait;
But, doom'd to swell their bubbling stream no more,
The jumping captives glitter on the shore!

So the sad votaries of Pleasure's wiles,
Who seek her varnish'd and pernicious smiles;
Caught by the gilded lure, too late they view
What woes for every transient joy ensue;
A direful pest their smiling goddess turns,
And the lost heart in pain reproachful burns.

BEAUTY

RICHARD VALPY 1754–1836

Nature, providently kind,
Arm'd with speed the trembling hind;
Lions with tremendous claws
Chasms of teeth and knotty paws;
Fins to scaly fish she gave,
Sporting in the chrystal wave;
To the warbling feathered race
Wings to cleave th'aerial space;
Guardian horns the bulls protend;
Pointed stings the bees defend:
Man's for wit and art renown'd,
With celestial wisdom crown'd.
Nature's gifts I see assigned:
What remains for womankind?
What has tender women shar'd?
Beauty, surest, safest guard.
Beauty's charms resistless prove;
All must yield to conquering love.

WILLIAM GODWIN 1756–1836

Oh, Helen, have I seen thee for the last, last time!
It shall not be—Oh, what a thing is man!
More fell than tigers o'er their gasping prey,
With cool deliberate mind he searches out
The vein where sovereign sense resides, the point,
Where we are most alive to nameless anguish,
And skips, and laughs, and revels in our torture.

But, no, it cannot be, there is no man,
That holds this empire o'er me.
I'll rase each monastry throughout the realm,
I'll scatter flames and death on ev'ry side,
Churches shall blaze, and ruin mark my progress.
What shall I do? Oh, whither, whither turn me?
Lost, peerless, lovely, angel Helena.

THETFORD

GEORGE BLOOMFIELD 1757–1831

The poets, one and all, were wont to choose
Some fabled, fav'rite Goddess, as their muse.
But gratitude alone my mind inspires,
No other Muse my simple pen requires.
When erst in youth's gay prime and uncontrolled
O Thetford! round thy flow'ry fields I've strolled,
From Tutt-Hill's eminence and Croxton's height,
Have view'd thine ancient ruins with delight,
Thy sloping hills and wooded vallies gay,
Whose silv'ry Ouse meand'ring winds his way.
Though then, each lofty mound, each ruin'd tower,
Told but of war, and time's destructive power;
And thou, thy pristine grandeur long had'st lost,
Nor more of Kings, or mighty chiefs could boast;
Yet heartfelt joys beneath thy roots I found,
And peace, with all the social blessings crown'd.
To tune his reed, and sing they healing streams,
Then enter'd not the Bard's enraptur'd dreams,
But now the Muse exultingly may sing,
The well attested virtues of thy Spring;
Since erudition and clear truth unite
To chase all fear, and set the judgment right.

THE CALL OF THE GENTILES

SPENCER MADAN 1758–1836

REMEMBER Lord,
And save the Creature of thy plastic Hand,
Whether Thou view'st him wand'ring on the Waste
Of Polar Zembla, Continent of Ice!
Or breathing rude Idolatry and Vows
Of prostrate Adoration at the Shrine
Of Thibet's hapless Lama! Wretched being
Less free, less happy, less a God than e'en
His vilest Votary!—Yet not alone
To the swart Savage of the barb'rous East,
The beaded Hottentot, or naked Slave
Who toils, untutor'd, in the guilty Mine,
Reveal thy saving Arm! But turn, O turn
The blinder Infidel, of every Name,
Or gross Mahometan, or stubborn Jew,
Or desperate Atheist, who mocks thy Pow'rs
With purpos'd Insult. Turn them, Lord, and save
And win them to thyself! O quickly bring
To Sharon's Fold and Achor's happy Vale
Thy full united Flock!

ELIZABETH GOOCH *b.* 1758

I'LL barter happiness for wealth;
Divert my mind—recruit my health
Smile at a mighty train of foes
Suspense, the prince of human woes,
No more my timid soul beguiles;
For through my tears I'll show my smiles.

I fondly thought Contentment's bow'r
Sacred to Honour's sov'reign pow'r;
And that the vicious mind alone
Was banish'd from her modest throne.
But, ah! I feel the dire mistake,
And from the sweet illusion wake!
The heart, depraved by abject wiles,
Basks in the sunshine of her smiles:
Where Fortune's aid is not deny'd,
Contentment's share is soon supply'd;
While the best lesson Art can give
Consists in knowing—how to live!
    Farewell the philanthropic mind,
To Love and Honour, both, inclin'd.
Farewell the unsuspecting heart,
That bears in ev'ry pang a part!
For I, alas! will build no more
My pleasures on a sinking shore;
But, since the wayward world I've seen,
Be all—that I would not—have been!

MORE BREAD AND CHEESE

NATHANIEL BLOOMFIELD *b.* 1759

My Brothers of this world, of ev'ry Nation,
Some maxims of prudence the Muse would inspire.
Now restlessness reigns throughout every station;
The low would be high, and the high would be higher;
    Now Freedom's the word,
    That unsheaths ev'ry sword,
But don't be deceiv'd by such pretexts as these:
    'Tis not Freedom, nor Slavery,
    That calls for your Bravery;
Tis only a Scramble for more Bread and Cheese.

THE ROSES

ALICE FLOWERDEW 1759–1830

From Nature's book I live to draw
   The pure, the moral lay;
There's not a Flower that meets my eye,
   But wisdom doth convey.

Within my Garden's sweet retreat,
   Two beauteous Roses grew;
Alike their early buds disclos'd,
   Tints of the brightest hue.

Surrounded by each Flow'ret gay,
   One grew with tow'ring pride;
Though all around her brightly shone,
   None with her beauties vy'd.

Expanding fair, alas! she stood
   Two much expos'd to view;
The Sun's bright beams impair'd her charms,
   Ere yet matur'd they grew.

The blushing damask of her leaves,
   I saw it early fade;
Encircled by the gay she droop'd,
   And faintly sunk her head.

And thus, ye fair, the moral speaks
   Beware of Fashion's pow'r;
Nor in those circles pass your bloom,
   Where pleasure fills each hour.

The other Rose, with gentle mien,
   Shrinking from common view,
Shelter'd beneath a spreading elm,
   In calm retirement grew.

Its fragrance fill'd the balmy air,
  In glowing tints array'd;
Softly it drew th'admiring eye,
  And Beauty's worth display'd.

It flourish'd long, and gently sunk,
  Diffusing sweets around;
The dropping leaves unfaded fell,
  And scented all the ground.

So shall the Nymph, retir'd from view,
  With modest graces shine;
Nor shall her charms neglected be,
  Or unadmir'd decline.

Beneath the dear and shelt'ring roof
  Of kind parental care,
The Man of Worth will ever find,
  Beauty most lovely there!

TO THE PARCAE

HANNAH BRAND *b. circa* 1760

INEXORABLE Triad! tell us! where,
  In what vast Antre, or what Cypress grove,
Your gloomy Altars trembling mortals rear;
  And what the hallow'd Sacrifice ye love?

Two Sisters are we, who in life's rough way,
  Full early enter'd 'neath a baneful Star,
Together, though unbless'd with one bright ray,
  We bear the hardships of its constant war.

No dearer Friendship, and no separate Joy,
  Has e'er estrang'd us from each others heart,
No Strife has ever mingled its alloy,
  In Good, or Ill, each had a Sister's part.

Such, ye stern Parcae! are your Suppliants now;
   Seeking Protection from one dreaded Ill:
We ask not Wealth, nor Honours for our Brow;
   Unmurmuring we have liv'd without them still.

CLOTHO! thy Distaff at thy pleasure fill:—
   E'en though the flax with rugged Knots be cross'd;
LACHESIS! draw our Threads together still,
   We heed not, whether long, or short thou draw'st:

When, to their length, th'appointed Threads are spun,
   Them to the fatal Shears together guide:
Swiftly, O ATROPOS! thy task be done,
   The Sister Threads at the same Stroke divide.

ATROPA

LA FAUSSE AVARE

SAMUEL ASHBY 1761–1833

Phyllis protests, no kisses she bestows;
Yet oft' she's kissed, if seeing is believing!
Phyllis is sly, and well the baggage knows
How to return each kiss she is receiving.

THOMAS MOTT 1761–1788

'Tis silence all around—save when is heard
The Perched screech-owl's shriek, and raven's croak,
The sudden busy clack of neighb'ring mill,
And solitary bleat of straggling sheep.
The midnight hour is past! nor longer now
The glow-worm's lamp of love[1] illumes her track.
The moon's gone down—and soon the stars will fade,
And village chanticleer, from neighbouring roost,
Give greeting to the morn. Lov'd scenes adieu
Receding from thy shades, a tear drop falls,
To think that, in my wanderings, I may ne'er
Behold thee more. Lov'd scenes farewell—and chance
I bid thee now a long—a last adieu.

---

[1] I refer to the light in the tail of the Glow-worm. The Glow-worm is a female CATERPILLAR; the male of which is a FLY. The Caterpillar cannot meet her companion in the air. The winged rover disdains the ground. They might never therefore be brought together, did not this radiant torch direct the volatile male to his sedentary female.

from HORACE

ROBERT BRADSTREET 1764–1836

Blest is he, who far from business,
   With his herd, like man's first race,
Ploughs his own paternal acres
   Free from every interest base!
He at war's fierce trumpet starts not,
   Dreads not Ocean's anger loud;
Comes not near the clamorous Forum
Nor the great man's threshold proud.
But the vine's maturer offspring,
   Joys with poplar tall t'espouse;
Or, amid the deep vale lowing,
   Sees his wandering cattle browze.
Or, the useless branch removing,
   Grafts the bough of fair increase;
Presses in pure jars the honey,
   Shears the sheep's encumb'ring fleece.

When the blustering Jove in winter
   Stormy rain, and snow prepares:
Savage boars with dogs he urges
   Right against the tangling snares:
Slender nets for greedy thrushes,
   Joys on taper pole to rear:
Or in gins, delighted captures,
   Alien crane, or timorous hare.

Thus, about to be a farmer,
   Did the us'rer Alphius say:
Call'd his money home in April
   Lent it out again in May.

SUFFOLK CHEESE

ROBERT BLOOMFIELD 1766–1823

UNRIVALL'D stands thy country CHEESE, O Giles!
Whose very name alone engenders smiles;
   Whose fame abroad by every tongue is Spoke,
The well-known butt of many a flinty joke,
That pass like current coin the nation through;
And, ah! experience proves the satire true.
Provision's grave, thou ever craving mart,
Dependant, huge Metropolis! where Art
Her poring thousands stows in breathless rooms,
Midst pois'nous smokes and steams, and rattling looms;
Where Grandeur revels in unbounded stores;
Restraint, a slighted stranger at their doors!
Thou, like a whirlpool, drain'st the countries round,
Till London market, London price, resound
Through every town, round every passing load,
   And dairy produce throngs the eastern road:
Delicious veal, and butter, every hour,
From Essex lowlands, and the banks of Stour;
And further far, where numerous herds repose,
   From Orwell's brink, from Waveny, or Ouse.
Hence Suffolk dairy-wives run mad for cream,
And leave their milk with nothing but its name;
Its name derision and reproach pursue,
And strangers tell of "three times skim'd sky-blue".
To cheese converted, what can be its boast?
What, but the common virtues of a post!
If drought o'ertake it faster than the knife,
Most fair it bids for stubborn length of life,
And, like the oaken shelf whereon 'tis laid,
Mocks the weak efforts of the bending blade;
Or in the hog-trough rests in perfect spite,
Too big to swallow, and too hard to bite.

from THE REV. WILLIAM CLUBBE'S TRANSLATION

Caseus indigena his terris, O Mopse, per orbem
Terrarum totum similem non invenit ullum.
Fame per externas regiones transvolat aeque
Omnibus in populis agitans irasque jocosque:
O quam saepe jocum! *bilem* quam saepe dedisti!
Atque aptum Satyrae quis te nimis esse negarit?
O frugum tumulus! barathum insatiabile! et urbium
Maxima! qua florent artes, qua millia centum
Vix spirant hominum; denso qua turbine fumus
Suffocat et pejus nigris olet aura venenis;
Divitiis parens spernit qua fraena voluptas
Nec modus in rebus prudens agnoscitur ullis:
Tu LONDINE, velut torrens fluis omnia tecum
Quidlibet est pretii vastato ex rure reportans;
Quod reliquum est pretii pretiosius usque relinquens.
"Assibus heus quotquot, Mercator?" *Non minus asse
Londini pretio*, quisque audit rusticus emptor.
Londinum versus vitulos *Essexia* mittit,
Sturaque tarda fluit stipato onerata butyro:
Longius *Orwelli* distanti a littore et *Ozoe*
Londinum ruris devexa est gaza per undas.
Hinc illae lacrymae-furor hinc uxoris avarae
Expressi lactis parce distringere florem:
Dedecus hinc vestrum, Suffolcia; et inde jocus stat,
Qui color albus erat, vasi ter coerulus exit.
Tali ex materie quid ligno mollius ortum.
Expectare datur? Quae, Caseus, est tibi virtus
Quam non ulmorum gestit sibi dura vetustas?
Natus in extremam aetatem es, nisi culter acutus
Non siccum scindat; citius nam postea quercus
Qua restas cultri victorem agnoscet acumen.
Forsitan, et maneas porcis comedendus—at illis
Gutture voraci, nec duro dente domaris.

POOR LUCKLESS MARY

ELIZABETH COBBOLD 1766–1825

WHAT form in yonder dewy vale
   Gathers the worm-wood, rue and clary?
One late the pride of Wensley dale,
      Poor luckless Mary.

Her soul was pure, her heart was gay,
   And light her step as any fairy,
And sweetly beam'd the morning ray
      On smiling Mary.

Her Father's homely board she drest
   With simplest viands, neat though chary,
And he, at evening, grateful blest
      His darling Mary.

Alas! that fortune gave a lot
   To youth's fair prospects so contrary,
Beguil'd by love she left her cot,
         Imprudent Mary!

Quick changing as the clouds of morn,
   Her love forgot his promise airy,
And to the world's unfeeling scorn
         Deserted Mary.

With tears and agony of grief
   Her Father mourn'd his child unwary,
Till idiot stuper gave relief
         To sighs for Mary.

And when she view'd his pallid cheek,
   How fast the rose of hers would vary!
She look'd to Heav'n with aspect meek;
         Heav'n pitied Mary.

And now a Parent's age to cheer
   She sells the worm-wood, rue and clary;
They bitter herbs, thy bitterer tear,
         Shall bless thee Mary.

from AN ODE TO NIGHT

NATHAN DRAKE 1766–1836

FORTH from his den the Lion breaks,
   His form thick-hung with clotted gore,
Whilst full in front wild Slaughter shrieks,
   And Nature trembles at the roar;
Madd'ning he foams, and tears the ground,
   Scourging his sides with sullen joy;
Red his stern eye-balls gleam around,
   And flash, keen-searching to destroy.

Hark! o'er sad Afric's torrid waste,
    Floats the deep yell of wild despair,
Now death the writhing victims taste,
    And load with groans the passing air:
When thus they shadowy tints allure
    To savage deeds of hell-born hue,
That haunt thy dark, thy dread obscure,
    And blend with blood thy pearly dew;
Say then! shall Fancy add a thought
    From Superstition's baneful store,
And, mid thy gloom, with danger fraught,
    Plant one dire, dismal feeling more?

CARMEN SECULARE PRO GALLICA GENTE 1791

LAWRENCE HALLORAN 1766–1831

B<small>RING</small>, boy, with speed the sounding lyre;
Let Sappho's Muse my breast inspire;
I feel, I feel a sudden fire
    Dart thro' each trembling vein.

Raptur'd, I sing those wrongs redrest,
That fir'd a gen'rous Nation's breast,
Fetter'd too long; too long opprest
    With Slavery's iron chain.

I sing the Golden Age restor'd;
Themis again on earth ador'd;
While o'er the realm a bounteous Lord,
    His people's Father reigns.

Lo! Aristocracy o'er thrown,
(The direst Monster Earth has known)
Now pours in turn th'unpitied groan,
    And flies th'enfranchised plains.

Let the glad Matrons with delight
To noble deeds their Sons incite;
To assert their own, and Country's right,
    And guard their trembling age;

And the chaste Maid, with decent pride
Rejoic'd to be a Freeman's bride,
With Honor, Truth, and Worth allied,
    In Hymen's bands engage.

Illustrious Chiefs, and Barons bold,
Champions in Freedom's cause of old,
With wonder now a field behold,
    That Runimede excels;

While Paris (Wondrous as it seems)
Free as Augusta quaffs her dreams;
And Seine, more free than sacred Thames,
    With copious Current swells.

THE RECRUITING SERGEANT

JOHN WEBB *b.* 1767?

MAKE way, ye smiling crowds, those fifes and drums
Proclaim the gay Recruiting Sergeant comes,
With measured step he boldly strides along,
The gaze and wonder of the village throng.
While brandishing the burnished blade on high,
He views the crowd with supercilious eye;
No chief returned from glory's tented plain,
Though honour rank him with her titled train,
Though glory for his brow her wreaths prepare,
Assumes such state or moves with such an air.
But mark! when lucre prompts, he can unbend,
And treat each humble stranger as a friend;

With graceful ease can happy freedoms take,
Give each rough hand the frank and hearty shake;
Troll the light catch, and tell the frolic tale,
And freely push about the mantling ale.
Won by his lures, some youth devoid of art,
Unmindful of a maiden's aching heart,
Regardless of a father's manly sigh,
Or the big drops that drown a mother's eye,
Accepts the boon, and spends the golden fee
In the mad scenes of midnight revelry,
Till from the friends that loved him called afar,
To learn on distant plains the trade of war.

THE ABORIGINAL BRITONS

GEORGE RICHARDS 1768–1837

Rude as the wilds around his sylvan home
In savage grandeur see the Briton roam.
Bare were his limbs, and strung with toil and cold,
By untam'd nature cast in giant mould.

O'er his broad brawny shoulders loosely flung
Shaggy and long his yellow ringlets hung.
His waist an iron-belted falchion bore,
Massy, and purpled deep with human gore:
His scarr'd and rudely-painted limbs around
Fantastic horror striking figures frown'd,
Which, monster-like, ev'n to the confines ran
Of nature's work, and left him hardly man.
His knitted brows and rolling eyes impart
A direful image of his ruthless heart;
Where war and human bloodshed brooding lie,
Like thunders lowering in a gloomy sky.
No tender virgin heard th'impassion'd youth
Breathe his warm vows, and swear eternal truth:
No sire, encircled by a blooming race,
View'd his own features in his infant's face:
The savage knew not wedlock's chaster rite;
The torch of Hymen pour'd a common light;
As passion fir'd, the lawless pair were bless'd;
And babes unfather'd hung upon the breast.

SONG

H. F. R. SOANE 1768–1803

WE snapt the golden cord in twain
    That bound my love and me:
Till each exclaimed, Restore my chain,
    If this be Liberty.

Welcome the golden cord again
    That binds my love and me!
Till Life's last hour I'll hug my chain,
    If this be Slavery.

WILLIAM COLE 1769–1835

The dreadful scourge of war is o'er,
    No more the cannon's rattle
Echoes back from shore to shore,
    To tell the blood-stain'd battle
  Fill the goblet, fill it high,
  Heroes we'll toast twenty,
  For mirth sparkles in each eye,
  Now blest with Peace and Plenty.

Our Navy with their gaudy prows
    In triumph plough'd old Ocean
And leaders grac'd with laurel'd brows,
    Returning gain'd promotion,
  Fill the goblet, fill it high,
  Heroes we'll toast twenty,
  For mirth sparkles in each eye,
  Now blest with Peace and Plenty.

Now the sword is sheath'd, I trust
    Dies all secret faction,
In its scabbard may it rust
    Ere forc'd again to action.
    Fill the goblet, fill it high,
    Heroes we'll toast twenty,
    For mirth sparkles in each eye,
    Now blest with Peace and Plenty.

Thus blest with Plenty, blest with Peace,
    Long may we revere them,
May England's happiness increase,
    And we live long to share them.
    Fill the goblet, fill it high,
    Enliven all before us,
    To GEORGE, his gracious Majesty,
    And England's weal in chorus.

THE LOVERS

THOMAS GREENE 1769–1825

While in his arms the am'rous boy
The lovely Delia's charms embrac'd,
Clasp'd more than monarchs can enjoy,
And seiz'd her round her slender waist;
      Caress'd her,
      Possess'd her,
    And to his breast prest her;
      Sweetly toying,
      And enjoying
All with which kind heav'n had blest her:
"If I don't love thee beyond measure,
"Sweetest angel! dearest treasure
"Drifted on some barren shore,
"May I never never more
"Once renew this genial pleasure;

"May I on the burning sands
"Of torrid Afric's desert lands,
"Vainly calling on thy name;
"Parch'd with thirst and heat expire
"Panting, gasping in the fire;
"Fire less fierce than Cupid's flame."

He said and Cupid, proud to please,
Gave a favourable sneeze.
While beauteous Delia, sweetly coy,
Turning to the am'rous boy;
Grace, and buxom beauty turning,
And her yielding bosom burning
With those lips that lovers court;
Blushing at the wanton sport,
Bath's his eyes in luscious kisses,
Eyes that twinkled with desire;
Steep'd their little loves in kisses,
Quenching, kindling all their fire.
And is not this the height of joy?
Tell me, you little, titt'ring boy
Tell me, you little, smirking miss
Do you not long for joys like this?
Pedants and prudes so cold to blisses,
Envy you not such hugs and kisses? —ha?—

TO MY KNITTING PINS

DOROTHY COBBOLD 1770–1857

Heroic deeds and high achievements bold,
Let gifted bards in lofty strains unfold:
While I with grateful zeal in humble verse,
The praises of my Knitting Pins rehearse.
Ye four bright wires, so slender and so smooth,
How many wakeful nights y've helped to soothe!
Nor have ye fail'd, through many a darksome day,
To keep the potent fiend, Ennui, at bay;
Affording occupation mute and kind,
Taxing no powers of body or of mind;
Leaving them free their higher dues to pay
Fresh air to breathe—to meditate or pray.
Nor is your homely labour without use,
While, with unvarying twitch, you noose by noose
Draw in succession, till at length appears
A full-grown stocking! and let him who wears
Th' elastic web, in truth and justice own
'Tis warm and strong, though beauty it has none.
Then while the lofty mountain we admire,
Let not the gentle rill unpraised retire.

THE BULL FIGHT

JAMES DEARE 1770–1824

But no precautions more confirms their strength
Than from their minds to avert the stings of love,
For, seen, the female by degrees corrodes
And saps their vigour: hence nor shade delights
Nor pasture longer on their memory dwells.
Oft too her charms the flame of war illume,
And move her haughty lovers to the fight.

While o'er the lawn the beauteous heifer feeds,
They with alternate and repeated wound
Conflicting rage: a dark sanguineous stream
Laves their gored sides, and now, with hideous roar,
They rush again, each on his steadfast foe.
Thus from mid-sea the lengthened billow rears
Its foaming head, and, with increasing swell,
Rolls to the shore, and bursts amongst the rocks
With deafening sound nor less than mountain's bulk.
Deep boil the whirlpools, and the miry sand
Is cast aloft from ocean's turbid bed.

EPITAPH ON A DORMOUSE

JOHN FENN *b. circa* 1770

In paper-case, hard by this place,
   Dead a poor dormouse lies;
And soon or late, summon'd by fate,
   Each prince, each monarch dies:
Ye sons of verse, whilst I rehearse,
   Attend to th'instructive rhyme;
No sins had Dor, to answer for,
   Repent of your's in time.

THE HALESWORTH DUNCIAD

JOHN HUGMAN 1770-1846?

Dennant! great Censor-general of the stage,
I've read thy learned pamphlet page by page;
Good Heaven! what brilliant satire fires each line,
Flash after flash, how awful! how divine!
Eternal blessings light upon that head,
Whose deep researches harrow up the dead;
Whose heart undaunted combats ev'ry toil,
Consumes the daily light, the midnight oil;
Who takes the literary field with spears,
And barbed arrows of two thousand years.
I like the man, who with a God-like arm,
Secures the sheep, and keeps the wolves from harm;
Who from the pulpit notifies his rage,
And from the press completely damns the stage.
Not Agamemnon, at the seige of Troy,
Nor Hector, Priam's bullying, fighting boy;
Not fam'd Achilles, clad in scales of steel,
And vulnerable only in the heel;
Nor Hercules, I mean the sportive He,
Who us'd to tick and toy with Omphale,
Wrapp'd in the dread Nemaean lion's skin,
Was half so fierce without, or fierce within,
As you, our Champion, when you sallied forth,
Keen as rude Boreas from his native north,
With hosts of Moralists, to aid your tale,
Enow to turn the very devil pale.
Your ancient fathers of the Christian church,
Wielded full oft the moralizing birch;
Scourg'd well the players, and the audience too,
Till ev'ry mother's child look'd black and blue.
Then said, we do not relish, as you find,
These second-rate instructors of mankind;

We'll have no farces, you immoral elves,
Save what in wisdom we perform ourselves;
No tales of gallantry your wives shall hear
Except at matins, or at evening prayer.
Your daughter's inmost wishes we'll insure,
And by confessionals retain them pure;
With holy converse perfect all their charms,
Then grant some patient husband to their arms;
Some pious man, who seeks not carnal love,
But trusts for happiness to God above.
What more, ye ingrates! would you have us do?
Speak softly!—what! what get your children too!

TO A LADY WHO HAD A FINE PAIR OF EYES BUT A DISCORDANT VOICE

RICHARD BURNETT 1772–

Lucetta's charms our hearts surprize
  At once with joy and wonder;
She bears Jove's lightening in her eyes
  But in her voice his thunder.

LINES TO A BOY PURSUING A BUTTERFLY

MRS. COCKLE 1772–1836

Stay, thoughtless urchin, nor destroy
Yon insect's little hour of joy!
Yon lovely flutterer was born
To frolic thro' a summer morn,
To sip the dew from every flower
That blushes round Sophia's bower:
Now, on the Lily's snowy head
Behold its azure mantle spread;
Now, sudden starts the fickle thing,
And hovers on its burnished wing,
Its little task beneath the sky
But to be happy, and to die.

Poor Elf! how like yon gaudy fly
Thou sport'st beneath the summer sky!
A lovely mirthful thing art thou,
With thornless heart and cloudless brow.
Some ruthless hand may o'er thee come
And from thy beauty brush the bloom,
Even as thy hand would now destroy
Yon lovely insect's short-lived joy.

FROM THE PETITION OF AN UNINHABITED HOUSE

CHARLES VALENTINE LE GRICE 1773–1858

ONCE the firm Guardian of the racy wines
Against the wall my Cellar-door reclines
Unlock'd, unhing'd; while thro' the dark profound
The empty Pipe emits a mornful sound.
Of cork-less Carcases a dreary row
Moulder in catacombs, that gape below.
Sons of the social hour, shed sorrows here!
If e'er ye wept, weep o'er the Bottled Bier.
Why starts my Muse? why trembling turns her head?
Views she some friend amid the mighty dead?
She views thy corpse, O Port, and mourns thy spirit fled.

    Shelves unburthen'd with a plate,
    Chimnies yawning for a grate,
    Knives and forks without a handle
    Candlesticks without a candle;
    Nail'd-up doors, and hinges rusty;
    Here the Dry-Rot, foul and dusty,
    There the Mildew damp and musty;
    Cupboards wide, in cruel mockery,
    Oping doors to shew no crockery;
    Corn-less Binns, and horse-less Stables,
    Salt-less Salt-box, meatless Tables;

Chairs untouch'd by mortal bottom,
(If worms have not already got 'em,
Time may at his leisure rot 'em;)
Bats that stilly flit around,
Owls AT HOME in dose profound,
Skeleton of famish'd cat
Vainly watching for a rat;
All is cheerless, melancholy,
Save that now and then a Solitary COCK just struts about,
Gives a peep, and then struts out.

from the Italian
MATILDA BETHAM 1776–1852

WHILST zephyr sooths the angry waves
    Of Ocean into rest,
Each vessel is in safety borne,
    And every pilot blest.

But he indeed demands our praise,
    Who stems the tempest's force,
And midst the ire of hostile waves,
    Pursues his destin'd course.

THE BOWER OF PLEASURE
J. HAMILTON ROCHE *b. circa* 1780

WITHIN the Bower lies Pleasure sleeping,
    While near him mourns a blooming maid;
He will not wake, and she sits weeping,
    When lo! a stranger proffers aid.

His hurried steps—his glance of fire,
    The god of wishes wild declare:
Fond Pleasure wake! exclaim'd Desire,
    And Pleasure woke to bless the fair.

But soon the nymph, in luckless hour,
    Desire asleep was doom'd to view;
Try, Pleasure, try, she cried—your power,
    And wake Desire, as he woke you.

Fond girl! thy pray'r exceeds all measure,
    Distinct his province each must keep;
Desire must still awaken Pleasure,
    And Pleasure dull Desire to sleep.

REGRET

JOHN BENNETT 1781–1855

The grass grows,
    The hay charms,
The flower blows,
    The sun warms;
But never can my soul unfold,
My spirit's dead—my heart is cold.

The grass's mown,
    The hay drawn,
The flower borne,
    The sun gone;
What once I knew no more will be,
And all I loved is fled from me.

My tears rise,
    Sighs swell,
Hope dies,
    Joys fail:
Glad wishes now are at an end;
No comfort have I, nor a friend.

from the Spanish

CHARLES BUCKE 1781–1846

The days of our happiness gliding away,
A year seems a moment, and ages a day;
But Fortune converting our smiles into tears,
What an age a diminutive moment appears!

Oh! Fortune, —possess'd of so fickle a name
Why only in this art thou ever the same?
O change! and bid moments of pleasure move slow
And give eagle plumes to the pinions of woe.

P.S. FOR JESSE

JOHN MITFORD 1781–1859

Here I sit forlorn, and poke
   About my now deserted bower,
Very like Gray's owl at Stoke
   In his ivy-mantled tower.

I wish myself at Upton Park.
   Listening to your pleasant speeches,
How the Romans on the bark,
   Carved their names on Burnham Beeches.

I wish—but what's the use of wishes?
   All things here will end at last.
Life a kind of made-up dish is
   Whereso'er our lot is cast.

TO THE ORWELL

JOHN TALWIN SHEWELL 1782—1869

ORWELL, delightful stream, whose waters flow
   Fring'd with luxuriant beauty to the main!
   Amid thy woodlands taught, the Muse could fain,
On thee, her grateful eulogy bestow.
Smooth and majestic though thy current glide,
   And bustling Commerce plough thy liquid plain;
Tho' grac'd with loveliness thy verdant side,
   While all around enchantment seems to reign:
These glories still, with filial love, I taste,
   And feel their praise: yet thou hast one beside
   To me more sweet; for on thy banks reside,
Friendship and Truth combin'd; whose union chaste
Has sooth'd my soul; and these shall bloom sublime,
When fade the fleeting charms of Nature and of Time.

MY MOTHER

JANE AND ANNE TAYLOR 1783–1824, 1782–1866

Who fed me from her gentle breast,
And hushed me in her arms to rest,
And on my cheek sweet kisses prest?
                My Mother.

When sleep forsook my open eye,
Who was it sung sweet hushaby,
And rocked me that I should not cry?
                My Mother.

Who sat and watched my infant head,
When sleeping on my cradle bed?
And tears of sweet affection shed?
                My Mother.

When pain and sickness made me cry,
Who gazed upon my heavy eye,
And wept for fear that I should die?
                My Mother.

Who dressed my doll in clothes so gay,
And taught me pretty how to play,
And minded all I had to say?
                My Mother.

Who ran to help me when I fell,
And would some pretty story tell,
Or kiss the place to make it well?
                My Mother.

Who taught my infant lips to pray,
And love God's holy book and day,
And walk in wisdom's pleasant way?
     My Mother.

And can I ever cease to be,
Affectionate and kind to thee,
Who was so very kind to me?
     My Mother.

Ah, no! the thought I cannot bear,
And if God please my life to spare,
I hope I shall reward thy care,
     My Mother .

When thou art feeble, old, and grey,
My healthy arm shall be thy stay,
And I will soothe thy pains away
     My Mother.

And when I see thee hang thy head,
'Twill be my turn to watch thy bed,
And tears of sweet affection shed,
     My Mother.

For God, who lives above the skies,
Would look with vengeance in his eyes,
If I should ever dare despise
     My Mother.

POOP IN IPSWICH

NAT ABLITT 1784–1855

You must not poop in Ipswich, for so the doctors say,
You must go on to Rushmere to take the smell away;
We are so refined now, your pigs you must not slay
Pig's blood produce the cholera, and turn us all to clay.

You must not strew the land with soil, and blood and dung
For if you do, the crop will breed the cholera in your lungs;
Our Edward's now, are grown so wise, also our John's and Nat's;
The next thing I expect to hear we mar'nt eat fish or sprats.

You must not take a jalap now, to set your bowels right,
Else we must stop our noses up, it makes the air so light;
We have a law in Rushmere your horses may not poop
Upon our pretty gravelled roads, or they'll be put to coop.

Now gentlemen, you must provide a bag to every steed,
Or, if you travel on our road, we'll fine you in good speed.
If you commit a nuisance, yourself, or by your pony,
Whether Edward, Tom, or Billy, we'll make you pay your money.

Now, let our Butchers warning take, and hire Green's Baloon,
And send their offal clean away—at night—but not at noon.
Fools—
What now! I thought 'twas alcohol which poisoned all the men;
Oh, no, don't fear 'twas nasty smell 'twas neither wine nor gin;
People never poop'd in towns, when I to school did go,
Nor shall you now, my brethren, you never shall, no, no.

DR. E—

BERNARD BARTON 1784–1849

"A BULLYING, brawling champion of the Church;
Vain as a parrot screaming on her perch;
And, like that parrot, screaming out by rote
The same stale, flat, unprofitable note;
Still interrupting all discreet debate
With one eternal cry of 'Church and State!'
With all the High Tory's ignorance, increased
By all the arrogance that marks the priest;
One who declares upon his solemn word,
The voluntary system is absurd:
He well may say so; for 'twere hard to tell
Who would support him, did not law compel."

STABAT MATER

W. J. FOX 1786–1864

JEWS were wrought to cruel madness,
Christians fled in fear and sadness:
   Mary stood the cross beside.

At its foot her foot she planted,
By the dreadful scene undaunted,
   Till the gentle Sufferer died.

Poets oft have sung her story,
Painters decked her brow with glory
   Priests her name have deified:

But no worship, song, or glory,
Touches like that simple story
   Mary stood the cross beside.

And when under fierce oppression,
Goodness suffers like transgression,
   Christ again is crucified;

But if love be there, true-hearted,
By no grief or terror parted,
   Mary stands the cross beside.

WOMAN'S TONGUE

JAMES BIRD 1788-1839

Sweet Woman's tongue! I love to hear its chime
That drowns the heavier iron tongue of time!
Rich in its tones, and varied in its power,
Its accents falling like an April shower
Upon the snow-drops of man's heart, to cheer,
Warm, soften, cherish, animate, endear!

EXORDIUM

JOHN LAMB 1789-1850

Let us begin from Jove. Let every mortal raise
His grateful voice to tune Jove's endless praise.
Jove fills the heaven—the earth—the sea—the air:
We feel his spirit moving here, and everywhere.
And we his offspring are. He ever good
Daily provides for man his daily food.
Ordains the seasons by his signs on high,
Studding with gems of light the azure canopy.
What time with plough and spade to break the soil,
That plenteous stores may bless the reaper's toil,
What time to plant and prune the vine he shows,
And hangs the purple cluster on its boughs.
To him—the First—the Last—all homage yield,
Our Father—Wonderful—our Help—Our Shield.

THE LEAF

MARY KERR HART 1792-?

Forsaken, wither'd leaf, where goest thou?
Alas! in heedlessness I wander now;
The rude storm hath pass'd o'er the spreading tree
Where once, in beauty and serenity,
I hung. —'Twas all my shelter, all my stay
That cradling branch!—and now I'm borne away
By ev'ry idle wind, or zephyr's breath,
From mountain height into the vale beneath,
From forest to the plain: nor mingle sigh
With that wild driving wind that passes by:
I go, alas! where, wither'd—sear'd, all goes
The leaf of laurel and the leaf of rose!

WILLIAM THEW *b.* 1794

Some men imagine that a pretty wife
Insures consummate happiness in life:
Provided she's as blooming as the rose,
That's quite sufficient as the world now goes.
But beauty cannot long retain its charms,
It quickly fades within a husband's arms:
And they who marry for a *face*, will find
It little signifies without a *mind*.
For sense and beauty seldom are combin'd.

A TESTIMONY TO THE TRUTH

JOHN TAMPEN *c.* 1793

There's no true peace to be enjoy'd on earth,
Excepting that of walking in the path
Of God's commands, and keeping them in sight;
Good David said that this was his delight:
And, to his grief, he well knew what it was
To turn aside from great Jehovah's laws:
Corrupted nature led him oft astray,
But he ne'er said the fault was in the way.

Our walking in the way does not procure,
That grief and trouble we so oft endure!
But Oh! it is our trifling in that way,
Which often prove the cause of our dismay!
'Tis true, that our corrupted appetites,
Must constantly be cross'd from sensual rites.
In this world our passover can't be eat,
Without partaking bitter herbs with it;
But the enjoyment of the crown at last,
Will over balance all our suff'rings past.

Just is the Lord, and equal are his ways!
O let us then with joy repeat his praise!
His arm protects the soul that trusts his name!
None that rest on him shall be put to shame!

Then let us cast our all into his hands,
And strive to run the way of his commands:
May he direct, instruct, and guide us still,
Preserve and lead us to his heav'nly hill!
Equal, immortal praise to him is due!
Now and for evermore, amen, adieu.

MONODY ON THE DEATH OF ROBERT BLOOMFIELD

WILLIAM FLETCHER 1794–1852

Flowers, simple flowers from blooming hedgerows wild
For he was nature's own and simplest child;
And cull them fill'd with dew that weeps,
And strew them o'er the turf where genius sleeps.
The simple daisy and the violet there
May droop and wither in their soft despair
And woodbine sweet and blooming ashphodel

The faint anemone and lily's bell,
The primrose, cowslip and the may,
That blooms so innocently gay.
Nor be your voices silent, let them breathe
A requiem, whilst your hands enwreathe
His lowly tomb with nature's purest dowers,
Leaves of eternal green and fadeless flowers;
For he was one who lov'd to slowly stray,
Through all your pastoral haunts and while away
The hours of grief, or gloom of anxious care
In gentle musings, plucking here and there
A bud to blossom in immortal rhyme
Making earth's simplest things a source sublime
Of poesy, from whence he largely drew
Volumes of thought and cogitations new;
He studied nature in her varying look,
And all around was but a glorious book
Of mute intelligence, to it he clung
With all the enthusiasm of the young
Inspir'd boy-bard, and knit his very soul
To God, to nature, to the wondrous whole.

THE DYING CHILD

G. W. FULCHER 1795–1855

Come closer, closer, dear Mamma,
    My heart is filled with fears;
My eyes are dark, I hear your sobs,
    But cannot see your tears.

I feel your warm breath on my lips,
    That are so icy cold;
Come closer, closer, dear Mamma,
    Give me your hand to hold.

I quite forget my little hymn,
    "How doth the busy bee,"
Which every day I used to say,
    When sitting on your knee.

Nor can I recollect my prayers;
    And, dear Mamma, you know
That the great God will angry be,
    If I forget them too.

And dear Papa, when he comes home,
    Oh will he not be vex'd?
"Give us this day our daily bread;"
    What is it that comes next?

"Thine is the kingdom and the power:"
　　I cannot think of more,
It comes and goes away so quick,
　　It never did before.

"Hush, Darling! you are going to
　　The bright and blessed sky,
Where all God's holy children go,
　　To live with him on high."

But will he love me, dear Mamma,
　　As tenderly as you?
And will my own Papa, one day,
　　Come and live with me too?

But you must first lay me to sleep,
　　Where Grand-papa is laid;
Is not the Churchyard cold and dark,
　　And sha'nt I feel afraid?

And will you every evening come,
　　And say my pretty prayer
Over poor Lucy's little grave,
　　And see that no one's there?

And promise me, whene'er you die,
　　That they your grave shall make
The next to mine, that I may be
　　Close to you when I wake.

Nay, do not leave me, dear Mamma,
　　Your watch beside me keep:
My heart feels cold—the room's all dark;
　　Now lay me down to sleep:

And should I sleep to wake no more,
　　Dear, dear Mamma, good-bye:
Poor nurse is kind, but oh do you
　　Be with me when I die!

A SURFEIT OF SWEETS

THOMAS DALLING BARLEE *b.* 1796

'Tis sweet to hear the tuneful hum of bees,
Like zephyrs, whisp'ring thro' the trembling trees;
To see the moonbeams tip, with silvery light,
The ocean, slumb'ring in the arms of night;
To hear the music of a murm'ring rill,
Or tinkling sheepbell, when all else is still;
For weary Pilgrims, when oppress'd with heat,
To slumber calmly in a cool retreat;
But sweeter far, the seaman's danger o'er,
The smile that greets him on his native shore.

THE INFANT

AGNES STRICKLAND 1796–1874

I saw an infant—health, and joy, and light
Bloomed on its cheek, and sparkled in its eye;
And its fond mother stood delighted by,
To see its morn of being dawn so bright.
Again I saw it, when the withering blight
Of pale disease had fallen, moaning lie
On that sad mother's breast—stern Death was nigh,
And Life's young wings were fluttering for their flight.
Last I beheld it stretched upon the bier,
Like a fair flower untimely snatched away,
Calm and unconscious of its mother's tear,
Which on its placid cheek unheeded lay;
But on its lip the unearthly smile express'd,
'Oh! happy child! untried and early blest!'

THE BATHERS

RICHARD COBBOLD 1797–1877

Come, sail upon the Orwell's tide,
And note the seats on either side,
    With one who loves it well;
One, who has spent his infant days
Upon its margin, and who says,
    Each beauty he can tell.

Haste from the Quay and pass along,
By ships, wharfs, boats, and buoys, a throng
    Of nautical utilities;
Diminished, as we onward steer,
Our friends upon the Quay appear,
    Who interchange civilities.

Yon Gas-work has a noble shaft!
Come let us seat ourselves abaft,
    And note the lovely scene;
See right and left, in frolic pranks,
The happy bathers on the banks,
    Love to be cool and clean.

Stript of our outward marks of pride
Who can discern, when side by side
    A rich and poor man swim,
Which is the best: for oft I ween
A noble aspect might be seen,
    Beneath a ragged trim.

Boast not yourselves, ye mighty men,
In outward pomp, for surely then
    Your weakness ye betray;
Nor you in humblier state disdain
Your wealthier neighbours, nor arraign
    God's providential sway.

MOTHER'S LAST WORDS

MARY SEWELL 1797–1884

The yellow fog lay thick and dim
    O'er London city, far and wide;
It filled the spacious parks and squares,
    Where noble lords and ladies ride.

But thicker still, and darker far,
    The noisome smoke-cloud grimly fell
Amongst the narrow courts and lanes,
    Where toiling people poorly dwell.

Down seven steep and broken stairs,
    Its chill unwelcome way it found,
And darkened, with a deeper gloom,
    A low, damp chamber, under-ground.

A glimmering light was burning there,
    Beside a woman on a bed;
A worn-out woman, ghastly pale,
    Departing to the peaceful dead.

Two little boys, in threadbare clothes,
   Stood white and trembling by her side,
And listening to his mother's words,
   The youngest of them sadly cried.

"Ah, John!" she said "my own dear boy,
   You'll soon be in this world alone;
But you must do the best you can,
   And be good children when I'm gone.

"You'll walk behind my coffin, dears,
   There's little more I have to crave,
But I should like to have my boys
   Just drop a tear beside my grave.

"I've mended up your bits of clothes,
   It is not much you've left to wear,
But keep as decent as you can,
   And don't neglect the house of prayer.

"And never join with wicked lads
   To steal, and swear, and drink and lie;
For though you are but orphans here,
   You'll have a Father in the sky.

"I can't see plain, what you should do,
   But God, I think will make your way.
So don't go to the workhouse, dears,
   But try for work, and always pray."

The woman ceased, and closed her eyes,
   And long she lay, as if at rest,
Then opened wide her feeble arms,
   And clasped her children to her breast.

Then soared her soul from that dark room,
   Above the crowd of toiling folk,
Above the cross upon St. Paul's,
   Above the fog, above the smoke.

And higher, higher, up she went,
   Until she saw the golden gate,
Where night and day, in shining bands,
   The holy angels watch and wait.

LINES ON THE DEATH OF BERNARD BARTON

J. CLARKE 1798–1861

BEHOLD, the hand of cruel Death
Suspended Bernard Barton's breath!
A sudden stroke 'twas to the poet;
O! cruel Death, how could you do it.

An honest quaker you've laid down:
A loyal subject to the crown:
In Woodbridge many friends must feel,
The loss of one whose patron's Peel.

His utmost wishes were to please
A friend or foe, and live at ease:
May he now join the choirs above
In lasting harmony and love.

LIFE

WILLIAM BRANWHITE CLARKE 1798–1878

I LOOKED upon the broadly-blushing sea:
   The mid-day sun from his unclouded throne
   Was with a glow of glory, smiling down
Upon that emblem of immensity
And soon came bounding onwards, fair and free,
   A stately bark, —so gallant was her trim,
   No ocean-bird upon the wave could swim,
In prouder daring, or less heedful glee.

I gazed awhile. The gaudy ship was gone
    And all was vacant to my wildered eye.
"And thus", I cried "doth man's life journey on
    A vessel bound unto eternity!
A moment seen: whilst all things else remain
Unchanged and constant as this watery plain."

From THE LITANY IN BLANK VERSE

EDWARD COBBOLD 1798–1860

Be pleased to keep and strengthen in true faith,
In righteousness and holiness of life,
They servant WILLIAM, our most gracious King;
O rule his heart in thy faith, fear, and love;
So shall he evermore affiance have
In thee, and seek thy honor and thy glory;
Be his defender, keeper, and him give
The vict'ry over all his enemies;
We pray thee send thy blessing on our QUEEN,
And all the Royal Family preserve;
Then hear us, we beseech thee gracious Lord.

Illuminate all Bishops, Priests, and Deacons,
With perfect understanding of thy Word,
That by their preaching and their living, they
May shew and set it forth accordingly;
That it may please thee to endue the Lords
In Council, and all Nobles of our land,
With wisdom, grace, and understanding true;
And may it please thee both to bless and keep
The Magistrates, and ever give them grace
To foster justice, and to maintain truth;
Then hear us, we beseech thee gracious Lord.

Bless Thou and keep thy people, one and all;
Give to all nations unity and peace,
And let them dwell in concord; and give us
An heart to love and dread thee, and to live
With diligence according to thy laws;
Oh may it please thee, bounteously to give
Of grace to all mankind a large increase,
That they may meekly hear thy holy Word,
Receive and prize it with affection pure,
And if thy Spirit may bring forth the fruits;
Then hear us, we beseech thee gracious Lord.

Yea, if it please thee, bring into the way
Of truth all such as err, and are deceived;—
O strengthen such as stand;—comfort and help
The poor weak-hearted; raise up them that fall,
And lastly, beat down Satan 'neath our feet;
Then hear us, we beseech thee gracious Lord.

ELIZA ACTON 1799–1859

Nay twine the heath-flow'r wild for me,
   It best will suit my blighted lot;
For I am flung neglectedly
   Abroad, where fostering love is not
And Roses on my aching brow,
Too soon would lose their blushing glow;
While on my throbbing bosom laid,
The lily's bloom in death would fade!

To the young seraph Hope, be giv'n,
   In homage to her soft eyes hue,
The violet-buds, which stole from heav'n
   Its matchless depth of star-light blue.
Entwine, —the lyre of song to shade,
The scented myrtle's shining braid!
But weave for me, that flow'r alone,
In wildness on the desert thrown!

E. BARLEE 1799–1853

Do not tell me Lady fair,
With that face so full of care,
That my form and face are old,
And my blood like Winter cold.
Rather think, tho' hair be grey,
Like the hoary frost in May,
When like thee the Sun has come,
And dispelled the transient gloom,
All the fire of Spring remains,
Warm within these seasoned veins.

THE HOUR OF WOE

PERRY NURSEY 1799–1867

Oh! leave the violet in the vale!
Oh! pluck it not for me!
But fetch me now some floweret pale
That sorrow's type may be.
Sing on thou lonely nightingale
From yonder sheltering tree,
Still let me hear thy plaintive tale
Till grief my heart shall flee.
Come, types of grief, and sounds that flow
From sadness! —'tis the hour of woe.

Oh! leave the sweet rose in its bed
The rose so fresh and fair;
Full soon 'twould droop its beauteous head,
Placed on this breast of care.
No—nought that is to beauty wed
Can bloom and flourish there!
Then twine for me the nightshade dread
Meet emblem of despair.
Talk not of beauty now—ah no!
It is the sick'ning hour of woe.

Oh! leave the jasmine in the bower
The primrose in its shade!
Cull not for me one beauteous flower
That blossoms in the glade.
For Ah! grief's venom'd sting hath power
To cause e'en brightness fade;
And sadder grows pale sorrow's hour
When beauty is display'd.
Then mock me not with beauty now
It is the sick'ning of woe.

Nay, mock me with no beauteous sight,
For nought can pleasure bring
To this wrung heart that feels the blight
Of its own sorrowing.
Sing on thou lonely bird of night
Thy mournful numbers fling
Still on mine ear: —'tis pale starlight
Oh! gentle mourner, sing!
Come, types of grief, and sounds that flow
From sadness! —'tis the hour of woe.

HENRY STEBBING 1799-1883

To bear a burden up a hill,
To row a boat against the tide;
Without the wind to work a mill;
Upon a jaded horse to ride,
To strive to read without a light,
To search our way at dead of night,
All this it is, and something worse,
To live, and with an empty purse.

ON THE DEATH OF QUEEN CAROLINE

HARRIET GIRLING *c.* 1800

'Tis past! her woes, her trials, all are o'er,
Britannia's Queen now sleeps the sleep of death,
Her soul reposes on a happier shore,
Far from the reach of slander's poisonous breath

Yes, she is gone! far from this world of woe,
The heavenly mandate gladly she obeyed,
Denied her rights and honours here below,
She's gone where every wrong will be repaid.

  See a crown of glory now,
  Angels place upon her brow,
  And with songs of rapture high,
  Hail her to eternity.

ON HEARING THE FUNERAL BELL

RICHARD ROLPH *b.* 1801

Hark, Hark! that solemn bell, while she knells out her woe,
She speaks a soul is gone, and we must shortly go,
His mortal shafts grim death is whirling all around,
The king of terrors swift to cut us to the ground.

He stalks along the globe, yea, in the midnight hour,
He conquers feeble man, none can withstand his power,
Yea, sudden as a thief, he tears our life away,
Consigns us to the earth as his own lawful prey.

THE BARK

JOHN HANNAH 1802–1854

The sun brightly shines on the ocean,
And the billows so tranquilly lie,
They seem to be scarcely in motion,
Or but kiss the white pebbles and die.

There's a bark o'er the silvery waves dancing,
With pinions wide spreading and gay;
In the day-beam its gilt prow is glancing,
As it bounds o'er the waters away.

There's a cloud gathering black in the heaven;
There's a dark ruffled speck on the deep;
Lo! the sky with red lightning is riven,
And the strong pinioned winds fiercely sweep.

Where now is the bark that so gaily
Danced along on the calm sunny sea?
It has perished—as mortals do daily
In the midst of their pride and their glee.

SIR JOHN

GEORGE BORROW 1803–1881

From the Old Danish

Sir Lave to the island stray'd;
He wedded there a lovely maid:
"I'll have her yet," said John.

He brought her home across the main,
With Knights and ladies in the train:
"I'm close behind," said John.

They plac'd her on the bridal seat;
Sir Lave bade them drink and eat:
"Aye: that we will," said John.

The Servants led her then to bed,
But could not loose her girdle red!
"I can, perhaps," said John.

He shut the door with all his might:
He lock'd it fast, and quench'd the light:
"I shall sleep here," said John.

A servant to Sir Lave hied;
"Sir John is sleeping with the bride:"
"Aye, that I am," said John.

Sir Lave to the chamber flew:
"Arise, and straight the door undo!"
"A likely thing!" said John.

He struck with shield, he struck with spear
"Come out, thou Dog, and fight me here!"
"Another time," said John.

"And since thou with my bride hast lain,
To our good king I will complain."
"That thou canst do," said John.

THE NAMELESS GRAVE

SUSANNA MOODIE 1803–1885

"Tell me, thou grassy mound,
What dost thou cover?
In thy folds hast thou bound
Soldier or lover?
Time o'er the turf no memorial is keeping
Who in this lone grave forgotten is sleeping?"

"The sun's westward ray
A dark shadow has thrown
On this dwelling of clay,
And the shade is thine own
From dust and oblivion this stern lesson borrow
Thou art living to-day and forgotten to-morrow!"

CHARITY

JAMES WHITE 1803–1862

Prithee, what is Charity?
Is she one with holy eye,
Weeping near to Sorrow's bed,
Soothing sinners hour of dread?
She who points to Heav'n above,
She whose heart is filled with love,
She who feels no prudish fear
When the child of shame draws near;
She who bids her not despair,
For God will hear repenting pray'r;
She who does her alms unknown,
She who bends at Mercy's throne,
Hidden from all human eye,
Trust me—this is Charity.

But a little French Milliner filled with grimace,
Takes Charity's name and stands forth in her place,
Flaunting abroad in a furbelowed gown
She's the wonder and pride and the belle of the town—
O how she sighs at a story of woe!
A sigh's so becoming to bosom of snow—
Oh! how she begs, looking pretty the while,
Till hearts, and subscriptions, are gained by her smile;
She sits in her parlour, surrounded by beaux,
And looks so divine making poor peoples clothes.
Oh! Charity flaunts it in feather and plume
And smiles like an angel—in rouge and perfume.

TRACES

THOMAS WADE 1805–1875

Thy name upon the sands, my Spirit's bride!
Lo! I have writ; and the fast-coming sea
Advances, that will sweep it utterly
Out of all mark and meaning: but the tide,
And the sleek shore o'er which its waters glide,
Newly configurate and changed shall be
By that impressure, though invisibly,
And ever with the touch thereof abide:
And thus, thy name, thy beauty, and thy love,
Whose traces Time's obliterating ocean
Hath wash'd from out my action-smoothed mind,
Shall, with a fix'd effect, be intertwined
Therewith eternally, and deep inwove
With Time's own everlasting voice and motion.

Remote from Beelzebub, there is a place
As far as downward doth the Tomb extend,
Which not by vision, but by sound hath trace
Of a small brook, that thither doth descend
Along a hollowed rock which it hath worn
In its winding course, that gently doth impend.
My Guide and I upon that way forlorn
Entered to greet again the world sublime;
And, holding all repose but as in scorn,
He first, I following, did we upward climb,
Until I saw the gracious heaven unfold
Its beautiful things, thro' a round opening dim:
And thence we pass'd, the stars to re-behold.

THE EAGLE

JOHN WODDERSPOON 1807–1862

O! to be free like the eagle of Heaven,
That soars over valley and mountain all day,
Then flies to the rock that the thunder has riven,
And nurses her young with the fresh bleeding prey.
         No arrow can fly
         To her eyrie on high,
No net of the fowler her wings can ensnare;
         The linnet and thrush
         May live in the bush,
But the eagle's domain is as wide as the air!

SONGS

EDWARD FITZGERALD 1809–1883

Who that in his hour of glory
   Walks the kingdom of the rose,
And misapprehends the story
   Which through all the garden blows;
Which the southern air who brings
It touches, and the leafy strings
   Lightly to the touch respond;
And nightingale to nightingale
   Answering a bough beyond,
Nightingale to nightingale
   Answering a bough beyond.

        *   *   *

So for her who having lighted
   In another heart the fire,
Then shall leave it unrequited
   In its ashes to expire:
After her that sacrifice
Through the garden burns and cries:
   In the sultry breathing air:
In the flowers that turn and stare
   "What has she to do among us,
Falsely wise and frozen fair?"

Lo the golden Girasolé,
   That to him by whom she burns,
Over heaven slowly, slowly,
   As he travels ever turns;
And beneath the wat'ry main
When he sinks, would follow fain,
   Follow fain from west to east,
And then from east to west again.
   Follow would from west to east,
And then from east to west again.

EVENING AT RHODES

W. R. WRIGHT c. 1809

Fast spreads the gloom; no longer to the view
The waving olive shifts its varying hue;
The orange and her paler sister fade,
Involv'd alike in undistinguish'd shade;
Sweet are their odours still, but dimly seen
Their mingled fruits and flow'rs and vivid green;
Alone unchang'd the cypress yet remains,
And still her colour as her form retains.
Still is the landscape; nature sleeps around;
All motion dead, and hush'd is ev'ry sound;
Save where the unyok'd heifer roams at large
Or the rude goatherd tends his wand'ring charge;
And, as their bleatings faintly strike my ear,
In mingled notes the herdsman's strain I hear,
List'ning his carol, as in uncouth rhymes
He sings the warlike deeds of other times;
Or wildly modulates to simple lays
His reed—the Doric reed of ancient days.

NOVEMBER

ORLANDO WHISTLECRAFT 1810–1893

Now Nature lays aside her gaudy vest,
And in her russet garb again is dress'd
The vapours rise from agitated main,
And forming clouds, return in drenching rain;
The rivers rise and flood the quaggy meads,
The comfort of the herds the rustic heeds,
Which from the barren pasture now he takes,
Hies to the plain, and for the turnip seeks.
The boisterous gale with leaves bestrew the ground,
And Winter's foot-steps oft at morn are found;

Where bleaching spangles deck the with'ring spray,
Till Sol breaks forth and sweeps the gems away.
The fields are bare, and naked is the copse,
The songsters mute, and vegetation stops.
The foaming billows lash the sloping shore,
Again retiring with incessant roar;
Unable to resist the furious gale,
The Vessel's toss'd on Ocean's hill and dale;
In spite of all their weak attempts to save,
The crew exhausted, meets a watery grave.

WOMAN

GEORGE HUGHES *c.* 1817

From Heav'ns perennial fountains there flow
Rich streams of enjoyment to cheer us below;
But, of all the dear blessings vouchsaf'd from above
The dearest is Woman, the daughter of love!
Tho' fair be her features, yet fairer than these
The charm that incessantly labours to please!
And the beautiful beaming those features impart
Has its light from the lamp which glows pure at her heart.

Then, fairest created! in life's lovely morning
Forget not that inward and mental adorning,
Arraying thy natural grace with a charm
No blight can destroy, and no violence harm!
There are eyes that glance brightly, but falsehood they wear;
There are tongues that speak softly, but poison is there;
There are honied seductions, thine heart all subduing
They woo thee to love, but they end in thy ruin!
Oh! listen distrustful, when soft on thine ear
Fall strains that sincerity's semblance may wear,
If a cloud the fair face of thine innocence shades,
The rose of its loveliness momently fades!

THE ASCENT OF ELIJAH INTO HEAVEN

ESTHER PEARSON 1817–1833

The hour was come, Elijah, lingering still,
Now cast a farewell look upon this earth
This little earth, the scene of former woes
Then gazed upon Elisha, till at length,
His spirit burning with the boundless hope
Of 'joy unspeakable and full of glory,'
Upborne on seraph wings he soared aloft.
Elisha breathless watched th' amazing flight,
And caught his falling mantle, (emblem sure
That a like spirit rested on his head,)
Saw him ascend his fiery car, his eye
Beaming unutterable bliss. And now
The glorious vision lessened on his sight
Slowly ascending—while their breathing harps
Far in entrancing echoes died away.
But now, a sound, as of a rushing wind,
Or mighty cataract of air, approach'd
A cloud of glory veiled th' ascending pomp,
Which, carried by the whirlwind into heaven,
Seemed to his breathless gaze a dying star
A feeble speck faint glimmering—lost at length
In the far radiance beaming from the gates
Of its own heaven!

COCK ROBIN

PHILIP FREEMAN 1818–1875

Poor Robin thou canst fly no more,
Thy joys and sorrows are all o'er;
Through life's tempestuous storms thou'st trod
But now art sunk beneath the sod.

Poor Robin's dangers all are past
He struggled to the very last;
Perhaps he spent a happy life,
Without much trouble or much strife.

LINES FROM THE POETRY OF HOME

GOODWYN BARMBY 1820–1881

On cold Mount Athos, once some travellers found
A curious monk, in lonely ignorance bound:
He asked, O poor! O lorn! O wretched man!
Asked—What is woman? creed it if you can
Asked—What is woman?—the full soul of zest!
The body of delight—man's rapturous rest!
The limbs of love—affection's ardent arms!
The breast of beauty and the face of charms!
The closed completion of all ecstacy!
And what is more—the soul of symmetry!
The subtle spirit that awakes desire!
The breath—the pulse—the ever warming fire
That moveth man to inform and to create
To image forth himself and fill his fate
To aspire—arise! and unto whom is given
To lead him upward by foretaste of heaven!
"Asked what is woman?" Would such question come
From him who truly ever knew a home?

THOMAS HARRALL *c.* 1820

If Adam's Ale
Did all regale
Instead of beer and porter,
The temperance host
Might loudly boast,
And say "Well done brave water!"

For Adam's Ale
However pale
Is of intrinsic merit;
While drinking rum
Brought death to some
Who now the grave inherit.

THE WAVENEY

JEAN INGELOW 1820–1897

Listen to me—
There is a little river, fed by rills
That winds among the hills,
And turns and suns itself unceasingly,
And wanders through the cornfields wooingly,
For it has nothing else to do, but play
Along its cheery way:
Not like great rivers that in locks are bound,
On whom hard man doth heavy burdens lay,
And fret their waters into foam and spray.
This river's life is one long holiday
                All the year round.
Listen and long—
It hears the bells of many churches chime,
It has a pleasant time:
The trees that bow to it their branches strong,
Hide many birds that make its spring one song,

And orchard boughs let fall their flowery wealth,
To float away by stealth,
And land in tiny coves a mile below,
Or round and round the stems of rushes veer
Like snowy foam, but truly none is here,
So calmly gurgle on the waters clear
                        With endless flow.

THE ORPHANS

JAMES SPILLING *c.* 1824–1897

Come hither, gentle sister, we will rest beside the flowers
Which we have wove in garlands through the long sweet summer hours,
And while the evening star doth fling its tresses o'er the wave
We'll sit awhile and talk beside our mother's lonely grave.

Speak softly, little sister, for our mother lived the tone
Of childhood's prayer, low whispered round our Father's heavenly throne;
Speak softly, little sister, for her spirit from the dead
Doth bless us in these flowers that bloom above her earthly bed.

Thou couldst not hear her soothing voice that moment e're she died,
Nor watch the love-light of her eye fade faintly at thy side;
For in that hour when first I held thy little form on high,
I lost our darling mother's voice and closed her dying eye.

Yet will I teach thy childish tongue to lisp her sainted name,
And teach thy tender heart, that she its earliest love should claim.
Oh, hearken! sister Mary! in these tones thy mother spake!
Thou seest her deep blue eyes in mine! then kiss me for her sake.

Oh! promise in thy lightest hours thou'lt not forget that she
Who sleeps beneath, took leave of life in giving life to thee.
And when in this low ivied church thou wear'st the young bride's smile,
Forget not that thy mother's bier passed down that bloomy aisle.

Nay, do not weep, dear sister, for the eyes of God above,
In starlight smiles, shed o'er our hearts their promises of love.
Yet will I bless thee for that tear thy simple heart hath given,
Although I feel our mother moves amid the realms of heaven.

But oh! thou'lt not forget her until I am passed away,
For I will lead thee here, each eve, beneath the stars to pray,
And gather the sweet flowers that grow above our mother's head,
And cherish them as blessings o'er her orphan children shed.

from the French

C. FEIST *c.* 1825

Nightingales! that through the grove
Sweetly warble songs of love,
If your little bosoms swell
With the Bow-God's thrilling spell,
How should man, on land or sea,
Shun his subtle archery!

Happy flocks! that through the day
Sport your little lives away,
Your soft instinct's uncontroll'd
Or by rank, or sordid gold;
Innocence refines your bliss,
Man's the slave of artifice!

from THEOCRITOS

CHARLES DALLAS MARSTON 1824–1876

Now know I how severe a God is Love;
Some lioness sure suckled him, and nursed
His youth amid the thickets, who consumes
And darts his flames within my inmost core.

Oh, lovely to behold, yet all of stone!
Oh dark-browed maid, embrace thy swain that I
May kiss thee! for there is sweet delight
Even in an empty kiss. Why wilt thou make
Me tear so soon the garland which I wove
For thee, dear Amaryllis, having twined
Ivy and rosebuds with sweet smelling thyme?

MY BEAUTIFUL LADY

THOMAS WOOLNER 1825–1892

I love My Lady; she is very fair;
Her brow is wan, and bound by simple hair
    Her spirit sits aloof, and high
    But glances from her tender eye
      In sweetness droopingly.

As a young forest while the wind drives through,
My life is stirred when she breaks on my view;
    Her beauty grants my will no choice
    But silent awe, till she rejoice
      My longing with her voice.

Her warbling voice, though ever low and mild,
Oft makes me feel as strong drink would a child:
    And though her hand be airy light
    Of touch, it moves me with its might,
      As would a sudden fright.

A hawk high poised in air, whose nerved wing-tips
Tremble with might suppressed, before he dips,
    In vigilance, scarce more intense
    Than I: when her voice holds my sense
      Contented in suspense.

My Lady walks as I have watched a swan
Swim where a glory on the water shone:
    The ends of willow branches ride,
    Quivering in the flowing tide,
      By the deep river's side.

Fresh beauties, howso'er she moves, are stirred:
As the sunned bosom of a humming bird
    At each pant lifts some fiery hue,
    Fierce gold, bewildering green or blue;
      The same, yet ever new.

What time she walks beneath the flowering May,
Quite sure am I the scented blossoms say,
    "O Lady with the sunlit hair!
    Stay and drink our odorous air,
      The incense that we bear:

"Thy beauty, Lady, we would ever shade;
For near to thee, our sweetness might not fade."
    And could the trees be broken-hearted,
    The green sap surely must have smarted,
      When My Lady parted.

TO LOVE

JOHN CORDINGLEY *c.* 1827

I will not own thy sway, love,
    Nor call thee Deity;
I throw thy snares away, love,
    And bid the visions flee.
The many cares you bring, love,
    But weakness ne'er infected;
And readily thy sting, love,
    By prudence is detected.

Yet I will own the tie, love,
    Thy votaries enslave;
And steadily outvie, love,
    These visionary brave.
Stationed thus at bay, love,
    I'll have no care about thee;
But pass my life away, love,
    With thee as if without thee.

SINAI

HENRY DAY 1827–1893

    How sweet to view
From Sinai's loftiest ledge the setting sun
Light his red beacon on the myrrh-clad peaks
Of Horeb; —Wondrous scene! —mount piled on mount
In labyrinth, as if a storm-tost sea
Had stiffened into stone: no stir of air,
No sound to break the deep and solemn calm
Save where the wheeling vulture poises high
His airy flight, or where the rushing sand,
With sudden avalanche thundering 'mid the hills,

Sounds to the credulous Arab's listening ear
As though, through all its chasme, the reeling rock
Heaved to the crash of subterranean bells
Sonorous: Far to the West a weary cloud
Breaks into purple bars, through which the sun
With level ray looks lingering lovingly
O'er the long vales, and on the splintered peaks
And shapes of rock that stand against the sky
Like Giants flushed with battle: Woodland slopes
Greet not his parting beam: no woven sound
Of stream and breeze, by wood or fountain, hold
Mystic communion; Odour stealing winds
Withdrawn to other climes sigh through the vales
Of soft Hesperia, or, in summer isles
Aegean, o'er the sheeny myrtle-breadths
Breathe airs Elysian.

BOOK COLLECTING

ANN KNIGHT *c.* 1829

Charlotte takes pleasure in arranging
   Her well bound handsome books.
From shelf to shelf the volumes changing
   To see their prettiest looks.

This done and finish'd is her pleasure,
   For it is all can please;
She cares not for their inward treasure
   A part she seldom sees.

"She hopes and thinks they are amusing
   Indeed remembers well;
But reading much is so confusing
   Though Ann thinks she can tell."

True, Ann can best instruct the reader,
   She follows a better plan;
In puffing, Charlotte is the leader,
   In understanding, Ann.

And thus no ornaments requiring,
   No show her thoughts engage;
Charlotte the outside is admiring,
   But Ann the inward page.

THE IRON SHROUD

SARAH REVELL *c.* 1829

And what is life but an Iron Shroud,
   Which we enter the day of our birth?
Capacious, and fair in the eye of the crowd
They view the wide space with feelings proud,
   In the joy of their youthful mirth.

But the seasons appointed onward roll,
   Sure a tenth of the boon seems gone:
We catch the faint sound of a warning Knoll;
And among the fair lights, that beam'd bright on the soul,
   We are surely missing one.

Time circles on; —lo, strength declines,
   The ear or the sight, —where is it?
Nor longer the mental vigour shines,
For darkness is shutting its closing lines,
   We search, but ah! we miss it.

On Life we look with a tearful glance,
   How narrow its sphere is become!
Nearer, and nearer the walls advance;
Compress them once more, and their whole expanse,
   Is the shroud, in the silent tomb.

MY FATHER'S GRAVE

ROBERT WHYTEHEAD *c.* 1836

'Twas Autumn, and the soften'd ray,
  Fell peacefully on wood and wave;
When tracing slow the Churchyard way,
  I sought my Father's lonely grave.

My Father, —ah! how oft with thee,
  Clasp'd in thy hand, I've wander'd there;
As with meek Love and Piety,
  Thy footsteps sought the house of Prayer.

And pointing to the heaving sod,
  When thou did'st tell of things divine;
I little thought that where we trod,
  A grassy couch should soon be thine!

A SIGH

MARY ELIZABETH SQUIRRELL *b.* 1838–

A sigh—what is it? how doth it breathe of woe!
It hath a thousand silent tongues,
As one harmonious chord
Telling of burden.
Perhaps 'tis hurried from its confines by oppression,
Whose rigid hand hath scourged
A hapless victim;
And the quick trembling sigh has risen,
A pensive murmurer to convey the tale.
A sigh; 'tis like a plaintive chord,
Whose mournful melody vibrates the very soul;
Or like a trembling aspen, for the bosom heaves,
Heaves with a conscious throe:

And the poor life-bound heart,
Glad to be eased of her oppressive load,
Or to dispel one sombre shade,
Severs the silvery chord which binds the sigh,
And sends the pleader forth,
To seek among the sons of men of sympathy a part.

THE QUEEN

SAMUEL HART *c.* 1840

I was then on my travels, the day being fine,
These words I composed, then came to my mind.
I arrived at Halesworth, there was great preparation,
They were then celebrating Victoria's Coronation.

The Streets they were all decorated so grand,
And presently after, harmonised with the band:
They gave three cheers for Victoria the Queen,
As blooming young virgin, as ever was seen.

    Long may she live,
    And her charity give,
May peace ever more crown the nation,
    May hearts now rejoice,
    In her liberal voice,
And so leave no room for vexation.

She have now gained the crown,
Which have such great renown,
    May she be remembered for good,
May the Lord mark her way,
That she go not astray,
    Nor yet wander out of the road.

THE RACE

W. P. ISAACSON *c.* 1840

The race!
The glorious race! To see the noble barb,
Impatient for the contest, tear the ground
With fiercest rage, until the trumpet's blast
Give signal for the start then, at a bound,
Sweep o'er the turf—the skilful rider's hand,
His silken doublet rustling in the wind,
Applied, almost in vain, to curb the strength
That else must lose itself! Thus, side by side,
Mocking at fear, the gallant coursers run,
Struggling for victory, which doubtful hangs,
E'en as they near the goal, where horse and man
Alike their energies display—the rein
The whip—the spur—all active, midst the din
Of shouts from anxious thousands! each, in turn,
Proclaim'd the conqueror, until the one
With an impetuous rush, just clears the post
A neck before its swift antagonist!
O, 'tis a noble sport!

THE PRUDENT CHOICE

ANN ROLFE *c.* 1840

Give me a man of prudent age,
Who can a virtuous heart engage;
And as to person, air, or face,
Let them possess a manly grace—
Experienced and sedate withal,
In various changes that may fall;
Well educated and well bred,
Nor e'en by idle fancies led;

Possessing independent store,
To keep dull misery from the door—
If such a man as this there be,
He is the one that pleaseth me.

SUFFOLK

ROBERT HUGHMAN *c.* 1840

But come, my County, let me build thy claim
Upon a base of more enduring fame,
That thou hast earn'd thyself by art and toil
First honours in the culture of the soil.
That prime of occupations and the best,
Ordain'd divinely and divinely blest,
That peaceful life which Patriarchs employ'd,
Which Kings have lov'd and more than Kings enjoy'd.
Here, SUFFOLK, is thy theme for glory—here
For honourable pride the lawful sphere.
Then rest your fame, friends, on your faithful ploughs,
For here the staff of life abundant grows,
And blesses him that reaps and him that sows.
Here, crops of Barley, Buckwheat, Carrot, Turnip,
You yearly mow, or reap, or pull, or spurn up;
Here Beans, Pease, Coleseed, Artificial Grasses,
Feed horses, grunters, oxen, sheep and asses;
Here fleecy flocks upon the uplands feed,
Of hardy Norfolk or of South-down breed;
Your lowing Cow here crops the juicy mead,
Fam'd for full udder and for hornless head.
Now let me give my pencil all its force
To paint the powers condens'd within thy Horse.
Survey his honest front! the Highland Bull
Scarce boasts the honour of a thicker skull:
His neck, arch'd like a bow at fullest strain,
Shakes the thick glories of his shaggy mane;

Full and erect his firm-distended chest,
His body short, and like a sphere comprest,
With sturdy limbs well fit to carry all the rest:
Hind-quarter'd like an ox—his tail divides
The just proportions of his brawny sides,
And sweeps the dusty turnpike as he strides.
Sound in his lungs, and on his legs secure,
He, like the hound, though slow, is always sure.
SUFFOLK! one bumper to thy Horse, I say,
For he at every Show has borne the prize away.
My mouth in melting melodies would utter
Thy fair pretensions to superior Butter,
But to the sourness of a crab would squeeze,
And deprecate, detest, condemn thy Cheese!
Curs'd on the board of ev'ry mother's son,
Who scarce will own "'tis harder where there's none,"
Fitted for nought, the proverb flies abroad,
Except to bind the body or the road!

THE NEREIDS

SELINA GAYE 1814–1881

Did you ever see the Maidens,
See the Nereids, Water-Maidens,
Floating in and out the billows,
Playing with the crested breakers,
Chasing them to shore and sending
Froth and foam and tiny ripples
Laden all with Ocean treasure?
Little do our joyous children
Guess who sends the shells and seaweeds,
Which they gather on the beaches,
Which they find among the rocks, and
Take to build their tiny grottoes.
By the gentle Water-maidens
They are brought from ocean shallows,
Brought from shady depths of ocean,
Brought by all the azure wavelets,
Brought to please our joyous children,
Carried to their feet and stranded,
Left there by the waves which hasten
Back in hurry and confusion,
Lest they too be caught and captured.

THE RED POPPY

T. W. GISSING c. 1850

Erect and stately see the Poppies rise,
With crimson petals, and dark shining eyes;
They bloom above the cornfield's waving breast,
The Child's delight, and careful Farmer's pest.

JOSEPH TURNLEY c. 1850

Some drift along the turbid tide alone;
Some bound upon the beach triumphantly,
Dashing the sea-foam from their weary brows;
Whilst some are shatter'd like a tiny shell
Where surf and swell in angry waves break round,
Rousing the sea-bird in her airy nest;
And others, desp'rate, plunge to darkest chasms,
And o'er them roll the ceaseless, deafening waves.
The noble, mighty, and the fair there sink,
Then rest entomb'd where fretted pinnacle
And gleaming aisles are sculptured by the waves,
Those busy children of the mighty deep.

CRIMEAN VETERANS

JAMES CARR c. 1859

It is my humble view, I say!
That when such men come in our way,
It would be mean, remaining cold,
And most unworthy to withhold
Such eulogy as each possess
Though verging e'en on nothingness.

I ask what now our state would be?
And where our envied liberty?
If iron rule had but prevailed,
And barb'rous hordes our land assailed.

Where now had been our Monarch chaste?
With ev'ry lofty virtue grac'd!
Who, subjects' love encircles round,
Whose praises o'er the earth resound!
Whose name by ev'ry creed and sect,
Is held in most deserved respect!
Who, when our forces home returned;
To receive the honours each had earned,
Descended from her lofty seat
Each radiant heart to cheer and greet.

Ennobling then for men to stand
Receiving from their sovereign's hand
Those glittering tokens on their breasts
More welcome far than wealth's bequests.
When death has laid each brave heart low,
Offsprings' hearts with pride will glow,
When they record to ears unborn,
The scenes for which those stars were worn!

BEES WITHOUT A STING

JAMES DEER c. 1864

In my garden Bees are swarming
  Curious sometimes dangerous things;
There are others not alarming
  Useful Bees that have no stings.

B patient, B prayerful, B humble, B mild
B wise as a Solon, B meek as a child;
B cautious, B prudent, B trustful, B true,
B courteous to all men, familiar with few;
B temperate in argument, in pleasure, in wine,
B careful of conduct, of money, of time;
B honest, B holy, transparent and pure;
B humble, B Christ-like, and you'll B secure.

THE FOGGY, FOGGY DEW

ANON 1951

(redditum in versus Latinos ab A.G.H. et G.A.S., alumnis Scholae Bungaiensis, Id. Mai. MCMLI)

bracchia cum coelebs exercerem mea telis,
    contentam poteram solus habere domum.
forte mihi iuveni venit nitida obvia virgo;
    unde semel nata est unica culpa mihi.
propter eam constans patiebar frigora brumae,
    propter eam solis verbera saeva tuli.
ne laedant teneram caligo rosque puellam,
    delicias cingunt bracchia saepe proci.

quondam adiit thalamum cum somno languidus essem,
    et lecto visa est deposuisse caput.
adfata est lacrimis oculos suffusa nitentes,
    hercle! adeo lugens ut moritura foret.
cum luctu queritur magno sua fata puella;
    arripio in lectum: tuta puella mea est.
ne noceant tenerae caligo rosque puellae,
    delicias temere bracchia laeta tegunt.

sum coelebs hodie, nec solus stamina verso,
    nam mihi consors es, nate venuste, seni.
quandoque adversi conspexi lumina fili,
    me memorem, ut quondam, pulchra puella subit.
et repeto quoties sim passus frigora brumae,
    et quoties tulerim torrida flabra Noti,
ut, ne sint leto caligo rosque puellae,
    delicias cingant bracchia laeta meas.

PARNASSIAN MOLEHILL

THE BIOGRAPHICAL NOTES

INTRODUCTION

TO BOOK II

I HAVE divided these biographical notes into two sections: (*a*) those whose poems appear above and (*b*) such other Suffolk Poets as I have been able to find. For neither section can I claim to have carried out any great original research: what I have done is to collect and collate on a geographical basis information most of which is available in the standard books of reference and in biographical dictionaries—*The Dictionary of National Biography*, Foster's *Alumni Oxoniensis*, Venn's *Alumni Cantabrigiensis*, Calamy's *Non-Conformists' Memorial*, etc., etc.— and to these I have made no reference in my notes. Many of the authors have had published posthumous collections of their works combined with a life of the author by some pious editor and to these too I have made no reference nor in general to what must be the main source of information to any student of Suffolk literature, the Davy MSS in the British Museum. I have, of course, had to examine a number of collections of Suffolk books and I am indebted to the owners who have allowed me this privilege, in particular to Mr H. R. Lingwood, Mr S. F. Watson and the authorities at the Bury St. Edmunds and Ipswich Borough Libraries. In many books previous owners have written biographical details of the authors and where I have relied upon these I have quoted my source unless I have been able to verify the information elsewhere. As regards the bibliographical details I have examined myself copies of most of the books concerned, though for some I have had to rely on descriptions by other people or e.g. in the catalogue of the British Museum Library. I have not dealt with minor bibliographical points nor indeed can I even have found all the books published by all the authors: I can only hope to have whetted the appetite of some bibliophile who will complete the work started by Davy over a hundred years ago and who some day will publish an *Athenae Suffolciensis*.

C.

NAT ABLITT

According to *Nat Ablitt's History* in free verse in his *History, Poems and Writings of Nat Ablitt* Ipswich E. F. Barber, n.d. but circa 1850, he was one of the seven sons of Jacob Ablitt of Kesgrave. In his youth 'one day was to school and one day was to keep the sheep' so that 'a love of sheep was with him all his days'. He spent some time in Canada and the United States returning to live at Rushmere where he developed into a robust eccentric, pacifist and anti-clerical, observing nature, ready to enter into a controversial correspondence in the Press on almost any conceivable subject, from the administration of local charities to the distance from the earth to the sun, proving to his own satisfaction that this latter distance is but 144,000 miles. His death in 1855 aged eighty-one is commemorated on his father's tombstone in Kesgrave churchyard.

ELIZA ACTON

Eliza, daughter of John Acton, a brewer, of Hastings and later of Ipswich, was born at Battle in Sussex, 17 April 1799. As a young woman she was taken abroad for the sake of her health and while in Paris became engaged to an officer in the French Army: the engagement was broken off and she returned to England to publish her *Poems*, 12mo, Ipswich 1826, of which a second Edition was published in 1827, and to die a spinster. She was the author of a few poems in Fulcher's Sudbury Pocket Book and in 1837, when at Tunbridge Wells, presented Queen Adelaide with some verses commemorating her devoted attendance on her husband, King William IV, during his last illness. In addition, *The Voice of the North*, 8vo, London, 1842, addressed to Queen Victoria, is attributed to her. In 1845 was published *Modern Cookery*, 8vo, London, which was an immediate success, a second and third edition appearing in the same year, a fourth and fifth in 1846, and a large number of editions in successive years. Her last book, *The English Bread-book*, was published in 1857, two years before her death in Hampstead in February 1859.

WILLIAM ALABASTER

WILLIAM ALABASTER was born at Hadleigh in 1567. Educated at Westminster School and Trinity College, Cambridge, of which society he was a fellow, his first and best known publication was his Latin tragedy *Roxana*, 8vo, London, 1632, which had been acted in the hall of his college. In 1596 Alabaster accompanied the expedition to Cadiz as Chaplain to the Earl of Essex and while in Spain became a convert to Roman Catholicism, apparently writing and publishing on his return a pamphlet giving *Seven Reasons* for his conversion. No copy is known of this pamphlet, but Roger Fenton's *Answers to William Alabaster his Motives*, 4to, 1599, and J. Racster's *William Alabaster's Seven Motives Removed and Confuted*, 4to, 1598, show that some such pamphlet must have been issued. He seems to have been thrown into the Tower for his change of religion, but by 1607 he was abroad and published at Antwerp a strange treatise on cabalistic religion, *Apparatus in Revelationem Jesu Christi*, 4to, 1607. He published a number of other books and pamphlets on the same obscure subject, from one of which *Ecce Sponsus venit*, 4to, London, 1633, it appears that he went to Rome, was imprisoned by the Inquisition, but escaped and returned to England where he became reconverted to Protestantism: his *Apparatus in Revelationem* was placed on the index by the papal authorities. Once again a Protestant he seems to have been presented to the living of Thorfield in Hertfordshire, dying in April 1640. Some of his poetry was preserved in manuscript and published in Collier's *English Dramatic Literature*, 1879, and in *The Athenaeum* for 1903.

SAMUEL ASHBY

SAMUEL ASHBY was a printer and publisher at Bungay who died 1 October 1833, aged seventy-two, and with his wife Judith, is buried in the churchyard of Holy Trinity church in that town. He was a prolific writer of verse and published one large volume of 155 pages, *Miscellaneous Poems*, 4to, London, 1794, but it was as an author and often publisher of ephemeral pieces that he seems to have excelled. A strong, one might almost say violent, Tory, he wrote and published a number of political pamphlets and broadsides in verse and many others on topical subjects—the Volunteers, the Duke of Wellington, the King's Coronation, etc., etc., including a very touching little *Elegy to the Memory of a son*, 24pp, 4to, Bungay, 1811, while under the pseudonym of 'Bungaiensis' he contributed largely to the poetical columns of the local newspapers. Reading his political pieces one cannot but regret the passing of a more robust age, and hope that the future may bring less mealy mouthed political literature than that which in our days is inflicted on the long suffering electorate.

NICHOLAS BACON

NICHOLAS, the second son of Robert Bacon of Drinkstone in Suffolk and sheepreeve to the Abbey of St. Edmunds, was born in 1509. Educated at Bury St. Edmunds and Corpus Christi College, Cambridge, he graduated B.A. in 1527. A member of Gray's Inn, he was called to the Bar in 1533. In 1544 he shared in the grants made to the King's friends from the confiscated estates of the monasteries—Redgrave Hall, formerly belonging to the Abbey of Bury St. Edmunds, of which his father had been a servant, being part of his not inconsiderable share. In 1545 he was elected M.P. for Dartmouth, and in 1546 made attorney of the Court of Wards by Henry VIII and continued by Edward VI in the following year. Under Mary, in spite of his Protestantism, he retained his office and escaped persecution, but the accession of Elizabeth brought him into active political life. William Cecil, afterwards Lord Burghley, had been his intimate friend since their Cambridge days, and he, on being created Secretary of State, secured for Bacon in 1558 the post of Lord Keeper of the Great Seal. From that time on the Queen seems to have been content to leave the ordering of Church affairs in the hands of Cecil and Bacon, to whose statemanship is due the careful establishment of the reformed religion. For twenty years Bacon held the office of Lord Keeper, dying in London 20 February 1578/9. He was twice married, first to Jane Fernley of Creeting in Suffolk, by whom he had a son, Nicholas, from whom is descended the premier baronet of England, and secondly to Anne, daughter of Sir

Anthony Cooke and sister-in-law of his friend and patron Burghley, by whom he had two sons, the younger of them the illustrious Francis, by many said to be the author of the plays and poems usually ascribed to William Shakespeare. A few pieces of poetry by Bacon, *The Recreations of his Age*, came down in manuscript and were printed in 4to at Oxford in 1919.

JOHN BALE

JOHN BALE was born at South Cove in Suffolk on 21 November 1495. Educated at the Carmelite Convent at Norwich and Jesus College, Cambridge, he was at first a zealous Catholic and vehemently opposed the new learning. Converted to Protestantism by the teaching of Lord Wentworth, he renounced his vows and created a great scandal by taking to himself a wife. In 1534, when he held the living of Thorndon in Suffolk he was convened before the Archbishop of York for preaching a sermon denouncing Romish practices, while at the same period he published a number of poetical dramas on similar subjects, too many to be itemised here. A coarse and bitter controversialist, known as 'Bilious Bale' from his acerbity, he raised many enemies and was only saved from punishment in his early days by the protection of Thomas Cromwell. The fall of the latter left Bale with too many enemies to stay unprotected in England and he fled in 1540 to Germany with his wife and family, returning in 1547 on the accession of Edward VI, who presented him to the see of Ossory in 1553. As Bishop he showed himself an uncompromising Protestant, angering the Irish Priests by denouncing their superstitions and advising them to marry. On the death of Edward VI and accession of Queen Mary, Bale had again to go abroad, returning to England in 1559 on the accession of Elizabeth, an old and worn out man, and dying at Canterbury in 1563.

MRS BARBAULD

ANNA LAETITIA AIKIN, only daughter and eldest child of John Aikin, M.D., was born in 1743 at Kibworth in Leicestershire. In 1758 her father became a tutor at the famous dissenting academy at Wakefield where she lived for the next fifteen years of her life in the cultivated society which she there found. At the age of three she could read, and when quite a child was well acquainted with English Literature. At an early age she mastered French and Italian, so that her father was reluctantly compelled to teach her Latin and Greek, unusual accomplishments for a young lady in those days. In 1773 her first volume of poetry appeared, *Poems*, 4to, London, 1773, which met with immediate success. A second edition in 4to, with the same title page but reset type, and a third in 8vo appeared in the same year, followed by a fourth and fifth in 8vo in 1774 and 1775. This was followed by *Miscellaneous Pieces in Prose*, London, 8vo, 1774, of which she and her brother John were the joint authors. In 1774 she married the Rev. Rochemont Barbauld, a dissenting minister of French descent, whose father 'A Clergyman of the Church of England had sent him, rather injudiciously, to the dissenting academy at Wakefield, where he naturally imbibed presbyterian opinions.' Soon after their marriage they went to the Free School at Palgrave in Suffolk to which Mr Barbauld was appointed Headmaster and where they lived until 1785 when they moved to London. It was while at Palgrave that Mrs Barbauld's *Hymns in Prose* first appeared, known to later generations of children as the *History of the Robins*. In 1808 Mr Barbauld died insane and she was free to devote herself entirely to literary work, starting with an edition in fifty volumes of the Best English Novelists. In 1812 she produced a long and gloomy poem *Eighteen hundred and eleven*, 4to, London, in which she prophesied that some future traveller from the Antipodes would contemplate the ruins of St Paul's from a broken arch of Blackfriars Bridge—the original of Macaulay's New Zealander. This was universally criticized and was her last published work before her death in 1825 at Stoke Newington.

EDWARD BARLEE

EDWARD, son of the Rev. Charles Buckle, Rector of Worlingworth in Suffolk, was born at that village in 1799. Educated at St Johns College, Oxford, he graduated B.A. in 1821, as Edward Buckle. In the same year his father assumed the name and arms of Barlee and young Buckle is recorded as proceeding M.A. in 1830 under the name of Edward Buckle Barlee. In 1835 he succeeded his father as Rector of Worlingworth-cum-Southolt where he lived for the remainder of his life. Early in 1853 he went to Switzerland for a holiday having taken the Chaplaincy at Vevey for the summer: late in July he had a stroke, lingered for a few weeks and died 4 September 1853. He is buried in the cemetery at Vevey. He was in the habit of writing little poems to suit his mood or the occasion on the odd leaves of a scrap-book: these, edited by his son, appeared as *Idle Hours*, 8vo, London, 1854. According to Davy, the Rev. Charles Barlee (formerly Buckle) mentioned above was the anonymous author of *Elizabeth, or the Exiles of Siberia*, 12mo, London, 1822. The translation of this work seems to have been a favourite pastime of anonymous authors: there are several in the British Museum, none of which can definitely be ascribed to Charles Buckle.

THOMAS DALLING BARLEE

Thomas, youngest son of the Rev. William Barlee (formerly Buckle) was baptised at Wrentham in Suffolk 21 December 1796. According to Davy he went first to sea, but retired on account of ill health and took to the law for a profession. He practised for a time in Dawlish, but on the death of his father gave up his profession, living an invalid life on his small patrimony. His only known work is *Miscellaneous Poetry*, 12mo, Bath, 1837, in which both his name and the names of a number of relations included in the list of subscribers have been gallicised by the addition of an acute accent on the last 'e'.

GOODWYN BARMBY

Born at Yoxford in Suffolk in 1820, John Goodwyn Barmby seems to have developed Radical tendencies at an early age. At sixteen he would harangue small groups of agricultural labourers and at seventeen went to London where he became associated with a small group of revolutionary socialists. In 1840 he visited Paris and always claimed to have then been the originator of the word 'communism' in conversation with a French revolutionary. In 1841 he founded and became the first President of the London Communist Propaganda Society, the third cell of which was founded in Ipswich. In the same year he prepared and published in the *Educational Circular and Communist Apostle* the Society's official doctrine on Marriage in the New Common World. True to revolutionary form these early London Communists seem to have used new names for the months and the enumeration of the years started with 1841 as 'year 1'. In the same way, using the greek alphabet to set out the paragraphs of their matrimonial charter, these are arranged in an order unknown either to the Ancient Greeks or modern classical scholars, while the Charter itself is on conventional revolutionary lines.

> Man without woman and woman without man are two human halves, incomplete in being, imperfect in destiny.
> No woman can love more than one man at the same time. No man can love more than one woman at this same time, but the woman and man may each love various persons successively.
> Love is essential marriage.
> Love only rendereth marriage sacred.
> When love endeth marriage is dissolved and divorce begins.
> No persons should be forced to remain together in a state of nominal marriage or essential adultery when love has ceased between them.
> etc., etc.

For the next few years he was engaged in promoting Christian Socialism and universal brotherhood, revisiting France in 1848 as the Commissary of the Communistic Church to the friends of freedom in France. He later became a Unitarian Minister, the last twenty-one years of his ministry being spent at Wakefield. He remained a radical to the end, but turned from revolutionary pamphlets to somewhat pedestrian poetry, throughout which one can see traces of the old communist's view on the proper—or improper—relations between the sexes. In 1879 his health broke down and he returned to Yoxford, where he died at the Vines on the 18 October 1881.

His poetical works are as follows: *The Madhouse—a Poem*, 8vo, Stocking, 1839, *Poetry of Childhood*, 8vo, London, 1852, *Poetry of Home*, 8vo, London, 1853, *Poetry of Spring*, London, 1860, and *The Return of the Swallow*, 8vo, London, 1864. I have never seen a copy of *The Madhouse*, nor can I find any trace of one. There is a cutting from a newspaper containing a review of it in a copy of *The Return of the Swallow* in the Ipswich Library, and it is mentioned in *The Communist Apostle*, Vol. I. It was published under the name of John Goodwyn Barmby, thereafter he seems to have dropped his first christian name.

BERNARD BARTON

THE son of John Barton of Carlisle and Mary Done his wife, Bernard Barton was born 31 January 1784. The family were of yeoman stock from the Cumberland dales, but the grandfather had invented a piece of machinery for calico printing and had set up a small factory in Carlisle. John Barton, shortly before his marriage, had left the Church of England and became a member of the Society of Friends, and when the time came for him to go to school Bernard Barton was educated at a Quaker School in Ipswich. At the age of fourteen he was apprenticed to a shopkeeper named Samuel Jessup at Halstead in Essex, but in 1807, having married his employer's niece, he removed to Woodbridge and set up as a coal and corn merchant. The following year his wife died in giving birth to their daughter Lucy and Barton left Woodbridge to become tutor in the family of a Mr Waterhouse, a Liverpool merchant. In 1809 he returned to Woodbridge as a clerk in Messrs Alexander's bank, a position which he held for forty years. His first volume of poetry was published anonymously, *Metrical Effusions*, 4to, London, 1812, as was his second *Poems by an Amateur*, 4to, London, 1818, and with these began a lifelong friendship and correspondence with Robert Southey and Charles Lamb. It is said that the anonymity of his first two works was due to fear lest his employers should think he was neglecting his work, but his acknowledged *Poems*, 8vo, London, 1820, was praised by the critics and reached a fourth edition in 1825, so his employers' qualms (if any) were quickly soothed. The next eight years produced a spate of poetry and increasing fame: *Napoleon*, 8vo, London, 1822, which he was allowed to dedicate to King George IV, was followed by *A Widow's Tale*, 12mo, London, 1827, and *A New Year's Eve*, 8vo, London, 1828. By this time he had acquired very considerable popularity as 'the quaker poet', and in addition to his published works he was contributing largely to the various Pocket Books, Lady's Companions and other ephemera of the day. He seems in fact to have been writing so much as to endanger his health. For whatever reason the next few years his published works were but a few contributions to Fulcher's and other pocket books and diaries until *The Reliquary*, 8vo, London, 1837, followed in 1845 by his last major publication *Household Verses*, 8vo, London. In addition to the above he published a number of small pamphlets in verse, many of them printed in Woodbridge and most of them now very rare: *The Triumph of the Orwell*, 16pp, London, 1818, *Verses on the Death of Shelley*, 24pp, London, 1822, *A Day in Autumn*, 32pp, Woodbridge, 1820, *Tributory Verses to Robert Bloomfield*, 32pp, Woodbridge, n.d., containing verses by Barton, W. Fletcher and W. Branwhite Clarke, *Leiston Abbey*, 44pp, London, 1823, with verses by Barton, James Bird and W. Fletcher, *A Missionary's Memorial*, 24pp, London, 1826,[1] *Stanzas on the Opening of the East Suffolk Hospital*, single sheet, broadside, Woodbridge, 1836, *Sonnet for the New Church Bazaar*, Woodbridge, single sheet, broadside, n.d. but 1841, *Seaweeds gathered at Aldeburgh*, 4pp, Woodbridge, 1846 (this on his return from a visit to that town for his health), *A Memorial of J. T. Gurney*, 24pp, London, 1847, *Ichabod*, 12pp, Woodbridge, 1848, *Birthday Verses at 64*, 8pp, Woodbridge, 1848, *A Memorial of Major E. Moor*, 8pp, Woodbridge, 1848, *On the signs of the Times*, 4pp, Woodbridge, 1848. In 1846, on the recommendation of Sir Robert Peel, he received a Civil List Pension of £100 a year, a fit reward for one of whose works the *British Review* said: 'modern days have furnished no happier instance of this alliance of poetry with sound religion. Mr Barton, without awakening the passions, has found the means of touching the affections; the tear which he produces is chaste as the dew of heaven; the sympathy which he stirs is such as the angels may feel; the joy which he imparts is such as the father may share with his daughter—the son with his mother'. Barton died at Woodbridge 19 February 1849, and in the same year appeared in 8vo *Selections* from his poems and letters, edited by his daughter Lucy and with a memoir of the poet by her future husband, Edward Fitzgerald, whose marriage seems to have held joys exactly comparable to those imparted by his father-in-law's works.

---

[1] I have recently seen *A Poet's Appeal for the Asylum . . . at Stoke Newington*, single sheet, broadside, 1827.

JOSEPH BEAUMONT

Joseph Beaumont was born at Hadleigh in Suffolk 13 March 1615, the eldest son of John Beaumont, a woollen manufacturer and several times Mayor of that town which at that period was a Borough. Joseph early showed signs of intelligence and learning and his father was advised to send him to Westminster School but 'considering that giddy youth is pliable and soft to the impressions of vicious examples, could be prevailed upon by none of the most flattering inducements to place him at so great a distance from his own prudent care'. The boy was accordingly educated at Hadleigh Grammar School under William Hawkins, where he certainly was one of those who acted in the Headmaster's *Apollo Shroving* and possibly in his later play *Pestifugium* which was performed before the Cambridge runaways from the plague in 1630. From Hadleigh he went to Peterhouse, Cambridge, of which society he was elected a Fellow in 1636, having graduated B.A. in 1634. Like his father, a strong Royalist, he was ejected from his fellowship in 1644 and retired to his native town where as he says in the introduction to his *Psyche*, 4to, London, 1648, 'The turbulence of the times having deprived me of my wonted accommodations of study, I deliberated, for the avoidance of mere idleness, what task I might safelyest presume upon without the society of books: and concluded upon composing this poem'. Explorers and big game hunters have often done the same in similar circumstances, but the wiser of these have destroyed their efforts before returning to civilization. Beaumont so occupied himself until 1647 when the Bishop of Ely invited him to his palace as domestic chaplain, but his other verses remained in manuscript until after his death, being published under the title *Original Poems in English and Latin*, 4to, Cambridge, 1749. In 1650 Beaumont married the Bishop's step-daughter, heiress of a Mr Brownrigg, of Tattingstone Place, near Ipswich, and retired to lead the life of a country gentleman until the restoration, when he was appointed one of the King's Chaplains. In 1662, he was elected Master of Jesus College and on the death of Dr Hale in 1663, Master of his old college, Peterhouse, where he lived until his death 23 November 1699, having been Regius Professor of Divinity since 1670.

JOHN BENNETT

John Bennett is best known for his works on shorthand published by Cowells at Ipswich between 1825 and 1845. *Pitman's History of Shorthand*, Fourth Edition, says of Bennett's method: 'An unusual number of arbitrary words are placed to the letters, the average being five and three-quarters to each! And the system is so burdened with non-alphabetical marks for words, that it is no wonder we never heard of its being written by any other person than the author'. Bennett's poetical works are *Poems*, 12mo, Ipswich, 1830, of which a second edition was published in the same year, and *The Bells and Other Poems*, 8vo, Ipswich, 1831. He died in Ipswich 25 September 1855, aged seventy-four.

MATILDA BETHAM

Eldest daughter of the Rev. William Betham, headmaster from 1784 to 1833 of the endowed school at Stonham Aspall in Suffolk, and Mary his wife, daughter of William Damont of Eye, Mary Matilda Betham was born in 1776. Her education is said to have consisted mainly in having free access to her father's library at Stonham, but it developed in her an ardent love of literature, and especially of history. She taught herself miniature painting and exhibited some of her portraits at the Royal Academy, but did not achieve any success as an artist. As a poet she was thought highly of by her contemporaries; Lamb, Southey and Cunningham all warmly praising her *Lay of Marie*, 8vo, London, 1816. In her old age she lived in London where her wit, her love of literature, and the sweetness of her disposition made her a favourite not only of her contemporaries, but with the new generation. 'I would rather talk to Matilda Betham than to the most beautiful young woman in the world' said a young man of her in her old age. She died in London in 1852. Her other poetical works were *Elegies*, 12mo, Ipswich, 1797, *Poems*, 8vo, London, 1808, and *Vignettes in Verse*, 8vo, Ipswich, 1818.

JAMES BIRD

James Bird, the son of a substantial farmer, was born in Suffolk at Deerbolts Hall, Earl Stonham in November 1788. Educated at the local day school and subsequently at the Needham Market Grammar School, on leaving school at fifteen he was apprenticed to a miller in Earl Stonham, with whom he worked until the age of eighteen. In 1814 he set up for himself as a miller in Yoxford, marrying in 1816, Emma, the daughter of Hardacre, the printer and bookseller in Hadleigh. From this union sprang a family of sixteen children, of whom twelve survived their father. In 1819, he published his first volume of poems, *The Vale of Slaughden*, 8vo, Halesworth, T. Tippell, which achieved an immediate success, a second edition being published in the same year. As a miller, Bird was not successful, and relinquished the tenancy of his mill not only poorer than when he started, but heavily in debt. He then set up as a bookseller, and notwithstanding his ever-increasing family, was able by hard work and careful management, to pay off every farthing he owed. In his new venture he prospered and had moreover ample time for writing: *Machin, or the Discovery of Madeira*, 8vo, London, 1821, being quickly followed by *Cosmo, Duke of Tuscany*, 8vo, London, 1822, *The Exile*, 8vo, London, 1823, while his popularity was such that many of his verses appeared in the ephemera of the day. These were later followed by *Dunwich*, 1828, *Framlingham*, 1831, *The Emigrant's Tale*, 1833, and *Francis Abbott*, 1837, all in verse and published in London in 8vo. He was also the author of a drama in prose in two acts, *The Smuggler's Daughter*, 12mo, London, 1836. In 1838 he was discovered to be suffering from tuberculosis, dying 26 March 1839, at Yoxford.

GEORGE BLOOMFIELD

George, the eldest brother of Robert Bloomfield, was born at Honington in Suffolk in 1757. In 1770 he seems to have been in Thetford, but by 1777 he was working with his brother Nathaniel in London as a journeyman shoemaker for a Mr Chamberlayne of Cheapside, living in lodgings at 1s. a week. Like his more famous brother he seems to have had what little regular education he received from his mother, who had been a school mistress, and at the school of Mr Rodwell at Ixworth, while in later life he seems to have taken every possible opportunity to continue with his education by reading such books and periodicals as he could afford. In 1784 he left London and set up for himself in Bury St. Edmunds, where he died 24 January 1831. In 1821 was published by J. Smith of Cambridge a small poem of sixteen pages, *Thetford Chalybeate Spa*, by 'A Parishioner of St. Peter's'. According to a note by Walter Bloomfield in a copy of this work in the British Museum, it was written by George Bloomfield, a fact which is confirmed by statements in an autographed letter from the author, now in the West Suffolk County archives.

NATHANIEL BLOOMFIELD

An elder brother of Robert Bloomfield, Nathaniel was born at Honington 23 February 1759. At an early age he was bound apprentice to a tailor at Market Harling and when his time was completed, moved to London where he worked as a journeyman until 1800 when he started on his own as a master in a small way. Like the rest of this remarkable family he seems to have educated himself by buying such books as he could afford from cheap bookstalls and even this he could seldom do after his marriage in 1787, followed as it was by the inevitable crop of children. He was fortunate that his poetry was brought to the notice of Capel Lofft with whose assistance his *Essay on War*, 8vo, London, was published in 1803 and quickly followed by a second edition in the same year. This was his one flash of fame, after which he returned to obscurity and his subsequent history is unknown.

ROBERT BLOOMFIELD

Robert, the son of George Bloomfield, a tailor, was born at Honington, 3 December 1766. His father died when he was but a year old and the boy was educated by his mother, who kept the village school, and by a Mr Rodwell of Ixworth. At the age of eleven he joined his brothers George, a shoemaker, and Nathaniel, a tailor, in London, where the two older men lived and worked with four others in a garret in Fishers Court, Bell Lane. The boy Robert was engaged chiefly upon running errands for the men and in reading the newspapers to them, and in this way educated himself until he became a voracious reader of all the books he could lay hands on. Two small poems were accepted by the *London Magazine*, which encouraged the young man in the composition of his best known work *The Farmer's Boy*. This he composed while working at his brother's trade of tailor, carrying 50–100 lines in his head until the opportunity arose to put them on paper. The manuscript passed through several hands until it was seen by Capel Lofft, by whose efforts it was published in 4to and 8vo in 1800 with woodcuts by Anderson. The woodcuts have often been attributed to Bewick, but the artist's name is given on the title page of the rather rare first 8vo edition of 1800. The poem met with an immediate success: 26,000 copies are said to have been sold in less than three years, while the book was translated into French, Italian and even, by the enthusiastic William Clubbe, into Latin hexameters. Through the Duke of Grafton, Bloomfield received the post of undersealer in the Seal Office, but had shortly to resign owing to the ill-health which dogged his remaining days. In 1802 was published 4to *Rural Tales* followed by *Good Tidings*, 4to, London, 1804, on Jenner's discovery of vaccination. His remaining poetical works comprise *Wild Flowers*, 12mo, London, 1806, *The Banks of Wye*, 12mo, London, 1811, and *May Day with the Muses*, 12mo, London, 1822. He also published *Hazelwood Hall: a Village Drama*, 12mo, 1823, on the popular subject of the seduction of village maidens by wicked squires and a small, but now exceedingly rare, moral tale for children *The History of Little Davy's New Hat* 12mo, London, 1817. In 1806 he tried his hand as a bookseller, but soon became bankrupt, and in 1812 retired to Shefford in Bedfordshire where, with the aid of a pension of 1s. a day from the Duke of Grafton, he tried to support himself and his family by making Aeolian harps. He had long been interested in these instruments and in 1808 had produced in 4to *Nature's Music consisting of extracts from several authors; with practical observations, and poetical testimonies in honour of the harp of Aeolus*. By 1815 he had become hypochondriacal and half blind and he died at Shefford 19 August 1823, leaving a widow and four children.

THOMAS BLUNDEVILLE

Thomas, son of Edward Blundeville of Gunton, Suffolk, and Newton Flotman, Norfolk, succeeded to his father's estates in 1568, which he seems to have managed well and prudently. He was the author of numerous books and pamphlets on Horsemanship, Astronomy, Logic, etc., the earliest of which, *Three Moral Treatises*, 4to, London, 1561, is in verse.

OSBERN BOKENHAM

Osbern Bokenham was born in 1393, probably at Old Bockenham in Norfolk, and became a member of the Augustinian monastry of Stoke by Clare in Suffolk. Five years of his early life were spent at Venice, and he was later a frequent visitor to Rome and other parts of Italy. A man of considerable learning, he left in MSS a series of poems in English on the lives of twelve holy women and of the 11,000 virgins. This 'lyvys of Seyntys . . . . translayted into englys be a doctour of dyvynite clepyd Osbern Bokenham a suffolke man' is an interesting specimen of Suffolk dialect in the fifteen century and was printed for the Roxburgh Club in 1839. Bokenham seems to have died in 1447, the year in which the transcription of his *Lives of the Saints* was completed. *A dialogue between a Secular and a Friar* in English and Latin verse printed in Dugdale's *Monasticon Anglicanum*, 1600, has also been attributed to Bokenham, some of the passages of English verse closely resembling the *Lives of the Saints*.

GEORGE BORROW

George Borrow was born at East Dereham in 1803. His father was Captain and Adjutant of the East Norfolk Militia, and the family were constantly on the move throughout England, Scotland and Ireland following the Regiment, but must have returned to Norfolk by 1810 for at the age of seventeen Borrow was articled to a solicitor in Norwich. Here, encouraged by William Taylor, he started his literary career with *Faustus*, 8vo, Norwich, 1825, translated from the German of von Klinger and *Romantic Ballads*, 8vo, Norwich, 1826, a translation of a number of old Danish ballads. On the death of his father he moved to London to seek his fortune as a writer, but with scant success. Later, as agent for the British and Foreign Bible Society, he travelled through France, Germany, Spain, Russia and the near East, publishing *The Zincali, or the Gipsies in Spain* in 1841, and *The Bible in Spain* in 1843, which established his reputation as a writer and enabled him to pur-purchase a small estate on Oulton Broad. Here he lived for a number of years allowing the gipsies to pitch their tents and caravans on his land and mingling with them as a friend. At Oulton he published *Lavengro*, 1851, and *Romany Rye*, 1857, both somewhat idealized accounts of his travels through England in his youth and at Oulton he died in August 1881.

ROBERT BRADSTREET

Robert, son of Robert Bradstreet of Bentley and Higham in Suffolk, was born at Higham 27 July 1764 and baptised on 30 August in the same year. He was educated by the Rev. T. Foster of Halesworth, and at St. John's College, Cambridge, graduating B.A. in 1786. He lived for many years abroad, mainly in France, where he saw much of the French Revolution, of which he was at one time a strong advocate. He married in France, but soon and easily obtained a divorce under the revolutionary laws and on his return to England married in 1800 a Miss Adham of Masons Bridge near Hadleigh. For sometime he lived at Higham Hall, but later removed from thence and died at Southampton 13 May 1836. He was the author of *The Sabine Farm, A Poem*, 8vo, London, 1810.

FITZ-JOHN BRAND

A native of Norwich, where his father was a tanner, John Brand was born in 1746. Educated at Gonville and Caius College, Cambridge, he graduated B.A. in 1766, proceeding M.A. in 1772, in which latter year he published *Conscience, an Ethical Essay*, 4to, London, a poem which had been submitted for the Seatonian Prize. Having taken Orders he was appointed rector at St. Peter's Mancroft, Norwich, and rector of Wickham Skeith in Suffolk. A staunch Tory he published various papers on political economy designed to prove that the existing Tory associations were praiseworthy and useful, which attracted the attention of the Lord Chancellor, who presented Brand in 1797 to St. Georges, Southwark, where he lived until his death on 28 December 1808.

HANNAH BRAND

HANNAH, sister of Fitz-John Brand, was born in Norwich and for some years kept, with her sister Mary, a school in that town, but always seems to have had an ambition to go on the stage. She abandoned teaching and in 1792 appeared at Drury Lane in her own tragedy *Huniades*, which, itself a failure, seems to have been the beginning of a career equally unsuccessful as an actress and as a playwright. She had curious notions of her own ability and attributed her failure to the jealousy of Mrs Siddons and the Kembles, but as her biographer says: 'starched in manner, virtuous in conduct, and resolute in her objection to a low cut dress' she seems to have been doomed to failure from the start. 'Having failed as a teacher, an authoress and as an actress she lived for a time as a governess in Woodbridge, and later offered herself, and was accepted, as a governess in the family of a lady and her husband who, until the governess came upon them, had lived together tranquilly and with no other or greater interruptions than are found to occur in most families'. Miss Brand, however, encouraged such an affection in the lady of the house that she became so completely estranged from her husband that the two women left the house together and 'retired from Great Britain to a remote island in its dependencies where they lived together victims of self-reproach, of the greatest folly and the most unjustifiable perseverence'. This extraordinary woman, who died at Versailles 5 March 1821, was the author of *Plays and Poems*, 8vo, London, 1798.

WILLIAM BROOME

Born at Haslington, Cheshire in 1689, William Broome was educated at Eton and at St. John's College, Cambridge, where he graduated B.A. in 1711. He was appointed Rector of Stuston in Suffolk in 1713, and of Oakley in 1720. In 1728 he became Rector of Pulham in Norfolk, and in the same year was presented to the vicarage of Eye. Stuston, though, seems to have been his principal residence: it was there that he married Mrs Elizabeth Clarke, a widow, and there that all his children, with one exception, were buried. His *Miscellany of Poems*, 8vo, London, appeared in 1727, and eight books, the second, sixth, eighth, eleventh, twelfth, sixteenth, eighteenth and twenty-third, of Pope's Odyssey and all the notes are the work of Broome, who received £500 from Pope for the work. Broome also translated several of the Odes of Anacreon which were published in the *Gentleman's Magazine* under the pseudonym of 'Chester', while *The Oak and The Dunghill*, published anonymously by J. Roberts, folio, London, 1728, is usually ascribed to him. He died at Bath 16 November 1745.

CHARLES BUCKE

Charles Bucke was born at Worlington in Suffolk 16 April 1781. He went to London where he is said to have pursued his literary labours in the midst of great poverty until he found a patron in Thomas Grenville, who was believed to have paid him £5 a month. Bucke was the author of a number of books and plays, including *The Fall of the Leaf and other Poems*, 8vo, 1819. His tragedy *The Italians*, 8vo, London, 1817, obtained considerable fame, more by fortuitous publicity than from intrinsic merit. It was accepted by the committee of Drury Lane for presentation and billed to be performed with Edmund Kean in the principal part: for various reasons it was delayed until after the performance of Miss Porter's tragedy *Switzerland*, in which Kean acted so badly that Bucke withdrew *The Italians*. This public exposure of a famous actor created such a sensation that Bucke's tragedy had a rapid sale and passed through eight editions in a single year. He died at Islington, 31 July 1846.

J. B. BURGES

JAMES BLAND, son of George Burges, comptroller general of the Scottish Customs, was born 8 June 1752. Educated at Westminster and University College, Oxford, he was called to the bar at Lincoln's Inn in 1777. In 1787 he was elected M.P. for Helston and in Parliament steadily supported Wilberforce in his anti-slavery agitation. He was also a prison reformer and twice carried to a second reading his bill for the improvement of the conditions of those imprisoned for debt, but twice lost it through the opposition of the legal profession. In 1795 he retired from public life, received a baronetcy and devoted himself to literary pursuits. Princess Elizabeth is said to have prepared with her own hand a series of drawings to illustrate his *Birth and Triumph of Love*, 4to, London, 1796, and Richard Cumberland showed great interest in his *Richard the First*, 2 vols, 8vo, London, 1801, a tedious and voluminous poem of eighteen books in Spenserian metre. *The Dragon Knight*, 1818, and *The Exodiad*, 1807, the latter written in conjunction with Cumberland are his other poetical works. Burges was thrice married, in 1777, to the Hon. Elizabeth Noel, who died in childbed in 1779, secondly, in 1780 to Anne Montelieu, daughter of the Baron de Saint Hippolite, by whom he had ten children and who died in 1810, and thirdly, in 1812, to Lady Margaret Fordyce, with whom, as Lady Margaret Lindsay, Burges had fallen in love as a youth. The young lovers were separated and from this attachment sprang Lady Anne Lindsay's *Auld Robin Gray*, Burges being the Young Jamie of the Ballad. In 1821 he came into possession of Ixworth Thorpe in Suffolk, the estate of his friend John Lamb and assumed by Royal Licence the name of Sir James Lamb. He died 11 October 1824. Even in that age of indifferent poets his work was not considered to be of a high order, though the following little epigram attributed to Richard Porson gives him fourth place:

>Poetis nos laetamur tribus—
>Pye[1], Petro Pindar[2], Parvo Pybus[3].
>Si ulterius ire pergis,
>Adde his—Sir James Bland Burges.

---

[1] Henry James Pye, Poet Laureate.
[2] John Wolcot, who wrote as 'Peter Pindar'.
[3] Charles Small Pybus, M.P. for Dover.

RICHARD BURNETT

Richard, son of Charles Burnett, was born in London 20 October 1772. Educated at Leytonstone in Essex he was admitted sizar at St. John's College, Cambridge, in 1792. Migrating to Trinity College he graduated B.A. in 1797 and was ordained in the following year. Curate of St. Andrews, Bungay, for a time, he was appointed headmaster of Bungay Grammar School in 1805, and while holding this appointment published his *Various English and Latin Poems*, 8vo, Norwich, 1808. Curate of Woodchurch in Kent in 1819, Vicar of Bethersden in that county 1823–57, he is recorded as unbeneficed in the Clergy list of 1858, but nothing is known of the rest of his life.

EDWARD CALVER

All that is known of Edward Calver is that he was a puritan, while the inscription under his portrait on the frontispiece of one of his pamphlets describes him as 'Gent of Wilbie in the County of Suffolk'. His poetical works are *Passion and Discretion in Youth and Age*, 4to, London, 1641, *England's Sad Posture*, 8vo, London, 1644, *Calver's Royal Vision*, 4to, London, 1648, *England's Fortresse Exemplified*, 4to, London, 1649, and *Zion's Thankfull Echoes from the Cliffs of Ireland*, 4to, London, 1649, though others of his pamphlets are partly in verse.

I am indebted to a member of the administrative staff of the East Suffolk County Education Committee for a free translation:

Let not the world but three poets ascribe us,
In Pye and Wolcot and wee Pybus.
If wider choice your fancy urges,
Include with these Sir James Bland Burges.

H.G.

ANN CANDLER

A<small>NN</small>, daughter of William More, a working glover of Yoxford, was born 18 November 1740. In 1750 her father moved to Ipswich where Ann taught herself to read and write and studied all available books. In 1762 she married Candler, a working man from Sproughton and a heavy drinker who proved a most unsatisfactory husband. In 1777 he deserted her to enlist in the army and from then until the end of the century she seems to have spent most of her time in the Workhouse at Tattingstone, twins being the result of a short absence and visit to her husband in London in 1780: these were born 20 March 1781 and she wrote one of her poems on their death a few weeks later. While still in the Workhouse she composed a number of poems, the first of which to be published appeared in the Ipswich Journal in 1785, and later through the help of Mrs John Cobbold she was enabled to publish by subscription her *Poems*, 8vo, Ipswich, 1801. By 1802 she had left the Workhouse and was able to set up a home of her own. She died at Holton 6 September 1814.

JAMES CARR

S<small>AVE</small> that he was a boot and shoemaker with premises in St. Lawrence Street, Ipswich, nothing is known of James Carr beyond what can be gleaned from the introduction to his *Heroes Wreaths*, 8vo, Ipswich, 1857, that this little book of poems was inspired by the gallantry and devotion to duty shown by the Armed Forces of the Queen during the Crimean War.

ZACHARY CATLIN

Z<small>ACHARY</small> C<small>ATLIN</small> was probably the son of Robert Catlin, minister, of Rutland, and afterwards of Suffolk. Educated at Christ's College, Cambridge, he graduated B.A. in 1602, proceeding M.A. in 1605. Ordained priest in that year he was presented to the Vicarage of Thurston in Suffolk in 1609. He was the author of *Pub. Ovid. de Tristibus . . . translated into English by Zachary Catlin. Mr. of Arts, Suffolke'*, 8vo, London, 1639.

GEORGE CAVENDISH

GEORGE, the eldest son of Thomas Cavendish, was born in 1500: his mother was the daughter and heiress of John Smith of Podbrook Hall, near Cavendish. In 1526, young Cavendish entered the service of Cardinal Wolsey as gentleman usher, serving his master in good fortune and bad: the Duke of Norfolk said of him 'this gentleman both justfully and painfully served the Cardinal like a just and diligent servant'. After the death of Wolsey Cavendish was rewarded by Henry VIII with six of the cardinal's horses, a cart, 5 marks for his costs homeward, ten pounds of unpaid wages and twenty pounds for a reward. With this Cavendish returned to his home in Suffolk where he lived for the remainder of his life, dying in 1561 having inherited his grandfather's manor in 1524. During his retirement he wrote the life of his master, but the accession of Elizabeth—Cavendish was attached to the old faith—made it dangerous to publish a book which necessarily dealt with highly contentious matter and the work remained in manuscript until it was published for party reasons as the *Alegations of Thomas Wolsey*, 4to, London, 1641. This publication was intended to draw a parallel between Cardinal Wolsey and Archbishop Laud in order to justify the impeachment and execution of the latter and is so mutilated as to bear but little relation to the original manuscript. In 1815 the complete text was first published, edited by W. Singer in *Cavendish's Life of Cardinal Wolsey* in the second edition of which are included, under the title *Metrical Visions*, descriptions by Cavendish in verse of the various important personages of his time.

JAMES CHAMBERS

JAMES CHAMBERS was one of those queer eccentrics who in every age manage to pick up a scanty livelihood from the charity and curiosity of the more conventional members of society. Born at Soham in Cambridgeshire in 1748, the son of a leather-seller in tolerably good circumstances, he left home at the age of sixteen, from which time he never seems to have had any fixed abode or regular work, but travelled from place to place, sleeping under hedges and in barns, maintaining himself by the minimum of casual labour and by selling acrostics and verses on local people and local events. So he travelled with two or three dogs for company, one of which he would carry in his arms, until he felt a desire for a more settled life when, untrammelled by Town and Country Planning or local Bye-laws, he would build himself some rude shelter and there 'surrounded by the impure stench of the interior and a mass of filth which formed a mound at the door he would prefer his homely gear and solitary abode to the pomp and splendour of a more eligible sphere.' He thus seems to have settled for a time first at Haverhill, then at Woodbridge and finally at Earl Soham, from whence he removed to die at Stradbroke in January 1827. Of him Bernard Barton wrote: 'Ladies are somewhat fond of pet oddities. An old tattered, weather-beaten object, like old Jemmy Chambers, is the very thing to take their fancies. When they stopped to speak to the old man, to be sure, they would get to windward of him, as a matter of taste; for he was a walking dunghill, poor fellow, most of his wardrobe looking as if it had been picked off some such repositories, and his hands and face bearing evident marks of his antipathy to soap and water . . . His poetry was poor doggerel; but he himself, and the life he led, were full of poetry; —now sleeping in a barn, cowhouse, or cart-shed; at other in woods; but always "in the eye of nature".' Chambers' *Works* were published in Ipswich, 12mo, 1820, and in the British Museum is *The Goat, a caution against Inebriety*, Ipswich, 1796, in which Chambers is said to have been the author of *Reflections on Storms and Tempests*.

JAMES CLARKE

JAMES CLARKE, grocer and draper of Easton, was born in 1798 and became a diligent collector of antiquities of all kinds, particularly those found in Suffolk. A member of the British Archaeological Society, he was a frequent exhibitor at its meetings of coins, medals and other articles found in the county. His *Suffolk Antiquary*, 12mo, Woodbridge, 1849, a queer collection of poems on his various finds, is properly described by the author as 'doggerel rhyme'. He died 25 September 1861 and is buried in the churchyard at Easton.

WILLIAM BRANWHITE CLARKE

WILLIAM BRANWHITE CLARKE was born at East Bergholt in Suffolk 2 June 1798, and was educated at Dedham Grammar School and Jesus College, Cambridge. He took Orders in 1821 and held various clerical appointments at Ramsholt and elsewhere on the understanding that he should be free to travel the continent on geological excursions, during one of which he was present at the seige of Antwerp in 1831. During this period he published a number of scientific papers on meteors, electrical phenomena and geology, but also found time to follow his early bent towards poetry. While at Cambridge his *Pompeii* had gained second place to R. Babinton Macauly for the Seatonian prize in 1819 and was published in Ipswich in 8vo in the same year. This was followed by *Carmen Exequiale*, 24pp, Colchester, 1821, *The River Derwent*, 8vo, London, 1822, and an anonymous account in verse of some of his excursions abroad in *Recollections*, vi+24pp, Manningtree, 1828, while in 1825 appeared *Tributory Verses to the Memory of Robert Bloomfield*, pp 32, Woodbridge, B. Smith, with verses by Bernard Barton, W. B. Clarke and William Fletcher. According to Bernard Barton, Clarke wrote pleasing verse though the *Eclectic Review* maliciously wrote of him that they did not dispute his right to the title of M.A., the art of poetry only being excepted. In 1839, Clarke being in delicate health, was advised to take a long sea voyage and sailed to Australia, where he stayed for the remainder of his life, devoting himself to his clerical duties and geological research. The name of Clarke is intimately connected with the discovery of gold in Australia. In 1841, he first found gold in the alluvium of the river Macquarie and after a hasty survey calculated that in this district alone gold must exist over an area of seven or 800 square miles. He communicated this fact to the Government of New South Wales who enjoined him to silence, fearing the influence of the discovery on the rude population of Sydney. The facts, of course, could not be hidden and by 1846 Cornish tin miners were being advised to emigrate to Australia. In 1860 the Governors of the Australian colonies signed a certificate stating that the first discovery of gold was made in Australia by Clarke in 1841, and when he was elected F.R.S. in 1876 it was especially stated that it was in recognition of his discovery. Clarke made many geological surveys in Australia and

Tasmania and his collection of specimens was purchased by the government of New South Wales in 1876. He died suddenly at the age of eighty, 17 June 1878, while still at work amongst his fossils, a good advertisement to the health giving properties of a sea voyage.

WILLIAM CLUBBE

THE seventh son of the Rev. John Clubbe, Rector of Whatfield in Suffolk, William Clubbe was born in that village 16 April 1745. His father was the author of *The History and Antiquaries of Wheatfield*, 4to, London, 1758, a burlesque on the archaeologists of the time which was frequently reprinted. William Clubbe was educated at Gonville and Caius College, Cambridge, where he graduated LL.B. in 1769, being instituted to the rectory of Flowton in the same year and to the vicarage of Brandeston in 1770. He married Mary, the daughter of Rev. William Henchman of Earl Soham, and on her death without issue in 1808, removed from Brandeston to live with his brother Nathaniel, an attorney in Framlingham, where he died 16 October 1814. A keen Latinist, he translated into English Verse *Six Satires of Horace*, 4to, Ipswich, 1795, and *The Epistle of Horace on the Art of Poetry*, 8vo, Ipswich, 1797, and from English verse into Latin *Ver*, 12mo, Ipswich, 1801, being a portion of Robert Bloomfield's *Farmer's Boy*, followed by the whole of that poem rendered into Latin verse under the title of *Agriculae Puer*, 8vo, Ipswich, 1804. His other poetical works comprise *The Emigrants*, 8vo, Ipswich, 1793, *The Omnium*, 8vo, Ipswich, 1798, and *Three Lyric Odes*, 4to, Ipswich, 1806.

DOROTHY COBBOLD

DOROTHY, youngest child of the Rev. Henry Homer of Birdingbury, Warwickshire, was born 5 January 1770. She married in 1798 the Rev. Thomas Spencer Cobbold, rector of St. Mary-le-Tower, Ipswich, and of Woolpit, to whom his nephew, Richard Cobbold, was for a short time curate. Of their union there survived one child, Susanna Elizabeth, who married Rev. Luke Flood Page, afterwards Rector of Woolpit. Family tradition has it that when the Plurality Act was passed,

Mr Cobbold, being faced with having to give up one of his livings, offered the choice to his daughter, who chose Woolpit for her husband. Mrs Cobbold spent her widowhood at Woolpit in the house of her son-in-law, producing her *Domestic Rhymes*, 8vo, London, 1856, at the advanced age of eighty-six, in an effort to raise money towards the rebuilding of Woolpit Church spire, which had been destroyed by lightning, 17 July 1852. She died 1857 at Woolpit, where, in the chancel, is a stone to her memory.

EDWARD COBBOLD

EDWARD, the youngest child of John and Elizabeth Cobbold, was born at Ipswich in 1798. Educated at Trinity College, Oxford, and St. Albans Hall, he graduated B.A. in 1820, proceeding M.A. in 1823. He took Orders and was presented to the Rectory of Long Melford, which he held for the rest of his life, like others of his family, producing at intervals some small volumes of verse, *The Litany in Blank Verse*, 4to, Long Melford, 1833, *The Galley*, 8vo, London, 1835, and *The Georgics of Virgil in Heroic Couplets*, 8vo, London, 1852. In his latter years he seems to have suffered from financial and domestic worries and spent much of his time in London. Finally, one night in October, 1860, he took a room at Hatchett's Hotel in Dover Street, Piccadilly, his baggage consisting of a carpet bag containing a strange mixture of soiled socks, betel-nut and half smoked cigars. The following morning he was found lying on the floor, a razor clenched tightly in his hand and his head nearly severed from his body. (*Suffolk Chronicle*).

ELIZABETH COBBOLD

ELIZABETH KNIPE was born in London in 1766, the daughter of Robert Knipe, a prosperous Liverpool merchant. At an early age she showed that taste for literature and poetry which lasted throughout her life, and the same outward modesty combined with an unconscious self-assurance which seems to have been the foundation of her undoubted charm. As Eliza Knipe, she published her first volume *Poems*,

4to, Manchester, 1783, followed by *Six Narrative Poems*, 4to, London, 1787. Most of her childhood seems to have been spent in Manchester, with frequent visits to London, where she met Sir Joshua Reynolds, to whom her second volume was dedicated. In 1790 she was married to William Clarke, Comptroller of the Customs at Ipswich, a man much her senior in age, and published as Eliza Clarke, a romance in two volumes, *The Sword*, 12mo, Liverpool, 1791. Mr Clarke died within six months of their marriage, but in the words of her biographer, 'it was not to be expected that a woman possessed of such amiable qualities of the heart, and gifted with so many attractions of the mind, should long remain a widow, or should affect any undue delicacy on her hand being so soon again solicited by a person fully competent to appreciate her merits, and of sufficient wealth and liberality to indulge her taste for literature.' This satisfactory admirer was the philoprogenitive John Cobbold, of the Cliff Brewery, Ipswich, a widower with fourteen children, to which number, with her assistance, he was enabled to add another seven. An admirable wife and mother, a prolific versifier, a patron of music and the theatre and an amateur artist of great repute amongst her friends, 'although she was not visited by the higher circles of the county, yet everybody knew her for her talents and respected her' (*Memoirs of Captain George Evers, 12th Foot*, London, 1903), she seems to have made the Cliff and Holywells the centre of the intellectual life of Ipswich. Nor did she neglect the Sciences: an ardent naturalist she was a regular correspondent of Sir James Smith, the President of the Linnaean Society, and of James Sowerby, the conchologist, the latter of whom named after her one of the fossil molluscs of the Crag. She seems as well to have a genuine feeling of sympathy for the less fortunate members of the community and to have been liberal with her own time and her husband's money on their behalf.

In addition to those mentioned above her poetical works were: *The Mince Pye*, 4to, London, 1800, published under the pseudonym of Carolina Petty Pasty, *Valentine Verses*, 12mo, Ipswich, 1813, *Ode on the Victory of Waterloo*, 8vo, Ipswich, 1815, while a collection of her poems with an account of her life was published at Ipswich, 8vo, on large and small paper, 1825. She had also many contributions in the ephemera of the day, such as Fulcher's Sudbury Pocket Book. It is a pity that this admirable woman, who died 17 October 1825, did not write better poetry.

RICHARD COBBOLD

The twentieth of the twenty-one children of John Cobbold by Elizabeth, his second wife, Richard Cobbold was born at Ipswich in 1797. Educated at Bury St. Edmunds school and at Gonville and Caius College, Cambridge, he graduated B.A. in 1820. He entered the Church and after a short period as curate to his uncle the Rev. T. Cobbold at St. Mary-le-Tower, Ipswich, he was presented to the Rectory of Wortham in 1825, where he lived until his death 5 January 1877. He seems to have been the typical sporting country parson, fond of shooting and hunting, acting as Chaplain to the local Workhouse, demanding as his only stipend that the inmates should attend his church on Sundays, yet also to have inherited the literary and artistic tastes of his mother. His first novel *Margaret Catchpole*, 3 vols. 8vo, London, 1845, was for some reason a best seller, but the rest of his literary adventures were less successful. Among his poetical works were *Valentine Verses*, 8vo, Ipswich, 1827, and *Original Poetry*, 8vo, Ipswich, 1827: of these over 100 of the former and 600 of the latter were in the catalogue of the sale of his effects after his death in 1877. He also published anonymously and 'for the benefit of a family in distressed circumstances', *The Orwell*, 14pp, 1826 and, under his own name *A Father's Legacy*, 8vo, London, 1850, and *A Canticle of Life*, 8vo, London, 1855. Like his mother he tried his hand at painting and engraving: his *Valentine Verses* is illustrated by no fewer than 100 lithographs by his own hand, while the large paper edition of his mother's posthumous *Poems*, 1825, is embellished with lithographs by himself and others of the family of their mother's drawings. There is at Caius a portrait of Richard Harvey painted by Richard Cobbold and presented by him to that College. One of the most curious of his efforts is *Geoffrey Gambado, by A Humorist Physician*, 8vo, London, Dean & Sons, n.d. For this he made his own lithographs of Henry Bunbury's famous drawings and wrote his own text: some seventy odd of this work were catalogued for his sale. By his marriage in 1822, he had three sons, one of them the famous helminthologist, Thomas Spencer Cobbold (1828–1886).

MARY COCKLE

MARY, daughter of Charles Roope, medical practitioner of Pulham Market, Norfolk, was born in 1772. She married a Mr George Cockle, a surgeon, but they parted and, whether *post hoc* or *propter hoc* is unknown, in her *Important Studies for the Female Sex*, 1809, she says, 'remember that the matrimonial path is not, any more than another, strewn with *thornless* roses'. Thrown on her own resources she became a governess, part of the time it would seem to a family in the north of England since certain of the little pamphlets attributed to her in the British Museum catalogue were published in Newcastle as well as in London. For a time she was governess to the children of Mrs Jordan by the Duke of Clarence, by whom her services were recognized with a pension of £40 a year which, with her writing, enabled her to pass the latter part of her life in Ipswich, where her brother, George Roope, was barrack master. She published a number of little books of poetry including: *Fishes Grand Gala*, 16mo, London, 1810; *Lines on the death of Sir John Moore*, 4to, London, 1810; *Lines to Lady Byron*, 4to, London, 1817; *Reply to Lord Byron's Fare thee well*, 8vo, London, 1817; *Elegy on the death of George III*, 8vo, London, 1820. In addition an anonymous election song *The Banner of Blue*, fol., 1835, has been ascribed to her. She died in 1836, and is the subject of a very fulsome obituary in the *Ipswich Journal*.

WILLIAM COLE

WILLIAM COLE was the second son of John Cole, Gent, of Boyland Hall, Morningthorpe, Norfolk, and was born in 1769. For several years he farmed at Ubbeston Hall, Suffolk, but was unsuccessful as a farmer and retired to Norfolk where he died 23 February 1835 at New Bokenham. He was the author of *Rural Months, A descriptive Poem*, 8vo, Norwich, n.d., and *A Poetical Sketch of the Norwich and Lowestoft Navigation . . . by Wm. Cole, Clerk at these Works*, 8vo, Norwich, 1823.

EDMUND COOTE

Educated at Peterhouse, Cambridge, where he graduated B.A. in 1580, on 1 June 1596 Edmund Coote was appointed Headmaster of Bury St. Edmunds Grammar School, but resigned the mastership, 15 May 1597. As the resignation is accompanied by the long medieval formula about not doing so under stress of fear or being tricked into it, but spontaneously and freely, we can probably conclude that his resignation was an enforced one. Of his subsequent history nothing is known. His *English Schoolmaster*, 4to, London, 1627, seems to have been a standard school book for over 100 years, the thirty-seventh edition being published in 1673 and the forty-fifth in 1737. The book was devised to teach reading and writing not only to Grammar School boys but to everybody, and judging by the rarity of the earlier editions it must have been not only popular but extensively used. In this, his only publication, there are a few pieces of poetry, one of which is here reprinted.

MATHEW COPPINGER

Lowndes *Bibliographer's Manual* says of Mathew Coppinger, the author of *Poems, Songs and Love Verses*, 8vo, London, 1682, that he was a player and was subsequently hanged. Coppinger indicates that he was one of the Suffolk family of that name, but I have been unable to find any further details, save that he was executed 27 Feb., 1695.

JOHN CORDINGLY

According to Clarke's *History of Ipswich* John Cordingly was 'a native of Ipswich' and may have been the person of that name who was a timber merchant there in 1855. He was probably the son of William Cordingly (d. 1832) and his wife Amy (d. 1805) who were parents of Amy who died October 1826 aged thirty-nine. All of the above have verses on their headstones in St. Peter's Churchyard which suggests that some relation's Muse had been aroused and in his *Poems*, 8vo, Ipswich, 1827, John Cordingly has a verse *On the Death of a Sister, Oct.* 1826.

GEORGE CRABBE

George, son of George Crabbe of Aldeburgh, in Suffolk, collector of salt duties, was born in that town 24 December 1754. George, the younger, received but little regular education, though he was for a time at the Grammar School at Bungay, and later at Richard Haddon's school at Stowmarket. In 1768 he was apprenticed to a doctor at Wickhambrook, who treated him as little better than a labourer, and in 1771 he was transferred to Mr Page, a surgeon in Woodbridge, where he first met his future wife, Sarah Elmy, then living with her uncle, a substantial farmer of Parham. He started writing poetry for various magazines, and in 1774 appeared anonymously *Inebriety*, 4to, Ipswich, a piece now of exceeding rarity. In 1775 he returned to Aldeburgh, first as apprentice to Mr Maskill, and later in practice on his own as a surgeon, but with little financial success. In these circumstances Miss Elmy refused to marry him, though still engaged, and he left for London to earn his living by his pen. *The Candidate*, 4to, London, 1780, was a failure, and Crabbe was in the gravest financial straits when Edmund Burke came to the rescue and persuaded Dodsley to publish *The Library*, 4to, London, 1781, which was a success and the whole profits of which were generously given to the author by the publisher. Burke advised him to take Orders and backed by Dudley North of Little Glemham and Charles Long of Saxmundham, Crabbe was ordained Deacon by the Bishop of Norwich in 1781, and Priest in 1782. Burke obtained for him a Chaplaincy to the Duke of Rutland and at Belvoir Castle he completed *The Village*, 4to, London, 1783, followed by *The Newspaper*, 4to, London, 1785. By this time his fortunes had so improved that he could marry Miss Elmy and his eldest child was born at Belvoir in 1784. He published nothing more until *Poems*, 8vo, London, 1807. The next few years were spent at Muston in Northamptonshire (1789–92), Parham (1792–96) and Great Glemham (1796–1801) leading the life of a well-to-do country parson, writing a little and mainly engaged on botanical work. The list of plants in Loder's *History of Framlingham* was compiled by Crabbe. A good friend of the poor, for whose benefit he still practised surgery, a moderate Tory, suspicious of excessive zeal and 'enthusiasm', he seems to have been on good terms with all classes, but his laxity in regard to residence finally attracted official notice.

Though Rector of Muston from 1789 he had lived mainly in Suffolk, holding the curacies of Parham, Gt. Glemham and Sweffling, and in 1801 the Bishop of Lincoln insisted that he should return to his rightful cure. By the intervention of Dudley North he was allowed four more years leave of absence which he spent at Rendham, Gt. Glemham House, of which he was tenant, having been sold by Mr North in 1801. In 1805 he returned to Muston finding that in his absence his parishioners had somewhat naturally deserted the established church and non-conformity was flourishing. This he attacked with more zeal than prudence and was pleased to be offered the living of Trowbridge by the Duke of Rutland in 1814, where he died 3 February 1832. Crabbe's other poetical works are: *The Borough*, 8vo, London, 1810, *Tales*, 8vo, London, 1812, and *Tales of the Hall*, 2 vols, 8vo, London, 1819.

SAMUEL CROSSMAN

SAMUEL, the son of Samuel Crossman of Bradfield in Suffolk, was born in 1624. Educated at Pembroke College, Cambridge, he took Holy Orders and was appointed to the Rectory of Little Henny in Essex, from which he was ejected for non-conformity in 1662. He subsequently again conformed, became one of the King's Chaplains, and was made Dean of Bristol in 1683. Dying in that City 4 February 1683/4 he was buried in the Cathedral. He published a number of sermons and one volume of poetry *The Young Man's Meditation*, London, 1664.

ROBERT DALLAS

ROBERT CHARLES, son of Robert Dallas, M.D., of Dallas Castle, Jamaica, was born in that island in 1754. Educated at Musselburgh, on the death of his father he went to Jamaica, but finding that the health of his wife was suffering from the climate, he returned to Europe, living mainly on the continent. On the outbreak of the French Revolution he emigrated to the United States, but was disappointed in that country and returned once more to Europe when, according to Davy, he lived for some years at Fornham and Bury St. Edmunds. A prolific writer, his poetical works were *Miscellaneous Writings*, 4to, London, 1797, and *Adrastus . . . and other Poems*, 8vo, London, 1823, but he is best known by his connection with Byron. His sister had married George Anson Byron, an uncle of the poet, and Dallas introduced himself by a complimentary letter on the publication of *Hours of Idleness*. After Byron's death Dallas prepared for publication an account of the poet's life from 1808 to 1814, but the executors obtained an injunction against the publication of any of Byron's letters. Dallas died immediately afterwards in Normandy, 20 November 1824, and was buried at Le Havre, while his book on Byron was published in 8vo in the same year as *Recollection of the Life of Lord Byron from the Year 1808 to the End of 1814*, without the letters and edited by his son A. R. C. Dallas.

CHARLES DARBY

CHARLES DARBY was admitted to Jesus College, Cambridge, in 1652 as of Suffolk and graduated B.A. 1655/6, proceeding M.A. in 1659. A fellow of his College from 1657 to 1666, he was in 1664 presented to the rectory of Kedington in Suffolk, where he was buried 19 September 1709. According to Davy he was the author of the anonymous *Bacchanalia*, folio, London, 1680, in which are described scenes such as at times astonished some of us during the latter years of the recent war, and *The Psalms in English Metre*, 1704.

HENRY DAY

HENRY, son of Henry Thomas Day, Vicar of Mendlesham in Suffolk, was born in 1827. Educated at Harrow and Trinity Hall, Cambridge, he graduated LL.B. in 1854. In 1849 he gained the Chancellor's Medal for English verse with his *Titus at Jerusalem*, 8vo, Cambridge, 1849, and in 1857 submitted his *Sinai* (published in 8vo at Burton-on-Trent in the same year) for the Seatonian Prize. This poem was, in fact, chosen for second prize by the adjudicators, but since Day was LL.B. and not M.A. they were 'prevented from rewarding by a Prize the author of a

Poem which they considered to be of much merit.' Curate of Bedfield in Suffolk 1851–52 and of Drayton in Bucks, 1852–55, he was in the latter year appointed Headmaster of the Grammar School at Burton-on-Trent, dying in that town 10 August 1893.

JOHN DAY

THE son of John Daye or Daie the printer, John Day the younger was born in London in 1566. He became a commoner of St. Alban Hall, Oxford in 1582, and was elected a fellow of Oriel College in 1588. After taking Orders he had the reputation of being the most frequent and noted preacher in the University. In 1605–08 he travelled on the continent, during which time he became strongly attached to Calvanism. On his return he was appointed Vicar of St. Mary's, Oxford, in 1609, but missing the Provostship of his college on the resignation of William Lewes, he left his living and fellowship and was presented to the rectory of Little Thurlow in Suffolk, where he died 10 January 1627/8.

He published a number of sermons, etc., a few of them including some original poetry.

JAMES DEARE

JAMES RUSSELL DEARE, son of Philip Deare, one of the Commissioners for auditing public accounts, to whom is dedicated his translation of the *Georgics*, 8vo, London, 1808, was ordained priest before coming into residence as a Fellow Commoner at Christ's College, Cambridge, in 1793. In the following year he was presented to the Vicarage of Luton, Bedfordshire, which he held until 1798 when he became Vicar of Bures in Suffolk. He remained at Bures until his death 11 September 1824, aged fifty-four.

JAMES DEER

The introduction to *Occasional Poems by The Thatcher of Risby*, 20pp, Bury St. Edmunds, n.d., but circa 1864, is signed by 'Charles Allix Wilkinson, Domestic Chaplain to the King of Hanover, officiating pro. tem. at Risby', who states that the author was James Deer of that parish.

NATHAN DRAKE

Son of Nathan Drake an artist, Nathan Drake the younger was born at York in 1766. He graduated M.D., at Edinburgh in 1784 and first started practice in Sudbury in 1790, where he formed a life-long friendship with John Mason Good. Drake moved to Hadleigh in 1792, married in 1807, and lived a happy, useful and uneventful life until his death in that town in 1836. In early life he published a small volume of poetry *Poems*, 4to, London, 1793, but fortunately did not repeat the experiment, confining himself to writing a number of essays and criticisms which were favourably received at the time and indeed make pleasant reading to-day; *Essays Biographical, Critical and Historical*, 1809–10, *Winter Nights*, 1820, *Evenings in Autumn*, 1822, and *Mornings in Spring*, 1827, were amongst the better known. A friend of Capel Lofft the elder, he was a great admirer of Robert Bloomfield and organized a subscription for that poet amongst his friends in the Hadleigh district as a token of their appreciation of the *Farmer's Boy*.

ARTHUR DUCK

In 1730 was published *The Thresher's Miscellany*, 8vo, London, a parody on the poems of Stephen Duck the Wiltshire ploughboy poet and protegé of Queen Caroline. In the introduction is an account of the author's life in which he is stated to have been Ipswich born, 'conceived in sin and brought forth in iniquity in 1680, so that I am double the age of my cousin Stephen Duck and have ploughed harrowed and threshed twice as long, and all to no purpose.' According to the Davy MSS Arthur Duck was a real person, but it is more probable that the name is a pseudonym and the biography fictitious.

CHARLES FEIST

Thoughts in Rhyme by An East Anglian, 8vo, London, 1825, is said to have been by Charles Feist, a member of Fisher's company of actors, who subsequently turned school master and kept an academy on Mill Hill, Newmarket, His other poetical works were *Elegiac Lines on the Death of Queen Charlotte*, 8vo, Halesworth, 1818, and *Useful Rhymes for Youth Betimes*, 8vo, London, 1837.

OWEN FELLTHAM

Owen, the second or third son of Thomas Felltham, of Mutford and Mary his wife, the daughter of John Ufflete of Somerleyton, was probably born in 1602. According to two pedigrees in the British Museum he married Mary Clopton of Kentwell Hall, Long Melford. At the age of eighteen he published his *Resolves Divine, Morall and Politicall*, 12mo, London (n.d. but 1620?), moulded somewhat on Bacon's Essays. The eighth edition of 1661, the first in folio, contains a number of poems and was several times reprinted. He seems to have been secretary or chaplain to the Earl of Thomond of Great Billing in Northants, where he died and was buried in 1688, leaving instructions in his will that the cost of his funeral should not exceed £30.

JOHN FENN

According to his *School-master's Legacy and Family Monitor*, 12mo, Woodbridge, 1843, John Fenn had been at that time for fifty-eight years a schoolmaster. He is said to have kept a school at the house now known as 'Athenrye' in Woodbridge, and when Christopher Crofts was appointed Headmaster of Woodbridge School he delayed opening for so long that the foundation scholars were sent to Mr Fenn's school.

EDWARD FITZGERALD

Edward, third son of John Purcell of Bredfield House, Woodbridge, and his wife Mary, daughter of John Fitzgerald, was born at Bredfield 31 March 1809. In 1818 Mr Purcell, on the death of his father-in-law, assumed the name and arms of Fitzgerald. Educated at King Edward VI Grammar School, Bury St. Edmunds, and at Trinity College, Cambridge, where he studied Persian under Professor Cowell of Bramford, Fitzgerald lived practically the whole of his life in Suffolk and, except for a few years at Wherstead Lodge, within a few miles of Woodbridge and the Deben. His chief friends seem to have been George Crabbe, Vicar of Bredfield, Author of *Natural Theology*, London, 1840, and son of the poet, and Bernard Barton; his first publication being the memoir of Bernard Barton in the collection of poems and letters published immediately after that poet's death in 1849. Unconventional and somewhat of a recluse he spent much of his time cruising in his yacht up and down the East coast, but after the death of his skipper 'Posh' in 1877, his love of the river died too, and he was driven to console himself with his garden. He died suddenly on 14 June 1883, and is buried at Boulge. Of his friendship with 'Posh', of his marriage with Lucy Barton, and of his life in general much, and more revealing of themselves than of their subject, has been written by Freudian and salacious biographers: Fitzgerald's fame will rest on his translation of the Quatrains of the Persian astronomer poet, published as *The Rubáiyát of Omar Khayyám*, 8vo, London, 1859. At first a failure, this book soon achieved great popularity, four editions appeared during the translator's lifetime, and it has been many times since reprinted. With the exception of *Six Dramas of Calderon*, 8vo, London, 1853, his other poetical works were all published anonymously: *Agamemnon*, 4to, London, 1876, and *The Mighty Magician*, 8vo, London, n.d. (1877).

GILES FLETCHER

Son of Giles Fletcher, the ambassador and poet, and brother to Phineas Fletcher, Giles Fletcher the younger was born in London probably in 1588. He was educated at Trinity College, Cambridge, where he graduated B.A. in 1606, and became a fellow of his college in 1608. In 1618 he was presented to the Rectory of Alderton in Suffolk where he died in 1623. It is said that his 'clownish, low-parted parishioners valued not their pastor according to his worth, which disposed him to melancholy and hastened his dissolution.' In 1603, his *Canto upon the death of Eliza* was published in a volume of academic verse issued in Cambridge to celebrate the accession of James I; his chief work was *Christs Victorie and Triumph*, 4to, Cambridge, 1610.

JOSEPH FLETCHER

SON of Thomas Fletcher, a merchant of London, Joseph Fletcher was born, according to his epitaph in Wilby Church, in 1577. Educated at St. John's College, Oxford, he was presented in 1609 to the Rectory of Wilby in Suffolk, where he died in 1637, being buried in the Church. On 4 December 1618, after the death in child-birth of his first wife, Grace, daughter of Hugh Ashley, Vicar of St. Margarets Ilketshall, Fletcher wrote two elegiac poems, one in Latin and one in English in the register, where they still may be seen. His *Historie of the Perfect Cursed Blessed Man*, a very rare volume of poetry, was published in London, 1628. *Christes Bloodie Sweat*, London, 1613, has also been attributed to him.

WILLIAM FLETCHER

WILLIAM FLETCHER was born in 1794 and was admitted sizar at St. John's College, Cambridge, in 1821, as 'of Suffolk.' There is no record of his having resided and he was appointed headmaster of Woodbridge School in 1822. Ordained deacon in 1824 and priest in 1826, he was licensed perpetual curate of Charsfield in 1829. In 1832, Christopher Crofts succeeded him as headmaster and in the same year he was presented to the vicarage of Stone in Buckinghamshire by Dr. Lee, on the nomination of the Royal Astronomical Society, of which he was a member. Rector of Foscot, Buckinghamshire, 1839–43, and Vicar of Harwell, Berkshire, 1843–52, he died at Malmesbury 24 March 1852.

During his period at Woodbridge he published some small fragments of verse jointly with Bernard Barton and James Bird in *A Short Account of Leiston Abbey*, 4to, London, 1823, and jointly with Bernard Barton and William Branwhite Clark in *Tributory Verses to the Memory of Robert Bloomfield*, 32pp, Woodbridge, n.d. While at Stone his literary output on subjects as far apart as astronomy for children, the treatment of the deaf and dumb and Church reform, was greater, but all in prose.

ALICE FLOWERDEW

ALICE, the second wife of Daniel Flowerdew, was born at Bury St. Edmunds in 1759. After the death in 1801 of her husband, who had held a Government appointment in Jamaica, she kept a Ladies' Boarding School at Islington. She later removed to Bury and subsequently to Ipswich where she died 23 April 1830 and is buried at Whitton. 'Her superior attainments rendered her eminently qualified for the station in life which she filled: she died universally respected and lamented by her family and friends' (*Ipswich Journal*). Her *Poems on Moral and Religious Subjects*, 12mo, London, 1811, has an advertisement for 'Mrs. and the Misses Flowerdew's Establishment for a limited number of pupils', and the third edition contains her well known harvest hymn *Fountain of mercy God of Love*, altered to *Father of mercies*... in Hymns A. & M.

W. J. FOX

WILLIAM JOHNSON FOX, the son of a small farmer, was born at Wrentham in Suffolk 1 March 1786. Soon after Fox was born his father gave up farming and moved to Norwich where the boy started work, first as a weaver and afterwards as a bank clerk. He educated himself by his own effort, wrote occasionally for the local newspaper and finally in 1806 secured admission to the Independent College at Homerton, taking charge of a congregation at Fareham in 1810. By 1812 he had become a unitarian and in 1817 as minister of the Parliament Court chapel had acquired a great reputation as a preacher, to which was added during the following years an equally great reputation as a writer and journalist. His marriage in 1820 to Eliza, daughter of James Florance, a barrister, was a failure, and a separation was arranged in 1839: his advocacy of divorce in *The Monthly Repository*, of which he was owner and editor, caused him to be disowned by his brother Unitarian ministers and he preached from thenceforward as an independent. His services, for which he himself wrote a number of hymns, attracted a large congregation, including many reformist members of Parliament, and his sermons dealt more and more with current secular problems, the Corn Laws, Education, the Coronation, etc., etc. Inevitably he turned to politics, drew up in 1840 the Address to the Nation of the Anti-Corn Law League, became one of the leading orators of that association and was elected to Parliament as M.P. for Oldham in 1847, for which constituency, save for a defeat in 1852, followed by a victory later in the same year, he held without opposition until his death 3 January 1864.

PHILIP FREEMAN

Philip, son of Edmund Freeman of the Cedars, Combs, Suffolk, was born in that village 3 February 1818. He seems to have been a precocious child, his *Poems and Prose written by a child*, a small pamphlet of twenty-four pages being printed at Woodbridge in 1829. Educated at Trinity College, Cambridge, he graduated B.A. in 1839, and later became reader in theology at the College built on the island of Cumbrae in the Clyde by George, fourth Earl of Glasgow, who spent much of his patrimony on building churches and who would today probably be said to be suffering from a guilt complex. In 1865, Freeman was made archdeacon of Exeter, and in 1869 when the British Association met in that town, he protested in energetic language against the views expressed by Huxley on evolution and 'Darwinism'. He was the author of a number of works on theology and kindred subjects, and, in addition to his earliest venture, one book of poetry, *Sunday, a poem*, 1851. In 1875 he met with an accident while getting off a train and died 29 February, being buried in Thorverton churchyard near Exeter.

G. W. FULCHER

George William Fulcher was born at Sudbury in 1795, where he carried on the business of printer, publisher and bookseller. He took an active interest in local affairs, was several times Mayor of the Borough and a Magistrate. As a member of the Board of Guardians he was outraged by the inhumanities of the 'new Poor Law', and in his *Village Paupers*, 8vo, London, 1845, tried to rouse the public feeling on behalf of the unfortunate inhabitants of the Workhouse. Many of his poems were published in his *Sudbury Pocket Book*, first issued in 1825 and which continued year by year until his death, attracting as contributors Bernard Barton, William and Mary Howitt, James Montgomery and many other lesser known writers. Of his *Dying Child*, which first appeared in the Pocket Book for 1832, Bernard Barton thought very highly and wrote: 'Marry, an thou writest such stanzas, I shall fight shy of figuring in thy pages as a foil to their Editor's own contributions'.

SELINA GAYE

Selina Gaye was the author of a number of moral tales and sketches and one volume of poetry, *The Maiden of the Iceberg*, 8vo, London, 1867. In a copy of her *Courage and Cowards* in the Ipswich Reference Library is a MSS note in a contemporary hand, 'daughter of the Rev. John (sic) Hicks Gaye, Incumbent (sic) of St. Matthews, Ipswich', but this must, I think, be a mistake. Miss J. C. N. Willis, a grand niece of Miss Gaye, tells me that the authoress of the *Maiden of the Iceberg* was Selina (1814–81) daughter of Charles Seamen Gaye and sister of the Rev. Charles Hicks Gaye (1803–82), rector of St. Matthews, Ipswich, and afterwards of Swilland. The latter had a daughter, Selina, by his second wife Jane, daughter of Henry Howard, R.A., and had it not been for this 'family' information I should have been disposed to attribute this work to her.

HARRIET GIRLING

Harriet, daughter of the Rev. D. Packard, Rector of Middleton in Suffolk, married Richard Girling, a farmer of Westleton, and at the time of the publication of her *Original Poems*, 8vo, Norwich, n.d. (but 1848?) was living as a widow in Yoxford.

THOMAS GISSING

Thomas Wooler Gissing is probably better known as the father of George Robert Gissing (1857–1903), the author of *Demos* and other novels, than for his own literary and scientific attainments. He seems to have been a keen botanist, a correspondent of Hooker, Bentham and others and his *Wakefield Flora*, 8vo, 1867, is a competent piece of work for a man largely self-educated. His poetical works are all published under a pseudonym. Of two acknowledged poems by Gissing in the *New Suffolk Garland*, one was first printed in *Miscellaneous Poems, by T.W.G.*, 12mo, Framlingham, 1851, the other in *Margaret and other Poems, by an East Anglian*, 8vo, London, 1855, and I have seen in a bound volume of Suffolk books from the Glyde collection an angry letter from Gissing to Glyde complaining of a mistake in one of the poems reprinted. A few of the poems in *Margaret* first appeared in *Metrical Compositions, by T.W.G.*, 12mo, Framlingham, 1853. According to a MS note in the above-mentioned collection, Gissing 'was a chemist who at the time these poems were published was in business at Wakefield, Yorkshire. He was born, I think, at Framlingham, and apprenticed to a Mr Taylor, Chemist, Fore Street, Ipswich, and after being an Assistant for a time he commenced business for himself at Wakefield. He was a good botanist and published a work on the *Ferns and Mosses* in the neighbourhood of that town. In early life he was politically a Chartist, and theologically an Agnostic. Writing this in 1895, I may say that he has been dead many years.'

WILLIAM GODWIN

WILLIAM, son of John Godwin, dissenting Minister of Wisbech, was born in that town 3 March 1756. In 1758 the family moved to Debenham in Suffolk, but an Arian minority in the congregation opposed their Minister, who removed to Guestwich in Norfolk in 1760. William Godwin was brought up upon strict puritanical principles and had an attack of smallpox in 1768, having refused from religious scruples to be inoculated. After a period of schoolmastering he became minister at Stowmarket in 1780, where his faith in Christianity was shaken by a study of the French Philosophers, and in 1783 he moved to London and took up literature as a career. He dropped the title of 'Reverend', became one of the more ardent supporters of the French Revolution and published his best known book *Political Justice*, 8vo, London, 1793, which made him famous as the philosophical representative of English Radicalism. It is said only to have escaped prosecution because the Government supposed that little harm could be done by a three-guinea publication. He published a number of political and literary essays, some children's books and *Antonio, a tragedy in verse*, 8vo, London, He died in London 7 April, 1836.

ELIZABETH GOOCH

ELIZABETH, the daughter of William Villa Real of Edwinstow, Notts, was born in 1758, and according to her autobiography, *The Life of Mrs. Gooch*, 3 vols, 8vo, London, 1792, 'reduced to a level with the most unfortunate class of human beings' by the machinations of her mother-in-law, a designing governess who had married as his second wife the kindly, but weak, Sir Thomas Gooch, third Bart. of Benacre Hall, Suffolk. As a very young, and it would seem precocious, girl, Elizabeth was prevented from eloping with the local G.P. and taken for a season to Bath, where she was hurried into marriage in 1775 with Sir Thomas's second son, William Gooch. Shortly after the birth of her second son in 1778 she seems to have been guilty of some trifling indiscretion with her music teacher Rauzzini, as a result of which she was taken by her husband to Lille, where she was to be placed in a convent. Unfortunately he left her in lodgings in that town 'remarkable for the number of officers continually in garrison there, and who were of a country so much distinguished for its gallantry.' It was, however, an Englishman, a Mr Semple, who became her first lover, and she stayed on at Lille until her husband arranged for an English lawyer to visit that town and obtain the necessary evidence for a divorce, a M. du Buq being the co-respondent. The method used to produce the evidence would today make the King's Proctor's hair stand straight on end, and the evidence itself sufficiently unconvincing to cause the House of Lords to throw out the Bill, though a second Bill seems to have been passed in 1781. M. du Buq was followed by many others, English, French and German, most of noble birth, one at least Royal—in fact the authoress, if her own account is to be believed, must have been one of the most popular *poules de joie* known to the army of pre-revolutionary France. By 1792 she seems to have been living a chaste if lonely existence in London, punctuated by visits to a debtors' prison, rescued at intervals by the generosity of her former lovers; of her subsequent history nothing is known, though she published a number of books both original and translations from the French—a language in which her early life must have given her a remarkable and idiomatic proficiency. Her one book of poetry was *Poems on various Subjects*, 4to, London, 1793.

CHARLES GOODALL

According to Davy, Charles Goodall, son of Charles Goodall the elder (1642–1712) Physician to the Charterhouse, was born at Bury St. Edmunds in 1671. Educated at Eton and Merton College, Oxford, he died at Oxford 11 May 1689 and is buried in the college chapel. 'A most ingenious young man' he was the author of *Poems and translations . . . by a late scholar of Eaton*, 8vo, London, 1689.

JOHN GOWER

John Gower is described by Caxton in his edition of the poet's *Confessio Amantis*, published in 1483, as 'squyer borne in Walys', but it seems probable that he was of the Kentish family of that name, born in about 1327 and the John Gower who was lord of the Manor of Kentwell in Suffolk in 1368. A friend of Chaucer, for centuries the two were looked upon as the two earliest poets of eminence in England, but modern critics have been less kind, J. R. Lowell writing: 'Gower has positively raised tediousness to the precision of a science . . . Love, beauty, passion, nature, art, life, the natural and theological virtues—there is nothing beyond his power to disenchant.' *Confessio Amantis*, his only poem in English, in its first version was dedicated to Richard II and in its second to Henry IV, and in 1393–94 'un esquier, John Gower' is mentioned among Henry's retainers. In his old age he lived at the Priory of St. Mary Overies, Southwark,[1] where he died in 1408 and is buried in St. Saviour's, Southwark, where his tomb shows him with his head resting on his three major works, *Confessio Amantis* referred to above, *Speculum Meditantis*, a French poem first printed in 1899 in Macaulay's edition of Gower's works, and *Vox Clamantis*, a Latin elegiac poem first printed for the Roxburgh Club in 1850.

THOMAS GREEN

Thomas Green was born at Monmouth 12 September 1769, the only son of Thomas Green of Wilby, the author of a number of political pamphlets and editor of *Euphrasy*, a magazine published at Ipswich in 1769 in defence of the established church. Thomas the younger was educated at Ipswich School and privately, was called to the Bar and practised for a short time on the Norfolk Circuit. On his father's death in 1794 he gave up his profession and retired to Ipswich, devoting himself to literary work. He is best known from his diary in which he discusses and criticizes the books he reads from day to day, extracts of

---

[1] St. Mary Overies = St. Saviour's, Southwark = the present Southwark Cathedral. St. Mary Overies became at the Reformation the Parish Church of St. Saviour's, Southwark.

which were published anonymously under the title *The Diary of a Lover of Literature*, 4to, Ipswich, 1810. Further extracts were published in the *Gentleman's Magazine* in January 1834–June 1843, some years after his death on 6 January 1825. A few of his poems are printed in Maw's Ipswich *Chaplet*, 1807, and the *Suffolk Garland*, 1818, while a small collection of poems called *The Micthodion* is attributed to Green by Ford in his *Life of Thomas Green*, and by Mitford in the *Gentleman's Magazine*. *The Micthodian, or Miscellaneous Poems on Various Subjects* was printed 'for the author' by Punchard and Jermyn, 12mo, Ipswich, 1787, with a dedication *To the Ladies of Suffolk* and as being by 'J. T. Spenser, Esq.' It seems to have gone to three editions in the same year: I have seen a copy with 'Third Edition' on the title page, but no second edition. In the following year appeared *The Micthodian or a Poetical Olio, by a Young Gentleman*, 12mo, London, H. Gardner, 1788, dedicated to 'Her Most Gracious Majesties Maids of Honour.' This too was printed by Punchard and Jermyn, and the text seems to have been kept in form though the dedication is a page shorter than that to 'The Ladies of Suffolk' so that the pagination of the 'List of Contents' is wrong.

CHARLES VALENTINE LE GRICE

CHARLES VALENTINE, son of the Rev. Charles Le Grice, Rector of St. James, Bury St. Edmunds, was born in that town on St. Valentine's Day 1773. Founder's kin to Thomas Guy, he was admitted to Christ's Hospital in 1781 where for nine years he was educated with Samuel Taylor Coleridge and Charles Lamb, spending much of his holidays in the latter's home. Lamb, in his essays on Christ's Hospital, refers to the 'wit contests' between Coleridge and Le Grice comparing Coleridge to the Spanish galleon and Le Grice to the English man-of-war. From the Committee minutes Le Grice seems to have been indiscreet in speech and restless under discipline, but he was allowed to proceed to Trinity College, Cambridge, and received an allowance from the Hospital. He became a Scholar of his College in 1795, and graduated B.A. in 1796 proceeding M.A. in 1805. Soon after taking his degree he went as tutor to William Nicholls of Treriefe near Penzance, and married his pupil's widowed mother in 1798, having been ordained in the previous year. Young Nicholls died in 1815, aged twenty-six, of 'ossification of the body' and on the mother's death in 1826, the family property passed to Le Grice. From 1806–31 he was incumbent of St. Mary's, Penzance, and the remainder of his life was spent on his property at Treriefe, where he died 24 December 1858. He was the author of a number of small pieces in prose and verse; the chief of the latter being *An Imitation of Horace's First Epistle written and printed at Trinity College, Cambridge*, 1793, 8vo, Penzance, 1824. *The Petition of an Old Uninhabited House* (anonymous), 8vo, Penzance, n.d. (but 1811), second edition 1823, third edition 1858. In addition Boase and Courtney's *Bibliotheca Cornubiensis* records a large number, upwards of a score, of small pieces of poetry published at various dates on single sheets, many of them reprinted in the third edition of the *Petition of an Old Uninhabited House*, others in the *Gentleman's Magazine* at various dates.

JOSEPH HALL

JOSEPH HALL was born at Ashby-de-la-Zouch 1 July 1574, son of John Hall, agent to the Earl of Huntingdon. A Scholar and afterwards a fellow of Emmanuel College, Cambridge, he graduated B.A. in 1592. He first made some reputation as a writer with his Satires, *Virgidemiarum, Sixe Bookes, First three Bookes of Toothlesse Satyrs*, London, 16mo, 1597, followed by the *Byting Satyres* in 1598, his only poetical works. These the Archbishop of Canterbury ordered to be burned on account of their licenciousness, 1 June 1599, together with books by Marston, Marlowe and others, but Hall's Satires were reprieved a few days later. About this period Hall took Holy Orders and was presented to the living of Hawstead in Suffolk, where he stayed until 1608. He was consecrated Bishop of Exeter in 1627 and translated to Norwich in 1641. A moderate churchman, sympathetic with the puritans, he was much harassed by the spies of Archbishop Laud while at Exeter, but his very moderation was his strength and he succeeded in reducing all the clergy in his diocese to conformity. A strong exponent of the rights of the Episcopacy he was one of the thirteen Bishops impeached and thrown into the Tower in 1641. All his estates were declared forfeit and later, by the Act for the sequestration of the property of malignants (April 1643), all his goods were seized 'not leaving so much as a dozen of trenchers or the children's pictures.' His goods were purchased by sympathizers and returned to him and he continued with great courage to hold his place, preaching regularly though frequently threatened and insulted. The Cathedral was wrecked and desecrated with the greatest profanity and finally Hall himself was expelled from his palace and retired to Heigham just outside Norwich, where in 1652 he instituted John Whitefoot, Senr., into the Rectory and where he died 8 September 1656.

LAWRENCE HALLORAN

LAWRENCE HYNES HALLORAN or O'Halloran seems to have been born in Ireland in the year 1766 and was for a time master of Alphington Academy near Exeter, where he first assumed the character of a clergyman, though it is doubtful if he was ever ordained. He served as Chaplain on H.M.S. *Britannia* at the Battle of Trafalgar, and afterwards became master of a Grammar School in Cape Town and Chaplain to the forces in South Africa. Here he got involved in a duel between two Army officers and as a punishment was posted to the outpost at Simon's Bay. In reply he resigned his office and published *Cap-abilities: or South African Characteristics. A Satire*, 1810, for which he was banished from the Colony. He returned to England and took curacies in various parts —Bath, Lechlade, Bursley and, according to Davy, in 1813 and 1814 under the name of Lawrence Blakeney was curate of Thorndon in Suffolk. In 1818 under the name of O'Halloran he was convicted of forgery and transported to Australia where he established a very successful Grammar School at Sidney, in which town he died 8 March 1831, aged sixty-five. He was the author of *Poems*, 8vo, Vol. I, 1790, Vol. II, 1791. *Poems on Various Occasions*, 4to, Exeter, 1791, *An Ode on his Majesty's Visit to Exeter*, 1791, *Lachrymae Hibernicae, a ballad*, 1801, *A Poem on the Battle of Trafalgar*, 8vo, London, 1806, *A Pair of Odes for the New Year*, 4to, 1814 (the latter as Lawrence Blakeney) and as Philonautilus *The Female Volunteer, a drama*, 1808.

JOHN HANNAH

Eldest son of John Hannah of Creetown in Kircudbrightshire and Mary his wife, daughter of John Brait, farmer of Chapelton, John Hannah was born at Creetown, 10 November 1802. His father was the eldest son of John Hannay, a builder, but a whimsical preference for the reversibility of the letters induced him to change his name to Hannah. John, the younger, was brought up with his mother's relations at Chapelton, where he seems to have acted as ghillie to the local laird, from whom he acquired a love of literature. The family business of Mr Hannah proving insufficient to support his large family, John left Scotland in 1823 and settled at Diss, where he worked as an itinerant packman travelling on foot and trading from house to house in the neighbouring villages. In 1828 he started in business at Ipswich, and at first with some success, but later seems to have met with misfortune and moved to Burton-on-Trent, where he died 2 February 1854. His *Posthumous Rhymes*, 8vo, Beccles, 1854, was privately printed and first issued with a memoir of the author by S. W. Rix. According to a note by James Read in a copy of this first issue in the British Museum, great offence was given by this record that Hannah had at one time followed the lowly trade of packman, the book was withdrawn and re-issued without the memoir.

THOMAS HARCOURT

Thomas Harcourt, whose real name was Whitbread, was born in Essex in 1618. He was sent to the college of the Jesuits at St. Omer and came on the English mission about 1647 being in the Suffolk district in 1649. He worked in England for thirty-two years and was twice superior of the Suffolk district. Titus Oates, having been expelled from two of the colleges of the society, applied to Harcourt for admission to the Order and on being refused is said to have uttered the threat that he would be either a Jesuit or a Judas. Harcourt was finally arrested at the house of the Spanish ambassador in London 29 September 1678 and after being convicted of complicity in the 'popish plot' on the perjured testimony of Oates, Bedloe and Dugdale, was executed at Tyburn 20 June 1679. His two poems *To Death*, and *To the Soul* are printed in *The Remonstrance of Piety and Innocence*, 12mo, London, 1683.

SAMUEL HARDING

Samuel, son of Robert Harding of Ipswich, was born in that town, probably in 1618. Educated at Exeter College, Oxford, he graduated B.A. in 1638. He is said to have died 'about the beginning or in the heat of the civil war.' His tragedy *Sicily & Naples*, 4to, London, 1640, was published in defiance of the author's wishes by a friend who signs himself 'P.P.'

THOMAS HARRALL

I have found Thomas Harrall most elusive for a man who was obviously well known in his day. Davy says that he was a stout Tory and for some years was editor of the *Suffolk Chronicle* of Ipswich. That paper was later acquired by some Whigs when Harrall moved to Bury where he started the *Bury Gazette*. He finally moved to London where he 'lived by his pen.' His poetical works are *A Monody on the death of Mr. John Palmer, Comedian*, 8vo, London, 1798, *Claremont*, 4to, Ipswich, 1818, and *The Apotheosis of Pitt*, 8vo, Bury, 1822, the introduction to which is signed 'Westley Parsonage near Bury'.

SUSANNA HARRISON

A native of Ipswich, Susanna Harrison was born in 1752, one of a large and poor family. At the age of twenty she became a confirmed invalid and though without a regular education taught herself to read and write, developing some talent for religious poetry. Her *Songs in the night*, 8vo, Ipswich, 1780, was issued anonymously as by a 'young woman under deep affliction', but the author's name was revealed in an acrostic in the second edition, which appeared in 1781. She died 3 August 1784, and is buried in Tacket Street burial ground. Her poems reached a fifteenth edition in 1823. She also wrote *A Call to Britain*, published as a broadside of which many thousands of copies were sold in a short time.

MARY KERR HART

According to the introduction to her *Heath Blossoms*, 8vo, W. Hill, Ballingdon[1] n.d., but probably 1830, Mary Kerr Hart was an infant when her mother died in 1792, and the daughter of the sixth Marquess of Lothian. Lord Lothian was, according to Burke's Peerage, twice married, firstly in 1793 and secondly in 1806, so one must presume that Mary was born on the wrong side of the blanket, though he seems to have acknowledged her as his daughter. In 1814 she was married to a Mr Hart of Edwardstone Lodge in Suffolk, who was recommended as a suitable and wealthy husband by Sir Thomas Gooch and Sir William Rowley and by whom she had two sons. Within a few years of this marriage her husband was declared lunatic and bankrupt and, this being before the Married Woman's Property Act, her small settlement of £1,000 was seized by the creditors. Left penniless and apparently disowned by her husband's family and fatherless, she had 'the still greater misfortune to inherit PATRICIAN blood: the nature of which is to boil under the lash of persecution, and rush like an impetuous torrent to meet and repel its force; scorning the lessons taught by servility and the world that "la poverta e un infamia!" ' The unfortunate woman's only hope lay in her pen: *Heath Blossoms*, dedicated to Mr R. A. Dundas, M.P. for Ipswich, was published by subscription, and upwards of 300 subscribers' names are recorded. A second edition, 16mo, Southampton, seems to have been published in 1835, *Enignettes*, 12mo, London, appearing in the same year. By that time the eldest child must have been an 'earner', so one can only hope that she won through.

---

[1] Ballingdon-cum-Brundon a suburb of Sudbury in Suffolk where a 'William Hill, printer' is recorded in White's Directory of Suffolk of 1844.

SAMUEL HART

SAMUEL HART describes himself in his *Poem on the Coronation and marriage of . . . Queen Victoria*, 12pp, Woodbridge, n.d., but early nineteenth century, as 'Curer of corns and bunions, Scalt-heads, Rheumatism, Scrofula and various other complaints incident to the human frame. Poems and Pieces composed and arranged on any occasion.' In a copy in the British Museum is written in a contemporary hand—'Samuel Hart lives at Kettleburgh and is quack-doctor and verse maker in that Parish and neighbourhood.' He seems to have been the son of James Hart of Letheringham, miller, and the many contemporary gems of tombstone poetry in Kettleburgh churchyard must be his. His only other publication in the British Museum is a single sheet printed by Loder of Woodbridge addressed 'To the Afflicted' and consists of 'Extraordinary cases of . . . various complaints incidental to the human Frame, cured by S. Hart, the Poet etc., Kettleburgh.' In this are recorded the grateful thanks of various patients cured of their several ills, deafness, biliousness, corns, rheumatism, etc., while Sarah Weavers and S. Emeny of Kettleburgh both record their 'gratitude for your glorious eye-water.' We today can only read, with gratitude, his verse.

STEPHEN HAWES

STEPHEN HAWES was probably born in Suffolk and is presumed to be the Stephen Hawes whose will was proved at the Archdeaconry Court of Suffolk, 16 January 1523, and who left his property, all in Aldeburgh, to his wife Katherine. Educated at Oxford, he was Groom of the Chamber to Henry VII and was also apparently an officer of the court to Henry VIII. His most important work *The Passetyme of Pleasure* was first printed by Wynkyn de Worde in 1509, who was also the printer of his other works: *The Conversyan of Swerers*, 1509, *The Exemple of Vertu*, 1512, and *The Comfort of Lovers*, n.d. The *Passetyme of Pleasure* or the *History of Graunde Amoure and la Bel Pucel*, is an elaborate allegorical poem of about 6,000 lines and owes much, as Hawes himself acknowledges in the dedication, to Lidgate 'the chefe orygynel of my learning'. His other works are chiefly remarkable as bibliographical rarities.

WILLIAM HAWKINS

Nothing is known of the birth or ancestry of William Hawkins, though from internal evidence in one of his Latin Poems it has been suggested that he was born at Oakington or Long Stanton in Cambridgeshire. In 1619 he matriculated as a sizar at Christ's College, Cambridge, graduating B.A. in 1622/3 and proceeding M.A. in 1626. He was ordained at Peterborough in 1625 and in the following year became master of the Grammar School at Hadleigh in Suffolk. In 1627 was published his *Appollo Shroving*, 4to, London, a play written for his scholars and acted by them on Shrove Tuesday 1626/7. It has always been assumed that he became curate to Dr Goad of Hadleigh, and was succeeded at Hadleigh School by William Avis in 1627, but since in his *Eclogae Tres Virgilianae*, 4to, London, 1631, and *Corolla Varia*, 8vo, London, 1634, he is described as Master of Hadleigh School this cannot have been before 1634. On 14 September 1630, his eclogue *Pestifugium* was recited by two of the Scholars in the presence of some members of the University of Cambridge who had fled to Hadleigh to escape the plague, and on 6 April 1632 another eclogue *Corydon Aufuga* was similarly recited before the visiting Bishop of Rochester. It has been said that it was their mutual love of Latin verse which induced Dr Goad, Rector of Hadleigh, to appoint Hawkins his curate, sometime between 1634 and 1637, in which latter year Mr William Hawkins, Curate, died, probably of the plague, which was raging in Hadleigh at the time.

JOHN HENLEY

John, son of the Rev. Simon Henley, Vicar of Melton Mowbray, was born in that parish 3 August 1692. Educated at Melton Mowbray Grammar School and St. John's College, Cambridge, he graduated B.A. in 1712, proceeding M.A. 1716, in which year he was ordained and obtained a curacy in his native town. From his earliest years he seems to have been irritated at the methods of teaching prevalent at the time, and to have felt that he had a special vocation for introducing new methods of imparting both lay and secular knowledge. In 1721 he removed to London where he became reader at the church of St. George Martyr and where in his own words he 'preached more charity sermons, was more numerously attended and obtained more money for the poor than any other preacher.' His eccentricities, however, were too great for London and he was forced to retire in 1724 to the living of Chelmondiston in Suffolk. In a few years he returned to London where he rented rooms in which he preached a sermon every Sunday and read a lecture on some other subject every Wednesday. On one occasion one of these latter drew a large crowd of shoe-makers enticed by a promise that he would show them a new and quicker method of making shoes—this he explained during the course of his oration, was by cutting off the tops of boots. His ritual was gaudy and elaborate: he preached from a gold and velvet pulpit and Pope writes of him in the *Dunciad*:

> Oh great Restorer of the good old Stage,
> Preacher at once, and Zany of thy age!

Henley did not confine himself to preaching: for a time he was employed writing articles for Walpole at a salary of £100 in a periodical called the *Hyp Doctor*, he published many books and pamphlets on oratory, grammar and kindred subjects, and one book of poetry *Esther, Queen of Persia*, 8vo, London, 1714. He died in London 14 October 1756.

SAMUEL HENLEY

Samuel Henley started his career as professor of moral philosophy in William and Mary College, Williamsburg, Virginia, but on the outbreak of the American War of Independence returned to England and became an assistant master at Harrow School. In 1788 he was elected F.S.A. and in the same year published, as Rector of Rendlesham in Suffolk, his *Observations on the subject of the Fourth Eclogue*. He seems to have lived mainly at Harrow engaged in literary work and carrying on an extensive correspondence with the leading classics and antiquarians of the day. He published a number of books, one of which, *An Essay towards a new edition of the Elegiac of Tibullus*, 8vo, London, 1793, printed in Ipswich by G. Jermyn, contains some verse, while he 'occasionally wrote short poems for circulation amongst his friends' of which Davy records *Lines written at the Close of Winter*, 12mo, but n.d. His most interesting publication appeared in 1784, his English translation of *Vathek* by William Beckford (1759–1804) which was not published in the original French until 1787. In 1805 he was appointed principal of the newly established East India College at Hertford, retiring a few months before his death 29 December 1815, aged seventy-five.

GEORGE HUGHES

O F the Rev. George Hughes, author of *The Last Sigh of the Moor*, 4to, London, 1829, Davy says: 'This gentleman was for several years curate of Horningsheath, but removed to Hastings, where he died 17 October 1830 . . . I have no further particulars of him.' His other poetical works comprise: *Emmanuel, by a graduate of Oxford*, 8vo, 1817, *Horae Viaticae*, 8vo, London, 1818, *Madeline*, 8vo, London, 1818, and *Poems*, 8vo, London, 1822.

ROBERT HUGHMAN

According to family tradition, Robert, son of John Hugman, the author of *Poems by a Traveller*, changed his name to Hughman and kept a school at The White House, Yoxford, on the garden wall of which are incised the names of a number of the scholars. Davy says of him that 'Mr. H. being ashamed of his name, though it has been well known and respected in Halesworth for several generations, has changed it to Hughman and is the master of a very respectable school at Yoxford.' His *The Foil*, 8vo, London, 1843, and *Suffolk*, 8vo, Halesworth (n.d. but 1846) are no worse, though certainly no better, than some of his father's doggerel. Another poem, recited by the author to the Yoxford Farmer's Club, is printed in Glyde's *New Suffolk Garland*, 1866. There is in the British Museum *The Siege of Nicosia*, 8vo, Norwich, 1833, by 'Robert Hugman', according to Davy the same person before his change of name.

JOHN HUGMAN

Little is known of John Hugman the author of *Original Poems in the Moral, Heroic, Pathetic and other Styles, by a Traveller*, though he seems to have been a tanner who lived in Rectory Street, Halesworth, and he may have been the John Hugman who died in that town 30 November 1846, aged seventy-six. *Poems by a Traveller* first appeared in 1825 and there are in the British Museum copies of that date with Brighton, Cambridge, Clare and Colchester imprints.[1] The later editions seem all to have been printed and published by Tippell of Halesworth, and I have seen sixth, seventh, eighth, eleventh, twelfth, thirteenth, fifteenth, seventeenth and eighteenth editions with Tippell's imprint, the latest dated 1837. Hugman is said to have travelled the country peddling his books from town to town, which may account for the otherwise unwarranted number of editions of a collection of pretty poor doggerel. *The Halesworth Dunciad*, Halesworth, T. Tippell, 1808, was published during the controversy which raged at Halesworth in the autumn of 1808 on the question of the morals of the contemporary stage, a controversy which was fought out with pamphlets in prose and verse, printed and published by two rival printers in the town, W. Harper for the censorious, and Thomas Tippell for the defence. The battle was opened when the Rev. John Dennant, a non-conformist minister, announced that when next the Players came to town he would preach a sermon 'On Theatrical Amusements and the Impropriety of Professors of Religion attending them.' This produced *Audi Alteram Postem, Hear me first*, Halesworth, T. Tippell, 1808, from Dr Morgan, a physician in the town, in reply to which came *Five Minutes intrusion on your time before you go to the play*, Halesworth, Harper, 16 September 1808, anonymous but from Dennant, and on 22 September from the same *A letter to the writer of anonymous pamphlets in Defence of Plays*, Halesworth, Harper, this latter being signed by the author. Another from Dr Morgan was followed by a third from Dennant, dated 8 October, when Mr P. Jermyn, Attorney, entered the lists with *The Halesworth Review*, 14 September–14 October, printed by Tippell and ostensibly reviewing the first four

---

[1] Of these only the Brighton edition is a complete book in itself, the others being made up of a number of small pieces, separately printed but bound up with a common title page.

pamphlets, but with a Tippell and pro-stage bias. Mrs Douglas now entered the fray in verse with *Stanzas Objurgatory*, printed by Tippell and quickly followed by John Hugman's *Halesworth Dunciad* from the same printer and of course, on the same side. Fisher the comedian and *fons et origo* of the whole business then weighed in with a song on the stage printed as a broadside by Tippell, as did the Rev. Mr Scott, Catholic priest at Thorington Hall, with a letter in verse again from Tippell. In reply to this barrage came in verse *The Halesworth Dunciad Anatomized*, and in sedate prose *Gentle Strictures on the Halesworth Review*, both by Thornby, farmer of Wenhaston and a member of Mr Dennant's congregation, both, of course, printed by Harper. Hugman replied with two pamphlets in verse followed by Jermyn with the second and last issue of the *Halesworth Review*, 14 October–11 November 1808. The last shot was fired by Dennant in verse with *A Poem . . . or a Satire on Vanity, Dogmatism and Malice*, W. Harper and dated 28 November 1808.

WILLIAM HURN

WILLIAM HURN was born at Breccles in Norfolk 21 December 1754, the son of a substantial farmer. According to Davy, Hurn went for a time into the army, though *Brief Memorial of William Hurn*, 8vo, London, 1831, says that 'after a series of years chiefly occupied in the pursuit of literary and scientific acquirements he was admitted to Holy Orders in 1781'. Curate of Stowmarket and Rattlesden in Suffolk until 1790, in that year he was presented by the Dowager Duchess of Chandos (who had appointed him to be her Domestic Chaplain in 1788) to the Rectory of Debenham. Here he lived for twenty-two years, filling his church with a large congregation of worshippers from near and far, but finding himself more and more out of sympathy with the Established Church. Finally, in 1823, he left Debenham and the Church of England to become Minister to the Dissenting Chapel in Cuttings Lane, Woodbridge, where he died 9 October 1829, being buried in Debenham Church. He was the author of *Heath Hill, a descriptive Poem*, 4to, Colchester, 1777, *The Blessings of Peace, a Lyric Poem*, 1784, and a number of religious sermons and pamphlets.

JEAN INGELOW

Jean, eldest child of William Ingelow, a banker, was born at Boston, Lincs., 17 March 1820. In about 1834 the family moved to Ipswich where they became acquainted with the Rev. E. Harston, Rector of St. Stephen's Church in that town and afterwards Vicar of Tamworth. At an early age Miss Ingelow seems to have written, under the pseudonym of Orris, verses for the *St Stephen's Chronicle*, the organ of a literary group of young people in the town, and it may have been in that little paper that the verses on the death of Mr Harston's children appeared, verses which induced him to encourage and help her with her first published volume of poetry *A Rhyming Chronicle*, 8vo, London, 1860, published anonymously but as edited by Harston. Tennyson said of this publication that it had some 'very charming things' in it and that he would like to meet the author, but it was not until the publication of *Poems*, 8vo, London, 1863, that she was generally recognized as a poet of some merit. This work contains her best known poem *High Tide on the Coast of Lincolnshire*, and reached its fourth edition in the year of publication and its twenty-third by 1879. A second series of *Poems* appeared in 1876, and a third in 1885. Her other poetical works were *Home Thoughts*, 1865, and *A Story of Doom*, 1867. In addition she was the author of a number of novels and children's stories, but it is as a poet that her reputation stands highest. Before 1863 she removed to London where she lived for the rest of her life a friend of most of the poets, painters and writers of her time. She died at Kensington 20 July 1897 and is buried at Brompton cemetery.

WILLIAM ISAACSON

William Parr Isaacson, son of William Isaacson, solicitor of London, and Mary Louisa Parr, his wife, was a solicitor in Newmarket, and between 1844 and 1865 was Clerk to the Magistrates, Superintendent Registrar and Clerk to the Union. On his retirement he was made a Deputy Lieutenant of the County and a Justice of the Peace, dying in 1892 or shortly after. His only known published work was *Alice*, 8vo, Newmarket, 1841, a play in blank verse, the profits on the sale of which were given to the Newmarket Town Racing Fund. This fund was established to help trainers, jockeys and others connected with racing who had fallen on bad times and has now been superseded by the Bentinck Fund for Trainers and Jockeys, and the Beresford Fund for Stablemen.

ANN KNIGHT

According to Davy, Ann Knight was editor of *The Gleaner*, 12mo, Woodbridge, 1827, a small and anonymous anthology for children, containing also a number of the editor's own poems. Her *Mornings in the Library*, 12mo, London, 1828, is in prose but has introductory and concluding poems by Bernard Barton, who is said also to have helped her with *The Gleaner*. Davy says 'she is a widow, now (1829) residing at Woodbridge: her maiden name was Waspe and she keeps a school.'

JOHN LAMB

John, son of John Lamb, Perpetual Curate of Ixworth in Suffolk, was born in that village 22 February 1789. Educated at Corpus Christi College, Cambridge, he graduated B.A. in 1811, proceeding M.A. in 1814 and D.D. in 1827. In 1822, the last Whig to hold that office for over a hundred years, he succeeded Philip Douglas as Master of his College and died there 19 April 1850. His only poetical work, *The Phaenomena and Diosemaia of Aratus, translated into English Verse*, 8vo, London, 1848, is a somewhat pedestrian rendering of the works of one who has always been presumed to be that 'one of their own poets' quoted by St. Paul against the Athenian philosophers in Acts xvii, v. 28.

JOHN LANGSTON

John Langston, according to Calamy, was born in 1639. From Worcester Grammar School he went to Pembroke College, Oxford, in 1655, but does not seem to have graduated. At the Restoration in

1660 he held the sequestered curacy of Ashchurch in Gloucestershire, from which he was displaced by the returning incumbent. He went to London and kept a private school near Spitalfields and seems, with a short intermission, to have carried on with teaching until 1679, when he moved to Bedfordshire. During this period was published *Lusus Poeticus Latino-Anglicus*, 8vo, London, 1678, a school book in which he translated into English verse some of 'the more eminent sayings of the Latin Poets.' In 1686 he became Minister of the Congregational Church now meeting in Tacket Street, Ipswich, in the vestry of which is his portrait. He died 12 January 1704.

JOHN LIDGATE

JOHN LIDGATE, according to his own account, was born at Lidgate near Newmarket 'where Bacchus licour doth ful scarsly flete,' probably about the year 1370. He was admitted to the Abbey of Bury St Edmunds at the age of fifteen and ordained priest in 1397. He started writing verse at an early age and seems to have been inspired by Chaucer, whom he met sometime after 1390. Until 1413 he spent most of his time in London and was invited by the City Corporation to celebrate its various civil ceremonies in verse. After the accession of Henry VI, Lidgate seems to have acted as court poet and to have had a generous patron in Henry, Duke of Gloucester, the uncle of the King. The latter years of his life were apparently spent at Bury, where he died, probably in 1451. In his poems he repeatedly describes himself as Chaucer's disciple and seems during Chaucer's lifetime to have submitted his poems for his master's approval before release. His *The Chorle and the Birde*, 4to, *The Horse the Ghoos and the Sheep*, 4to, and *The Temple of Glas*, 8vo, were first printed by William Caxton, undated, but probably in 1477, 1479 and 1500 respectively, his *Courte of Sapyence*, 8vo, 1509, by Wynkyn de Worde and his *Testament*, 4to, by Richard Pynson probably in 1515.

CAPEL LOFFT

The son of Christopher Lofft, private secretary to Sarah, Duchess of Marlborough, and Anne his wife, sister of Edward Capell, the editor of Shakespeare, Capel Lofft the elder was born in London, 14 November 1751. Educated at Eton and Peterhouse, Cambridge, he left without a degree, became a member of Lincoln's Inn and was called to the Bar in 1775. On the death of his uncle, Edward Capell, he succeeded to the family estates at Troston in Suffolk and settled down to the life of a country gentleman A strong whig, 'this little David of popular spirit', as he is called by Boswell describing his visit to Dr Johnson, came to be regarded as a firebrand in Suffolk, where he was a leader of the reform party, taking part in the agitation against the American war, against the slave trade and in favour of parliamentary reform, while his name was struck off the roll of magistrates for trying to save the life of a poor girl who had been sentenced to death for a paltry theft: he seems, moreover, to have had in full measure the curious eccentricity in dress and antipathy to soap and water which are still today the hall-mark of the intellectual left. A good classical scholar, a great lover of literature and natural history, an amateur musician of some parts and a skilled astronomer, Lofft had an enormous correspondence with most of the literary characters of his time It was he who 'discovered' Robert Bloomfield and secured the publication of the *Farmer's Boy*, and subsequently some of the works of Nathaniel Bloomfield, Robert's less well known brother. Lofft himself was the author of a number of works, political, legal and literary, his poetical works being *In praise of Poetry*, 8vo, London, 1775, *Eudosia, a poem on the Universe*, 12mo, London, 1781, and *The 1st and 2nd Georgics of Virgil attempted in blank verse*, 1783 (not 1803 as stated in the D.N.B.). Lofft married firstly in 1778, Anne, daughter of Henry Emlyn of Windsor, the architect who restored St. George's Chapel, and secondly in 1812, Sarah Watson Finch, authoress of many of the sonnets in her husband's *Laura, an anthology of sonnets*, London, 1814, 5 vols, and by whom he had one son, Capel Lofft the younger. In 1818 he left Troston with his family for the Continent, travelling till 1822, when he settled in Turin, dying in Moncallieri, 26 May 1824.

THOMAS LYE

Thomas Lye, Lee or Leigh, was born at Chard in Somerset 25 March 1621. As Leigh he matriculated at Wadham College, Oxford in 1630, graduating B.A. in 1641. As Lee he migrated to Emmanuel College, Cambridge, where he proceeded M.A. in 1646, and as Lye in 1645 he succeeded Thomas Stephens as Headmaster of the Grammar School at Bury St. Edmunds, being dismissed and succeeded by Jeremy Wally in 1647. By 1651 he was minister at Chard, and in 1658 was elected minister of All Hallows, Lombard Street, being ejected under the Act of Uniformity in 1662. He was very popular as a teacher of young children and after his ejectment seems to have kept a school at his home at Clapham, where he died and was buried 7 June 1684. He was the author of a number of published sermons and devotional works and *A New Spelling Book*, 8vo, London, 1674, which contains some doggerel verse.

SPENCER MADAN

Spencer, son of Spencer Madan, Bishop of Peterborough, was born in 1758. Educated at Westminster and Trinity College, Cambridge, his *The Call of the Gentiles*, 4to, Cambridge, 1782, won the Seatonian Prize in that year, though he is probably best known for his translation of Grotius' *De Veritae*, which was also first published in 1782. Curate of Wrotham in Kent 1782–83, in the latter year Madan was presented to the Rectory of Bradfield Magna in Suffolk, which he held until 1786, when he was presented to the Rectory of Ibstock in Leicestershire, dying there 9 October 1836.

SIR JAMES MARRIOT

James Marriot, the son of an attorney of Hatton Garden was born about 1730. A scholar of Trinity Hall, Cambridge, he graduated LL.B. in 1751 and was elected a fellow of that society in 1756. In a day when influence rather than competence was the major factor in any man's career he was fortunate enough to gain the approval of the Duke of Newcastle, then Chancellor of the University, to his *Two Poems presented to the Duke of Newcastle*, 4to, London, 1755. In 1764 he was appointed advocate general and elected Master of his College in the same year, being made a judge of the Admiralty Court and knighted in 1778. From 1781–84 and 1796–1802 he represented the Borough of Sudbury in Parliament, causing great merriment by his attempt to justify the war with the American Colonies in saying that these were, in fact, already represented in the English Parliament by the member for Kent, since in the Charters of the thirteen provinces, they are declared to be 'part and parcel of the Manor of Greenwich.' He seems to have quarrelled with the fellows of his College and to have lived in Cambridge as little as he could, dying at his home at Twinstead Hall, near Sudbury, 21 March 1803. He contributed some verses to the University collections on the Peace of 1748, on the Death of Frederick, Prince of Wales in 1751 and on the new Queen in 1761: his *Poems, written Chiefly at the University of Cambridge*, 8vo, Cambridge, was published in 1760.

C. D. MARSTON

CHARLES DALLAS, son of Nathaniel Marston, solicitor, and great nephew of Charles Dallas, the friend of Byron, was born in the island of Jamaica in 1824. Educated at Eton and Gonville and Caius College, Cambridge, he graduated B.A. in 1849, proceeding M.A. in 1852. Curate of Bedfield in Suffolk 1849, he was presented to the vicarage of Houghton in Kent in 1850. He was subsequently Rector of St. Mary's, Bryanston Square, 1862–66, of Kersal, Manchester, 1866–73, and vicar of St. Paul's, Onslow Square from 1873 until his death 12 August 1876. While at Cambridge he composed the English Ode for the Quincentenary of his College in 1848: his only other poetical work is *Poems*, 8vo, 1849, written, according to the introduction, while he was at Bedfield.

JOHN MITFORD

John Mitford, a relation of his patron, Lord Redesdale, was born at Richmond in Surrey on 13 August 1781, the eldest son of John Mitford, a commander of one of the East India Company's ships. Educated at Tonbridge School and Oriel College, Oxford, he graduated B.A. in 1804, and in 1810 was instituted to the vicarage of Benhall in Suffolk. To this was added within a few years the rectories of Stratford St. Andrew and Weston, all of which livings he retained until his death. At Benhall he built a new parsonage in the garden of which he planted a great number of foreign and ornamental trees and shrubs and formed an extensive library mainly of English Poetry. In 1814, and again in 1816, he produced editions of the works of Thomas Gray, the earlier of which was the first accurate edition of the collected poems of that author. From 1834 to 1850 he was editor of the *Gentleman's Magazine*, yet found time to contribute much original poetry of his own as well as editing a number of Pickering's Aldine edition of the British Poets. His own poetical works are: *Agnes, the Indian Captive*, 8vo, London, 1811, *Lines suggested by a fatal Shipwreck near Aldborough*, 12mo, Woodbridge, 1855, and *Miscellaneous Poems*, 8vo, London, 1858. Many of his verses appear signed J.M. in the *Gentleman's Magazine*, others in the *New Suffolk Garland*, 1866. He obviously must have neglected his clerical duties, the more so since, for many years, he rented permanent lodgings in Sloane Street, and Charles Lamb described him as 'a pleasant layman spoiled.' During the winter of 1850 he is reputed to have caused to be built in his garden, and thatched, a large heap of snow which stood until the following Michaelmas. Returning from a visit to the Great Exhibition he is said to have told his parishioners that 'though everything in the world was said to be there one thing was missing, which he had, a thatched snow stack.' At the end of a long life spent in literary pursuits Mitford had a stroke and fell down in a London street. He never recovered from the shock and died at Benhall 27 April 1859, being buried at Stratford St. Andrew.

SUSANNAH MOODIE

Susannah, daughter of Thomas Strickland of Reydon Hall, Suffolk, was born in 1803. She married John Moodie, formerly of the 21st Royal North British Fusiliers, who had been badly wounded in Flanders in 1814. He had subsequently spent ten adventurous years in South Africa and was the author of *Ten Years in South Africa*, London, 1835, and *Roughing it in the Bush*, London, 1852. The newly married pair emigrated to Canada in 1832 where Moodie served as a captain of the Militia on the Niagara frontier in the insurrection of 1837. Mrs Moodie's first publication was *Enthusiasm and other Poems*, 12mo, Bungay, 1831, and, like her sisters, she turned to her pen when sickness and financial difficulties fell upon her family. Between 1852 and 1868 she published a number of minor works of fiction, the last of which, *The World before them*, London, 1868, was described by a reviewer as 'the handiwork of a sensible, amiable, refined and very religious lady ... innocent and negative.' She died in 1885.

PETER MOON

Peter Moon is presumed to have been a Suffolk man since his excessively rare poem *A short treatyse of certayne thinges abused In the Popysh Churche* was published by John Oswen at Ipswich in 1548. It has been suggested that Mistress Moon, the second wife of Thomas Tusser, was a relation of the poet.

THOMAS MOTT

Thomas, the son of Thomas Vertue of Burnham Market in Norfolk, was born there in 1761. Educated at Kings Lynn and at Palgrave under Mr Barbauld, he was admitted to Gonville and Caius College, Cambridge as a pensioner in 1779 under the name of Thomas Mott, having assumed that name in 1776 on inheriting property at Mendham in Suffolk from his relative John Thruston (formerly Mott). He married in 1784 Frances, daughter of the Rev. Robert Cremer, vicar of Wymondham and died 31 December 1788. His recorded poetical works are *The Strangers Return*, 8vo, Cambridge, 1813, and *The Sacred Period*, 12mo, Cambridge, 1822.

THOMAS MOUFET

THOMAS MOUFET, or Moffet, was born in London in 1553, the second son of Thomas Moffett citizen and haberdasher. Educated at the Merchant Taylor's School, Moffett matriculated as a pensioner of Trinity College, Cambridge, in 1569, but migrated to Gonville and Caius College in 1572, where he graduated B.A. While there he studied medicine under Thomas Lorkin and John Caius, and on leaving Cambridge pursued his medical studies at Basle where he received the degree of M.D. in 1578. The following year he visited France and Spain studying the culture of silkworms, the result of which was published in a poem *The Silkwormes and Their Flies*, 4to, London, 1599. In 1588, he became a fellow of the College of Physicians and was at this time in practice in Ipswich, but after a period as physician to the forces serving in France he settled in London in 1591. The latter part of his life was spent in Wiltshire as a pensioner of the Earl of Pembroke, by whose influence he was elected M.P. for Wilton in 1597. He died 5 June 1604, and was buried in Wilton Church. He was a competent doctor and an acute observer of all forms of insect life. He published a number of books on medicine during his lifetime, and his posthumous *Theater of Insects* appended to Topsell's *History of Four-footed Beasts and Serpents*, 1658, is one of the best of the early books on entomology.

THOMAS NASH

THOMAS NASH was born at Lowestoft in 1567, the son of William Nash, a minister in that town. Educated at St. John's College, Cambridge, he graduated B.A. in 1585, and by 1588 had settled in London. A bitter opponent of Puritanism he entered with spirit into the warfare of pamphlets which was waging at that time between the opponents and defenders of Episcopacy, apparently writing under the pseudonym of Pasquil. This general warfare finally developed into a private war between Nash and Richard Hervey, the astrologer, whose notoriously ineffective efforts at astrology Nash satirized in *A wonderful strange and miraculous Astrological Prognostication . . . by Adam Fouleweather, Student in Assetronomy*, 4to, London, 1591, followed later by *Pierce Pennilesse*, 4to, London, 1592, and *Have with you to Saffron-Walden . . . A full Answer to the Eldest Sonne of the Hatter-Maker*, 4to, London, 1596, the latter referring to Hervey's plebeian origin. The battle raged so strongly that in 1599 the licensers of the press intervened and the two authors were ordered to desist. In the same year was published *Nashe's Lenten Stuffe*, 4to, London, 1599, a panegyric on the red herring written after Nash had made a visit to Yarmouth, been hospitably entertained and been able to borrow some money. Apart from his many satirical pieces *Christ's Teares of Jerusalem*, 4to, London, 1593, and *The Unfortunate Traveller, or the life of Jack Wilton*, 4to, London, 1594, are his best known works, while his *Choise of Valentines*, a choice piece of pornography, was privately printed from MSS in the Bodleian and Inner Temple libraries in 4to in 1899. At the early age of thirty-four he died in 1601.

HENRY NORTH

HENRY NORTH, of Mildenhall in Suffolk, great grandson of Roger, second Lord North of Kirtling, was created a Baronet in 1660. He married Sarah, daughter of John Rayney, Esq., of West Malling in Kent, by whom he had one son (who died unmarried in 1695) and two daughters. The eldest daughter, Peregrina, married William Hanmer and was mother of Sir Thomas Hanmer, Bt., Speaker of the House of Commons, and editor of the well-known *Works of William Shakespeare*, 6 vols, 4to, London, 1743, to whom the Mildenhall estate passed on the death of his uncle. Hanmer in his turn died without an heir in 1746, when the estate passed to his nephew the Rev. Sir Charles Bunbury, fifth Bart, Rector of Mildenhall, whose grandson, Sir Henry Bunbury, published in his *Correspondence of Sir Thomas Hanmer*, 8vo, London, 1838, a few of Henry North's poems which had come down in MSS with the estate.

THOMAS NUCE

Thomas Nuce, a fellow of Pembroke Hall, Cambridge, in 1562, was rector of Beccles in Suffolk from 1575 to 1583 and from 1578 until his death in that village, in 1617, rector of Gazeley. While still at Cambridge he published *The Ninth Tragedie of Seneca, Called Octavia*, 4to, London, n.d. (but 1561), which was later reprinted as part of *Seneca his tenne Tragedies, translated into English*, 4to, London, 1581. Nuce was also the author of some English verse prefixed to John Studley's translation of Seneca's *Agamemnon*, 8vo, London, 1561.

PERRY NURSEY

Perry, son of Perry Nursey of the Grove, Little Bealings, and later of Foxhall, was born at Bealings 23 December 1799. The elder Nursey was trained as a surgeon, but married a Miss Simpson, a Ward in Chancery of considerable wealth, and gave up his profession to devote himself to painting. He acquired some small reputation as an artist, and a remarkable taste in christian names. Amongst his ten children were Poussin Hagard, Corinthea, Marietta Syrami, Fontaine Lavinia, Rosalba Violante, Claude Lorraine and Perry the younger. This latter was educated at East Bergholt and admitted as a Smith's pensioner to Corpus Christi College, Cambridge, in 1818, migrating to Sidney Sussex College in the following year. For some years he was curate of East Dereham and subsequently for more than twenty years curate of Burlingham St. Andrew and St. Peter in Norfolk. In 1863 he was presented to the living at Crostwick near Norwich, where he died in 1867 and is buried in the churchyard. His only publication was a small volume of poems *Evening, with other Poems*, 8vo, Norwich, 1829.

RICHARDSON PACK

The son of John Pack of Stoke Ash in Suffolk and his wife, daughter and heiress of Robert Richardson of Tudhoe, Co. Durham, Richardson

Pack was born 29 November 1682. Educated at the Merchant Taylor's School and St. John's College, Oxford, he left without taking a degree. Subsequently, he was called to the Bar, but preferring a more active life joined the army in March 1705. At the battle of Villa Viciosa his bravery attracted the attention of the Duke of Argyll, who obtained his promotion to major and remained his friend until his death. By 1714 he seems to have been on half pay living first at Stoke Ash and later in Bury St. Edmunds, but in 1725 he was back in the army as a major in Colonel Montague's regiment, dying in Aberdeen in 1728. A number of his poems were published by Curll, a notorious printer of pornographic poems, in various miscellanies and in the works of other writers. Pack's own published works being *Miscellanies in Prose and Verse*, 8vo, London, 1719, *A new Collection of Miscellanies*, 8vo, London, 1725, and *The Whole Works of Major R. Pack*, published posthumously in 1729.

WILLIAM PAGET

I HAVE included this author amongst our Suffolk Poets on rather slender grounds. My grandfather having been one of those who introduced into England the Little Owl—according to family tradition because in Holland, whence he obtained his specimens, the bird is said to kill bats in belfries—I have a strong and hereditary affection for the whole race: the beautiful lines here reprinted were irresistible. According to the author's introduction to his *Humours of the Fleet*, 46pp, London, 1799, William Paget was born in London and at first followed his father's profession of architect. He inherited an ample fortune, increased by a good marriage, but 'by indiscretions, too large dealings, and very great losses it was in a few years all run out.' He then took to the stage, spent some time in Ireland, and later lived at Ipswich for a short period where, as an admitted 'pot boiler,' he wrote his poem *A Voyage to Ipswich*, with prologue in honour of Admiral Vernon spoken at the Playhouse Ipswich. W. Paget, comedian, Ipswich, printed by W.C. (William Craighton) for the Author, 1741, size $7\frac{3}{4}'' \times 4\frac{3}{4}''$, Ipswich. Later he was flung into the Fleet Prison for debt, 'whence I never expect to return alive but ... by the last Insolvent Act ... was set at Liberty.'

ESTHER PEARSON

Esther Pearson was born at Bildeston 25 February 1817, the daughter of George Pearson, a deacon in the Baptist Church at Wattisham. Her mother, Susannah Pearson, 'an eminently gifted woman, possessing a vigorous mind and a strong predilection for literary pursuits' was well known in her own circle as the author of *Essays and letters affectionately addressed to the Church of Christ*. At an early age Esther Pearson wrote pieces, both in prose and verse on religious subjects, some of which were published in the *Spiritual Magazine* for June and December 1828. For three years at the boarding school of the Misses Oldring at Beccles, she was there stricken with consumption in May 1833, dying at Bildeston on 3 October in the same year. Her only publication *Buds of Hope*, 8vo, London, containing an account of her life, was published posthumously in 1855.

ROBERT POTTER

Robert Potter was born in 1721: educated at the Grammar School at Scarning and Emmanuel College, Cambridge, he graduated B.A. in 1741, but did not proceed to the degree of M.A. until 1788, when he was made a Canon of Norwich. In 1761 he was appointed Master of his old school at Scarning, but the inhabitants barred his entry by force as they wished the appointment of another master called Coe, who had been working the school for sometime. In spite of this inauspicious beginning—he was unable to enter his school until Sir Armine Wodehouse had read the Riot Act—Potter proved a good schoolmaster and remained at Scarning for twenty-eight years, occupying his spare time in translating into English verse the works of the Greek Tragedians: the Tragedies of Aeschylus were published in 4to in 1777, of Euripides 4to 1781, and of Sophocles, 4to, 1788. His other poetry was *Retirement*, 4to, London, 1748, *A Farewell Hymn to the Country*, 4to, London, 1749, *Holkham, A Poem*, 4to, London, 1758, *Kymber*, 4to, London, 1759, and *Poems*, 8vo, London, 1774. Some verses by Dr Johnson in derision of Potter's attempts at poetry were read at Mrs Thrale's house in July 1779, but the victim did not suffer in silence and published in 1783 *An Enquiry into some Passages in Dr. Johnson's Lives of the Poets*, and in 1789,

The Art of Criticism as exemplified in Dr. Johnson's Lives. Horace Walpole said that Potter's defence of Gray was 'sensibly written, civil to Johnson, yet severe.' In 1789 he was presented to the Vicarage of Lowestoft with the rectory of Kessingland, dying at Lowestoft 9 August 1809.

JOHN RANDALL

JOHN, son of Francis Randall of Eton, was born in that town in 1666. He was educated at Eton College and Christ's College, Cambridge, where he graduated B.A. in 1691, proceeding M.A. in 1694. He became an assistant master at the Grammar School at Bury St. Edmunds in 1690, where he was headmaster from 1707 to 1715. In 1718 he was appointed headmaster of Guildford Grammar School, a position which he held until his death in 1722. In his *Nomina quorundum e primariis olim regiae grammaticalis scholae Buriae Sancti Edmundi inter Icenos celeberrimae carminibus illustrata*, 1719, appears some verse, while his elegy on the death, from small-pox, of his son is quoted by J. W. Donaldson in his *Retrospective address read at the Tercentenary Commemoration of King Edward School, Bury St. Edmunds*, 8vo, London, 1850.

CLARA REEVE

CLARA, eldest daughter of Rev. William Reeve, Minister of St. Nicholas Ipswich, 1725–1755, was born at Ipswich in 1729. From an early age she was made to read the Parliamentary Debates and Greek and Roman history by her father, an old-fashioned whig. After his death in 1755, the widow with her three daughters moved to Colchester, where Clara's first book and only volume of poetry was produced—*Original Poems on Several Occasions*, by C.R., 4to, London, 1769. In 1777 was published her most famous work *The Champion of Virtue, a Gothic Story*, 8vo, London, 1777, a novel based on and, as the author avows, 'the literary offspring of Walpole's *Castle of Otranto*'. A second edition appeared in the following year, that and all the many subsequent editions being published under the title of *The Old English Baron*. Miss Reeve led a quiet and retired life and died at Ipswich 3 December 1807.

SARAH REVELL

A MANUSCRIPT note dated 24 November 1874 in a copy of *Gideon*, 8vo, London, 1829, printed by Bracket of Sudbury, says that the author was a Miss Sarah Revell who was living at Sudbury in 1829 but 'removed to Blackheath . . . where she died at an advanced age about 2 years since.' *Gideon* is published anonymously, and according to an advertisement at the end is by the author of *My Early Years*, 12mo, *Jane and Her Teacher*, 18mo, *George Wilson and his Friend*, 18mo, *The Lady at the Farmhouse*, 18mo, and *Maria's Reward*, 18mo. *Five Worlds of Enjoyment*, 8vo, Sudbury, G. W. Fulcher, 1857, is by S. Revell and has at the end an advertisement of 'works by the same author', which includes the above and *Gideon*. There is in the British Museum an anthology, *School Poetry*, 12mo, London, 1860, but Ipswich printed, edited by Sarah Revell, possibly the same person.

GEORGE RICHARDS

GEORGE, son of Rev. James Richards, curate of Halesworth, Suffolk, and afterwards vicar of Rainham, Kent, was born at Halesworth in 1768. Educated at Christ's Hospital and Trinity College, Oxford, he graduated B.A. in 1788, proceeding M.A. in 1791, and being elected a fellow of Oriel in the same year. In 1787 he obtained the Chancellor's prize for Latin verse and in 1791 obtained a prize in English Verse on the subject of *The Aboriginal Britons*, London, 4to, 1791, a second edition of which, also in 4to, was published in the same year. He was presented to the vicarage of Bampton, Oxon, in 1796 in which year he married Miss Parker, a sister of the Oxford Bookseller of that name. In 1820 he accumulated the degrees of B. & D.D. and was presented to the living of St. Martins-in-the-Fields. 'His exertions in that parish, his liberality in providing for the spiritual wants of his parishioners, and his general munificence, more especially that of erecting the present vicarial house at his own exclusive cost, and largely contributing to the new Chapel in Exeter Street, are matters of Public notoriety' (*Sucklings Hist. of Suffolk*). He died at Russell Square in 1837 leaving £5,000 to the Royal Society of Literature, the interest on which was to be applied to the publication of unedited MSS.

His other poetical works are: *Modern France, A poem*, London, 4to, 1793. *Matilda, the dying Penetant*, 4to, 1795. *Emma*, 12mo, 1804. *Odin*, 12mo, 1804. *Poems*, 2 vols., 8vo, 1804. *Monody on the death of Lord Nelson*, 4to, 1806. *Miscellaneous Poems*, 2 vols, 8vo, 1815.

HAMILTON ROCHE

JOHN HAMILTON ROCHE was the author of a number of small pieces of poetry, *Salamanca*, 4to, London, 1812, *Russia, A heroic Poem*, 4to, London, 1813, *France, a heroic Poem*, 4to, London, 1814, *The Sudburiad*, 8vo, Sudbury, 1813, including two appropriately published abroad, *Cathoerides, or Poems from Paris*, 4to, Paris, 1820, and *Les Amours des Muses*, 4to, Brest, 1826. He also published one novel, *A Suffolk Tale, or the Perfidious Guardian*, 2 vols, 12mo, London, 1810, but beyond the fact that John Hamilton Roche and Louisa Bath were married at Ixworth 8 August 1803, all that is known of him is Davy's statement that he was once 'a Captain in the Army, now (1816) residing in Sudbury.'

THOMAS ROGERS

THOMAS ROGERS was educated at Christ Church, Oxford, and graduated B.A. in 1573, proceeding M.A. in 1576. He was presented to the Rectory of Horningsheath or Horringer in Suffolk in 1581, dying in that village in 1616. He was the author of a large number of religious books and sermons, and according to Hazlitt was the author of *Celestial Elegies of the Goddesses and the Muses, deploring the death of Frances, Countess of Hertford*, London, 1598.

ANN ROLFE

ACCORDING to Davy, Ann Rolfe was 'wife of the butler to Mrs Shephard', presumably of Campsea Ashe. Her *Miscellaneous Poems for a Winter's Evening*, 8vo, Woodbridge, 1840, is by 'Mrs Ann Rolfe (late Mrs Plumb)' but I can find nothing of Mr Plumb.

RICHARD ROLPH

According to '*The Life of Richard Rolph, the blind peasant of Lakenheath*, 4to, Bury St. Edmunds, 1841, he was born at Lakenheath in Suffolk 8 May 1801, of poor but industrious parents and had what little schooling he received at the Wesleyan Sunday School. In his early youth he confesses that 'dissipation was my joy', and on becoming partially blind he became an itinerant fiddler with his younger brother leading him and playing the tambourine—indeed he 'became a Sabbath breaker ... selling shrimps on that sacred day.' By January 1831, he had become totally blind, when he gave up his wicked life, sold his fiddle and started composing spiritual poems which were written down for him by his friends. Of these I have only seen *A Poetical Discourse*, third edition, 8vo, Bury St. Edmunds, 1843, though this contains an advertisement for *Poetical Discourses, the Second Part*. Of his subsequent history nothing is known.

SAMUEL SAY

Samuel, second son of Gyles Say, sometime vicar of Southampton, was born in that town 23 March 1675. His father had been ejected from his living for non-conformity in 1662, but had continued as preacher to a dissenting congregation in the same town. Samuel was educated at Norwich and Thomas Rowe's Academy in London, where Isaac Watts was his fellow student and intimate friend. After a short period in Kent, Hampshire and Gt. Yarmouth, he settled at Lowestoft in 1707 as minister, where he stayed until 1725 when he became co-pastor with Samuel Baxter at Ipswich. In 1734 on the death of Edmund Calamy, he accepted the care of the congregation at Long Ditch, Westminster, where he remained until his death 12 April 1743 'of a mortification of the Bowells'. Two years after his death some youthful poems which he had left in manuscript were edited by William Duncombe and published as *Poems on several Occasions*, 4to, London, 1745, in the preface to which the editor says of the author 'he was a well versed in astronomy and Natural Philosophy, had a taste for Music and Poetry, was a good

Critic, and a Master of the Classics'. Samuel Say's only child married the Rev. Isaac Toms, a dissenting minister at Hadleigh, whose son, the Rev. Samuel Say Toms, was a minister to the congregation at Framlingham.

MARY SEWELL

MARY, daughter of John Wright, a Quaker farmer, was born at Sutton in Suffolk, on April 1797. In 1809 Mr Wright moved to Yarmouth where he set up in business as a ship owner and where in 1819 his daughter married, after a courtship of five years, Isaac, son of William Sewell of that town. Their only daughter, Anne Sewell (1820–78) was crippled for life by an accident in early childhood and in the intervals of sickness wrote *Black Beauty*, the autobiography of a horse, which has brought tears to the eyes of successive generations of children over the past seventy years. At the age of sixty, Mrs Sewell began seriously to write verse with the object of inculcating the moral virtues into all relations of human life—and so far as the circulation of her many little pamphlets is concerned, with enormous success. *Home Ballads*, privately printed in 1858 reached its fortieth thousand by 1889, while *Mother's Last Words*, 1860, which tells how two poor boys were kept on the straight and narrow path by the memory of their mother's last words, is said to have sold 1,088,000 copies. The Sewell's had left Yarmouth in 1822 soon after the birth of their daughter and finally settled near Bristol where most of Mrs Sewell's works were written. In 1867 they returned to Norfolk to live at Old Catton near Norwich, where she died 10 June 1884 and was buried in the Friends' Burial Ground at Lamas, though she had been baptised into the Established Church in 1835. Her numerous productions were collected in 1861 under the title of *Stories in Verse*, and again in 1886 as *Poems and Ballads*, in two volumes with a memoir of the author by Mrs Bayley.

CUTHBERT SHAW

The son of a shoemaker of the same name, Cuthbert Shaw was born at Ravensworth, Yorks, in 1739. For a time usher at Darlington Grammar School his first poem *Liberty*, 4to, 1756, was published in that town. He then seems to have joined a company of actors in the eastern counties and in 1760 was at Bury St. Edmunds where, under the pseudonmy of W. Seymour he published in 4to his *Odes on the Four Seasons*. He then moved to London, but having 'nothing to recommend him as an actor save his good looks, which were prematurely dulled by his excesses' soon left the stage and took to writing. His description of Johnson in *The Race, by Mercurius Spur, Esq*, 4to, London, 1766, is quoted by Boswell, who says of the author that he was 'alike distinguished by his genius, misfortunes and misconduct'. Tutor to the young Philip Stanhope who succeeded his godfather, the author of the *Letters*, as fifth Earl of Chesterfield in 1773, he died in London 'overwhelmed with complicated distress' 1 September 1771. A frequent contributor to the periodicals of the day, Shaw's other poetical works comprise *A monody on the death of a Young Lady who died in childhood*, 4to, London 1768, *Corruption a Satire*, 4to, London, 1769, and in 1770 *An Elegy on the Death of Charles Yorke, the Lord Chancellor* which was generally suspected to have been suppressed on the family paying a sum of money to the author.

RICHARD SHEPHERD

Richard, son of Henry Shepherd of Mareham-le-Fen, Lincs, was born in 1732. Educated at Corpus Christi College, Oxford, he seems to have gained some reputation as a poet with his *Ode to Love*, 4to, London, 1756, *Odes Descriptive and Allegorical*, 4to, London, 1761, and *The Nuptials*, 4to, London, 1761. Boswell thought highly of his poetry and says of an evening spent with Shepherd in 1763 'that night I passed the only pleasant hours during my stay at Oxford . . . finding him a quiet, modest, diffident man. He told me that he was fellow of a college, but that it was but a poor pittance which that yielded him: and besides that it kept him from an active life, which was the sphere he loved most: in particular the Army.' But Shepherd was destined for the church, taking Orders he became chaplain to Thomas Thurlow, Bishop of Lincoln, by whose nomination he was made Archdeacon of Bedford in 1783. F.R.S. in 1781 and D.D. in 1788, in 1792 he was presented to the Rectory of Wetherden in Suffolk, dying in that village in 1809. His other poetical works were *Hector*, 4to, London, 1770, *Bianca, a Tragedy*, 8vo, London, 1772, *Miscellanies*, 2 vols, 8vo, London, 1776, and *The Dying Hero*, 4to, London, 1779, the first of which, like the three first mentioned, was published anonymously.

J. T. SHEWELL

JOHN TALWIN SHEWELL was born in London, 26 January 1782, the son of Thomas Shewell of the Stock Exchange, and his wife Ann, daughter of John Talwin of Royston. Educated at Hitchin Grammar School and later at a Friends school at Wandsworth, he was apprenticed in 1796 to Isaac Liversedge, a Quaker merchant of Ipswich. He early showed a strong liking for literature and in particular for poetry and in 1808 was printed anonymously *A Tribute to the Memory of William Cowper*, 4to, Ipswich, J. Raw, which from the set up of the title page appeared to be by William Hayley and, until the recent revision, was in fact ascribed to that author in the B.M. catalogue. A second edition was issued in the same year by the same publisher as 'by J.T.S.' In 1802 Mr Liversedge died and Shewell was taken into partnership by the widow being joined in the business, which prospered under his management, by Edward Corder in 1821. In 1831 he retired, marrying in the following year Elizabeth Peckover of Wisbech. A deeply religious man, he had been recorded minister in the Society of Friends in 1829, and throughout his life he was prominent in the religious life of the town. His retirement was spent first at Orwell Lodge just outside Ipswich and later in Rushmere, to which village he removed in 1840 and where he died in 1869. An account of his life was published in Ipswich in 1870.

SAMUEL SLATER

SAMUEL, the son of the Rev. Samuel Slater of St. Katherine's in the Tower of London, was educated at Emmanuel College, Cambridge, where he graduated B.A. in 1647, proceeding M.A. in 1658. Rector of Nayland and afterwards lecturer at Bury St. Edmunds, he was summoned at the first assizes after the Restoration for refusing to read the Book of Common Prayer, being finally ejected under the Act of Uniformity in 1662. He moved to London where, in 1680, he became minister of the non-conformist congregation in Crosby Square, Bishopsgate, and where he remained until his death 22 May 1704. According to Calamy 'he was a grave, serious, and useful preacher, and always had a considerable stock of sermons before hand.' He published a number of sermons and *Poems*, 8vo, London, 1679, of which he says in the preface 'I was much taken with the learned Mr Milton's cast and fancy in his book *Paradise Lost*. Him I have followed much in his method, but I have used a more plain and familiar style'—a statement which cannot be disputed.

H. F. R. SOAME

HENRY FRANCIS ROBERT SOAME was born 16 October 1768, the only child of the Rev. Henry Soame of Thurlow Hall in Suffolk, and Susan, eldest daughter of Sir William Bunbury, Bart. He was educated at the Grammar School at Bury St. Edmunds, and at Trinity College, Cambridge, and died in India, a lieutenant in the 22nd Light Dragoons, in 1803. During his lifetime he published *An Epistle in rhyme to M. G. Lewis Esq., M.P.*, 12mo, London, 1799, while *Poetry by the late H. F. R. Soame*, 16mo, London, 1833, was printed after his death for Sir Henry Bunbury.

WILLIAM SMITH

WILLIAM SMITH was born in London in 1730, the son of a wholesale grocer and tea merchant. Educated at Eton and St. John's College, he was sent down from Cambridge for snapping a pistol in the face of a proctor and coming to London went on the stage, appearing first at Covent Garden in 1753. After a long and successful career as an actor he retired in 1788 to Bury St. Edmunds where he died September 1819. His first wife, whom he married in 1754, was a sister of the notorious fourth Earl of Sandwich and a great outcry was raised at the disgrace entailed by a lady in her position entering into such an alliance. Smith offered to retire from the stage if an annuity equal to the income he made from his profession was given to him, but this proposal was declined. Lady Elizabeth died in 1762 and Smith married again to a Miss Newson of Leiston in Suffolk, who survived him and forgave a solitary but notorious escapade when he took his leading lady to Paris in the spring of 1764. Known as 'Gentleman Smith', horse racing and hunting were his delight: he is said to have had a clause in his engagements that he should not be called upon to act on Mondays in the hunting season and he sometimes hunted in the morning and took relays of horses back to London so as to act at night, riding once, it is said, eighteen miles in an hour.

HUMPHREY SMYTHIES

HUMPHREY SMYTHIES was educated at Emmanuel College, Cambridge, where he graduated B.A. in 1743, proceeding M.A. in 1761. For a time Rector of Blewbury in Berkshire he was presented in 1781 to the Rectory of Alpheton in Suffolk, where his death is recorded 30 May 1806, aged eighty-two. He was the author of *Precepts, a Poem addressed to the Toasts of Great Britain*, 12mo, London, 1753.

JAMES SPILLING

ACCORDING to Glyde—'Mr Spilling was born in the Parish of St. Mathew, Ipswich, about 1824–25. His parents were poor, but through the interest of a subscriber he was placed as a scholar in the Blue Coat School in St. Mary Elms, then under the care of Mr Franks and his diligence and desire to acquire knowledge made him one of his Master's favourite pupils. On leaving school he was apprenticed to Mr Robert Deck, who resided on the Cornhill, Ipswich, well known in those days as a Bookseller, Printer and Stationer, and still better known politically as a Tory of the deepest dye. James Spilling remained with Mr Deck a short time after the expiration of his apprenticeship, but the tyrannical manner of his employer made him anxious to leave and he obtained work as a printer in the office of the *Suffolk Chronicle*. From there he removed to Mr J. M. Burton's, Cornhill, Ipswich, who engaged him as 'Reader', that gentleman being the publisher of the *Run and Read Library*. After two or three years he was engaged by the proprietors of the *Norfolk News* through the influence of a friend at Norwich. Mr Jack Tillet quickly proved his worth and he acted as sub-editor for many years. After Mr Tillet's death he was installed as Editor. He embraced the views of the New Jerusalem Church and frequently occupied the pulpit of one of their churches on a Sunday. His ability as a poet aided him greatly in expounding the principles of Emmanuel Swedenborg and the books that he published became very popular amongst those of his own Household of Faith. One of them *Charles Robinson* is to a considerable extent autobiographical. He was, however, probably best known for his dialogue stories—*Giles Trip to London* being the best known.' His poetical works were *The Spirit of the Seasons*, 8vo, London, 1850, and *Marriage Love*, 8vo, London, 1892.

WILLIAM SPRING

WILLIAM, son of Sir William Spring, Knight, of Pakenham in Suffolk was baptised 13 March 1613, at Stanton All Saints. Sheriff of Suffolk 1640–41, he was created a Baronet in the latter year, but in spite of this sign of his sovereign's pleasure was a strong parliamentarian serving on several important committees between 1643 and 1646. He married in 1642 Elizabeth, daughter of Sir Hamon L'Estrange of Hunstanton and dying at Pakenham 17 December 1654, left an only son William to succeed to the Baronetcy. *Suffolk's Tears*, 4to, London, 1653, contains a number of elegies on Sir Nathaniel Barnardiston, one by *William Spring Barronet*: this must, from the date, be the first baronet of that line.

MARY ELIZABETH SQUIRREL

Elizabeth, the daughter of Asaph and Martha Squirrel was born at Shottisham 10 March 1838. Her grandfather, Samuel Squirrel, was for thirty-eight years Baptist Minister at the adjoining village of Sutton. Delicate from birth, in 1852 she gained considerable notoriety by her alleged abstinence from food and drink for a period of 153 days. The case aroused great controversy: two committees of watchers attested to the fact that no fraud had been perpetrated, others affirming with equal fervour that the feat was impossible. A number of books and pamphlets on the case were published, in one of which *The Autobiography of Elizabeth Squirrel by one of her watchers* (Rev. W. A. Norton, rector of Alderton and Eyke), 8vo, London, 1853, is printed a number of her poems. The reports of the two committees were presented to a public meeting at the Corn Exchange, Ipswich, in 1852, which broke up in disorder. The family moved to Ipswich where she seems to have lived until 1857, but her later history is not known: she is said to have married and removed to London.

HENRY STEBBING

Henry, son of John Stebbing, was born at Gt. Yarmouth 26 August 1799. Educated at St. John's College, Cambridge, he graduated B.A. in 1823, and in 1825 was appointed evening lecturer at St. Mary's, Bungay, and in the same year perpetual curate of Ilketshall St. Lawrence. In 1827 he moved to London and was soon 'working for the booksellers from morning to night and sometimes from night to morning.' He edited, with the Rev. R. Cattermole, the *Sacred Classics* of England, some thirty volumes being published between 1834–36 while he himself wrote a number of religious tracts and books and also edited the works of Bunyan (1839), Josephus (1842), Milton's Poems (1851), and Robinson Crusoe (1859). His first poem *The Wanderers* was published in 1817, *The Minstrel of the Glen* in the following year, and *The Long Railway Journey*, 1851. With this literary drudgery, Stebbing combined much clerical work, dying in London, 22 September 1883.

THOMAS STEPHENS

THOMAS STEPHENS was admitted sizar at St. John's College, Cambridge, in 1629 as 'of Kent'. He graduated B.A. 1633/4 and proceeded M.A. in 1637, becoming D.D. in 1661. Headmaster of the Grammar School at Bury St. Edmunds from 1638–45 and again from 1647–63, he was presented to the Rectory of Lackford in Suffolk in the latter year, dying in that village in 1677. He published a few sermons, a commentary on the *Sylvae* of Statius, and *An Essay upon Statius, or the First Five Books of Statius his Thebais done into English Verse*, 8vo, 1648.

AGNES STRICKLAND

AGNES, second surviving daughter of Thomas Strickland and Mary Homer his second wife, was born in London 19 August 1796. In 1808 the family moved to Reydon Hall near Southwold, where the two elder children Elizabeth and Agnes were educated by their father. They early showed a taste for the study of history and when the death of their father in 1818 left the family in straightened circumstances, the two sisters turned to literature as a part of their means of livelihood. Agnes had published anonymously in 1817 in the *Norwich Mercury* a *Monody upon the Death of the Princess Charlotte of Wales*, and in 1827 appeared a metrical romance *Worcester Field*, 8vo, London, followed by *The Seven Ages of Women and Other Poems*, 8vo, London, 1827, and *Floral Sketches and other Poems*, 8vo, London, 1836. In conjunction with Bernard Barton she edited Fisher's *Juvenile Scrap-book* from 1837–39 and contributed two tales to the *Pic-nic Papers*, edited by Charles Dickens in 1846. In co-operation with her sister Elizabeth she then turned to prose, a number of children's books being followed by their well-known *Lives of the Queens of England*, the first volume of which appeared in 1840 and the twelfth and last in 1848. This was followed by a number of historical works *The Letters of Mary Queen of Scots*, 1842, *Lives of the Queens of Scotland*, 1850, *Lives of the Bachelor Kings of England*, 1861, etc., etc., all written in co-operation with her sister Elizabeth, but all with Agnes's name alone on the title page—the elder sister having an invincible objection to publicity. On her mother's death in 1864 Reydon Hall was sold and Miss Strickland removed to Park Lane Cottage, Southwold, where she died 13 July 1874, having been granted a Civil List Pension of £100 a year in 1870.

JOHN SUCKLING

JOHN, son of Sir John Suckling, Lord of Barsham and Shipmeadow, and member for Dunwich in the Parliament of 1601, was born at Twickenham 10 February 1608. Few English poets have lived a life so public and so full of vicissitudes. At the age of nineteen he wandered through France, Italy, Germany and Spain seeking education. He fought with the King of Sweden at Glogau and Magdeburgh and later with the greatest bravery in Silesia, leaving for England merely because he began to find war a tedious pursuit. The death of his father having left him an immensely rich man with large estates in Norfolk and Suffolk, on his return he spent much of his time in London and at court where cards and dice had an irresistible fascination for him and where he admits he prized 'a pair of black eyes above all the triumphs of wit.' In 1624 he had a quarrel with Sir John Digby, his rival for the hand of a daughter of Sir Henry Willoughby, a quarrel in which the poet tamely submitted to his opponent and seems to have taken an unmerciful thrashing without ever drawing sword. This loosened the tongues of his many detractors at court and he turned to the more sedate and intellectual companionship of such men as Lord Falkland, Robert Boyle and Thomas Stanley. He later returned to court where he became one of the leaders of the Royalist faction and 1639 he raised, at his own expense, a troop of 100 horse for Holland's abortive expedition into Scotland. Though there were no imputations against his personal courage, many scurrilous remarks were made about the lavish accoutrements of his men. In the following year he took part in a plot to secure command of the Army for the King, which being discovered, he had to fly to France and later to Spain where he fell into the hands of the Inquisition, was imprisoned and tortured. He was, however, released and returned to France where he died in 1642 at the age of thirty-four. Many stories are told of his death: his valet was said to have hidden a razor in one of his boots which severed an artery when he pulled it on:

other accounts tell of his murder in other ways and of his suicide, but the probability is that broken in body and mind by the tortures he had undergone in Spain, reduced in fortune and dreading poverty, he poisoned himself and 'died vomiting.'

During his lifetime he published *Aglaura*, 4to, London, 1638, and *The Ballad of a Wedding*, 4to, London, 1640, but seems to have taken little care of his other works which were collected and published after his death as *Fragmenta Aurea*, 8vo, London, 1646.

HENRY HOWARD, EARL OF SURREY

Henry Howard, Earl of Surrey, the eldest son of the third Duke of Norfolk, was born about 1517. Much of his early childhood was spent at his father's house Stoke Hall in Suffolk, but from 1530–32 he was educated at Windsor with Henry the Eighth's natural son, Henry Fitzroy, Duke of Richmond. At one time, Anne Boleyn seems to have urged the king to marry Princess Mary to Surrey, but she changed her mind and Surrey was married in 1532 to Frances Vere, daughter of the fifth Earl of Oxford, though on account of their youth, husband and wife did not live together until 1535. 'The most foolish proud boy that ever was in England,' Surrey was constantly in trouble, fighting, quarrelling, and in 1543, for breaking the windows of the citizens of London by shooting pebbles at them with a stone bow. Between 1543 and 1546 he was engaged in the French War, acquitting himself with great bravery and being reprimanded by the King for exposing himself to needless danger. In December 1546 Henry was known to be dying, and speculation was rife at court as to whether the King would select Norfolk or Lord Hertford to be Protector during the minority of Prince Edward. Surrey chose this moment to assert his right to include amongst his quarterings the arms of Edward the Confessor. For this he was accused by the Hertford faction of high treason, brought to trial, convicted and beheaded on Tower Hill, 11 January 1546/47. His body was first buried at All Hallows, Barking, but removed to Framlingham in 1614. During his lifetime much of his verse was circulated in manuscript, but it was not printed until Richard Tottel published *Songes and Sonettes* in 1557.

JOHN TAMPEN

All that is known of John Tampen is that he applied for membership of the Stoke Green Baptist Church on 3 April 1793, was baptised in Belstead Brook on 26 April and joined the Church on 5 May 1793. According to the introduction to his *Testimony of Truth*, Ipswich, J. Bush, Pt. I., 1796, he was 'though rich in faith, yet a poor helpless cripple, and in consequence never likely to be capable of doing anything to attain a livelihood; he has been in this situation near three years, though before that time, as he was young, so also healthy and strong.' A *Testimony of Truth* was published anonymously 'By a Prisoner of Hope': the author's name is only revealed by the acrostic in the last ten lines.

JANE AND ANNE TAYLOR

Isaac Taylor (1789–1829) was born in London and after being educated at Brentford Grammar School started work in the studio of his father Isaac (1730–1807) a well-known engraver. In 1781 he married at Islington, Ann Martin, and with her moved in 1786 to Lavenham in Suffolk, where he continued at his profession of engraver, producing, amongst many other works a series of engravings of Suffolk Mansions. A strong non-conformist, in 1796 he received a call to act as Pastor to an independent congregation at Colchester, and after some years in that town, removed to Ongar in 1810, where as Pastor he spent the remaining years of his life. 'The Taylors of Ongar', as the family were later known to distinguish them from the contemporary literary family the 'Taylors of Norwich', father, mother, Anne (1782–1866), Jane (1783–1824), and Isaac (1787–1865) were prolific writers, and between them produced an abundance of educational and devotional works in prose and verse. Mrs Taylor was the author of a number of little manuals on conduct and behaviour, all of which had a widespread sale: *Advice to Mothers*, 12mo, London, n.d., *Practical hints to Young Females*, 12mo, London, 1815, and *Correspondence between a mother and a daughter* (Jane) *at School*, 12mo, London, 1817, are the best known but there were many others, all exceedingly popular in their day. Of the daughter's productions, *Original Poems for Infant Minds*, 12mo, London, by Jane and Ann with a few poems by Isaac, was published in 1804: the well-known poem *My Mother* appeared in this and was one of Ann's contribution. *Rhymes for the Nursery*, 12mo, London, followed in 1806, again a joint compilation, containing Jane's *Twinkle, Twinkle little star*. *Limed twigs to catch young birds*, 8vo, London, 1808, *Hymns for Infant minds*, 8vo, London, 1810, and *Original Hymns for Sunday Schools*, 12mo, London, 1810, are amongst the better known of the books by the two sisters, most of which were frequently reprinted. *Hymns for Infant Minds* was probably the most successful, running to upwards of a hundred editions, the fourth of which has as frontispiece an engraving by Jane of a child kneeling by its mother's grave, after a drawing by her brother Isaac. In 1812, Ann was living at Ilfracombe with Jane and Isaac where she received a letter from the Rev. Joseph Gilbert, minister of the Fish Street Chapel at Hull, asking if he might visit her with a view to matrimony. The two had never met, but they had mutual friends, and Gilbert had apparently been impressed by her writings—though it must have been difficult to choose between the authors of *My Mother* and *Twinkle, twinkle*. She seems first to have sent him to Ongar where he made a good impression on her parents, and on hearing of their approval she allowed her would-be lover to visit her at Ilfracombe. They were married in 1813 when the literary partnership between the two sisters came to an end. A nineteenth-century brood of children slowed down the spate so far as Anne was concerned, but it wanted more than annual child-bearing altogether to silence a Taylor and she contributed more than a quarter of the hymns in Dr. Leifchild's collection of *Orginal Hymns*, published in 1842. Jane's productions continued: *Display*, 12mo, London, 1815, *Essays in Rhyme on Morals and Manners*, 12mo, London, 1815, were followed by a series of regular contributions in prose and verse to the *Youth's Magazine*, but she fell into a decline and died at Ongar 13 April 1824.

WILLIAM THEW

THE sixth son of an Ipswich lawyer, William Thew was born in that town 6 November 1794. In his youth he suffered so severely from an impediment in his speech that successive schoolmasters despaired of ever being able to educate him, and with this disability his declared intention of adopting the stage as a career not unnaturally incensed his father and amazed his friends. In the autobiographical introduction to his *Poems*, 8vo, London, 1825, he tells how he conquered his stammer by reciting poetry with two pebbles under his tongue, declaiming Richard III to the waves at Brighton on stormy days in order to teach himself to speak both loud and clear. So sure was he of his powers as a tragedian that he offered to compete for 100 guineas a side with Richard Kemble before any jury chosen by the latter, though unfortunately without success. Of his subsequent history nothing is known.

EDWARD THURLOW

EDWARD, son of the Rev. Thomas Thurlow, successively rector of Little Ashfield, Suffolk and Thurston, Long Stratton and Knapton in Norfolk, was born 9 December 1731. His early education was at the Grammar School at Scarning in Norfolk where he acquired the character of an incorrigibly bad boy and from which he was removed to the Perse School at Cambridge. At Gonville and Caius College he distinguished himself by his idleness and insubordination, and he was removed for misconduct without a degree in 1751. In spite of this inauspicious beginning, Thurlow had a remarkable career: called to the Bar in 1754, M.P. for Tamworth 1765, Solicitor-General 1770, and Lord Chancellor 1778, being raised to the peerage as Baron Thurlow of Ashfield, Suffolk, on his advancement to that office, an advancement due very largely to pressure from the King, to whom Thurlow had endeared himself by his constant support of the rights of the mother country against the American Colonies. Many are the stories of Thurlow's bluntness in his private conversation, which seems to have been well larded with oaths and minor obscenities; Glyde tells of many of them in his *New Suffolk Garland*. Nevertheless, he was fond of the company of men of letters, Dr. Johnson respected his conversational powers and at one period he was able to relieve George Crabbe from some pecuniary difficulty. He never married and on his retirement from office in 1792 was created Baron Thurlow of Thurlow, Suffolk, with remainder to the heirs male of his nephew Edward Hovell-Thurlow in whose *Moonlight*, 4to, London, 1814, appeared some of the Lord Chancellor's poems. Lord Thurlow died at Brighton 12 September 1806, and is buried in the Temple Church.

JOSEPH TURNLEY

Of Joseph Turnley's *Popery in Power, or the Spirit of the Vatican*, 8vo, London, 1850, the *Gentleman's Magazine* says 'it is a work distinguished both in its poetry and prose by a fiery bitter antipathy to Rome.' According to Davy, the author was for a time an attorney at Yoxford, but moved to Ipswich 'where he did not find his profession a lucrative one'.

THOMAS TUSSER

Thomas Tusser was born at Rivenhall in Essex probably in 1534. Educated at Eton he was elected to King's College, Cambridge, in 1543, migrating later to Trinity Hall. After serving ten years as 'a musician' to Lord Paget, he married and settled down to farming at Brantham in Suffolk, which he found much harder work than music and where he wrote his *Hunreth Good Poyntes of Husbandrie*, 4to, London, 1557. This work *Married unto a Hundreth Good Poyntes of Huswifery* in 1570, and enlarged to *Five Hundreth Pointes of Good Husbandry* in 1573, was the standard agricultural text book from then until the end of the seventeenth century, being reprinted and amplified in numerous successive editions.

Shortly after his book was first published he moved to Ipswich, where his first wife died and thence to West Dereham in Norfolk. Ill luck, or possibly merely a theoretical knowledge of farming evidently dogged his footsteps: he moved to Norwich, tried farming in Essex, thence to Cambridge, and finally to London, where he died in a debtor's prison in 1580.

THOMAS TYMME

Thomas Tymme seems to have been educated at Cambridge, possibly at Pembroke Hall, though he never graduated. He was appointed Rector of Hasketon in 1575, where he died being buried there 29 April 1620. Under the patronage of such influential persons as the Earl of Sussex, the Earl of Devonshire and the Archbishop of Canterbury, he produced numerous translations, mostly of theological works, his only known verse appearing in *Three parts of Commentaries of . . . Civil Warres in France*, 4to, London, 1574.

RICHARD VALPY

The eldest son of Richard and Catherine Valpy of St. John's Parish, Jersey, Richard Valpy was born on that island 7 December 1754. Educated first in Normandy and later at Southampton Grammar School, Valpy was subsequently removed to Guildford Grammar School and while still there published by subscription *Poetical Blossoms*, 4to, Guildford, 1772. In the following year he went to Pembroke College, Oxford, where he graduated B.A. in 1776, proceeding M.A. in 1784 and D.D. in 1792. In 1777 he was appointed second master of Bury St. Edmunds School, leaving in 1781 to be head master of Reading School. He continued in this office until 1830 with conspicuous success, raising the school to a very high standard. His school text books, especially his grammars, achieved a wide popularity and in spite of a reputation of being one of the hardest floggers of his day he inspired his pupils with an intense personal affection. In 1787 he was presented to the rectory of Stradishall in Suffolk, but seldom lived there and died at Kensington 28 March 1836.

THOMAS WADE

Thomas, the son of Searles Wade of Woodbridge, was born in that town in 1805. He seems to have gone early to London where he published his first book of poems, *Tasso and the Sisters*, 8vo, London, 1825. For some time after this he seems to have given his attention chiefly to drama, *Duke Andrea* (1829) and *The Phrenologists* (1830) succeeded mainly through the fine acting of Charles Kemble, but the *Jew of Aragon*, though supported by both Charles and Fanny Kemble was literally howled from the stage on account of its pro-Jewish bias. Wade now became a frequent contributor of poetry to the *Monthly Repository*, and these contributions, with other poems, appeared in *Mundi et cordis carmina*, 8vo, London, 1835. He next published a number of short poems in pamphlet form, all now of great rarity, including *The Contention of Death and Love*, 1837, *Helena*, 1837, *The Shadow Seeker*, 1837, *Prothanasia. and other poems*, 1839. In 1845 or 46 he translated Dante's *Inferno* into English and in the original metre, a few lines of which are quoted by Buxton Forman in his *Literary Anecdotes of the Nineteenth Century*. For the latter years of his life Wade lived in Jersey, where he died 19 September 1875.

SAMUEL WARD

SAMUEL, son of John Ward, minister of Haverhill, was born in that town in 1577. Nathaniel Ward, who emigrated to Massachusetts and was responsible for the first code of laws established in New England, was one of his brothers: another was John Ward, rector of St. Clement's in Ipswich. Samuel was educated at St. John's College, Cambridge, graduating B.A. in 1597 and was appointed one of the first fellows of Sidney Sussex College in 1599. After lecturing for a time in Haverhill he was in 1603 elected Town Preacher by the corporation of Ipswich and occupied the pulpit of St. Mary-le-Tower for some thirty years. In 1622 he was prosecuted for nonconformity by Bishop Harsnet, but was released after examination though he was again committed to prison by Archbishop Laud in 1635. Having obtained his release he retired for a time to Holland, returning to Ipswich in 1638 and dying there in 1640. As a mark of respect the corporation allowed to his widow and eldest son Samuel the annual stipend of £100 enjoyed by their late preacher. Ward was the author of a number of religious books and tracts, and of *A most elegant and Religious Rapture composed by Mr. Ward during his episcopall imprisonment... englished by John Vicars*, London, 1649.

JOHN WEBB

John Webb in the introduction to his *Haverhill*, 8vo, London, 1810, says of himself that as 'one born in the vale of obscurity, he never experienced any of the benefits that result from education: his days have been spent in scenes of honest industry, and his leisure intervals diverted to amusive and instructive studies ... Most of these poems were written while the author moved in the humble sphere of a Journeyman Weaver.' The name Webb is not uncommon in Haverhill, and the author is difficult to identify: he may have been the John Webb who married Mahitabel Brown, 17 March 1793, since one of his poems is *To Browne Webb, aged one year: object of paternal joy*. He died before 1859, the year in which the second edition of *Haverhill* was published as by 'the late John Webb.' There are in the British Museum ascribed to 'Kenrick Prescot' two volumes of poetry, *Mildenhall*, 1771, and *Poems*, 1772, both obviously amateur printed. A MSS note in the first says 'The author of this poem is John Webb, a journeyman weaver of Haverhill: and he seems to have been also his own printer. He has also written a Biographical History of Haverhill which, however, has not been printed.' This seemed so unlikely that I examined the copies of these two works in the University Library at Cambridge and found them to have belonged at one time to William Cole (1714–82) the Cambridge Antiquary, and both of them contain MSS notes by their former owner. In *Poems* is written: 'Sent to me by Dr. Prescote (*sic*) Master of Catherine Hall, Cambridge, Wm. Cole 1772. Printed by his son Charles at his private press', and in *Mildenhall*: 'this book ... was sent by Dr. Prescot whose son printed it in a little private Press in his own Chambers in St. Catherine's Hall.'

ORLANDO WHISTLECRAFT

The son of James Whistlecraft and Susan Brooke his wife, Orlando Whistlecraft was born at Thwaite 11 November 1810. Educated at Stowmarket and afterwards at Ipswich under Robert Burcham Clamp, rheumatic fever and infantile paralysis left him useless for normal work and obliged him to look to his pen for a livelihood. For a while he acted as amanuensis to the blind Dr. Robert Hamilton of Ipswich, but he is best known for his works on the prognostication of the weather and for *Whistlecraft's Almanack*, which was published annually for many years during the middle of the last century. Most of his works contain original —and topical—verses. In 1891 he was interviewed by the *East Anglian Daily Times* when an appeal was put forth on his behalf: 'He has now been bedridden during the last six years in consequence of an accident in which his leg was broken. Mrs Whistlecraft endeavours to make ends meet by keeping a small general shop, but the profits arising from this small source are not sufficient to keep the wolf from the door ... The aged weather prophet, whose prognostications were once held in high repute, says very pathetically that he has outlived his friends.' He died in 1893 and is buried in the churchyard at Thwaite.

Orlando should not be confused with 'William and Robert Whistlecraft, of Stowmarket in Suffolk, harness and collar-makers', the pseudonym under which John Hookham Frere published in 1818 his well-known *Prospectus and Specimen of an intended National Work*, afterwards known as *The Dwarfs and the Giants*.

JAMES WHITE

JAMES, son of John White of Dunmore, in the county of Stirling, was born in Midlothian in 1803. Educated at Glasgow University and Pembroke College, Oxford, he graduated B.A. in 1827, and in 1832 he was curate of Hartest-cum-Boxted in Suffolk. In that year he published anonymously *The Village Poor-house, By a Country Curate*, 12mo, London 1832, the second edition of which was published in 8vo in 1833 as 'by the Rev. James White, late Curate of Hartest-cum-Boxted, Suffolk'. This little work, dedicated to Brougham the Lord Chancellor, was described by Davy as 'a poem in which he rails at every respectable grade of Society and attributes all the misery and vice of the poor to the grinding oppression of the rich, especially the clergy. Whether it is due to the spirit of the work, or to the dedication prefixed, one cannot determine', White was presented in 1833, by the Lord Chancellor, to the Vicarage of Loxley in Warwickshire. In 1839 he married Rosa, only child of Colonel Popham Hill and on the death of his father-in-law succeeded to his not inconsiderable estate. He then resigned his living and retired to Bonchurch in the Isle of Wight where he died 26 March 1862. In retirement he turned his attention to literature and published a number of Scottish historical tragedies one of which *John Savile*, 8vo, London, 1847, was acted at Sadlers Wells in that year. His only other poetical work was *Church and School: a Dialogue in Verse*, 12mo, London, 1839.

ROBERT WHYTEHEAD

ALL that I have been able to find of Robert Whytehead is that he was perpetual curate of St. Peter's, Ipswich, at the time when his *Poems for the Afflicted*, 12mo, Ipswich, n.d. (but 1836), was published.

JOHN WODDERSPOON

A NATIVE of Bath, where he served on the staff of the *Bath Journal*, and a journalist, John Wodderspoon came to Ipswich in 1837 at the age of thirty to help run the *Suffolk Chronicle*. John King, the editor, gave Wodderspoon the task of running a new 4d monthly, *The Suffolk Literary Chronicle*, in the sixth issue of which he started a series of Historic Sites of Suffolk. The *Literary Chronicle* died with its fourteenth number, but Wodderspoon's *Historic Sites* was published in book form in 1839, followed by his *Memorials of Ipswich* in 1850. His only volume of poetry was *Three Poems*, 12pp, Norwich, 1856, though a few of his poems appeared in the *Literary Chronicle*. After a spell on the *Morning Post* his health deteriorated and he returned to East Anglia in 1849 as reporter and sub-editor of the *Norwich Mercury* where he spent the remainder of his life. In 1862 he deputed J. F. Smith, reporter, to cover a Sunday lecture by Professor David Anstead. Smith was a Sabbatarian: he took out a summons alleging 'offensive language' over this assignment, and while Wodderspoon was instructing his solicitor he collapsed 8 November 1862 and 'died by the visitation of God accelerated by great mental excitement.'

THOMAS WOOLNER

Thomas, son of Thomas Woolner of Hadleigh in Suffolk, was born in that town 17 December 1825. His father moved to London where the son, who had shown much promise with drawing and modelling, was placed as a pupil in the studio of William Behnes the sculptor. In 1847 Woolner met Rosetti through whom he became one of the original 'pre-Raphaelite Bretheren' and as such in 1850 he contributed to *The Gem* two poems, *My Beautiful Lady* and *My Lady in Death*. The first of these was accompanied in *The Gem* by an etching by Holman Hunt and was later separately published in 1863, obtaining great celebrity. His other poetical works comprise *Pygmalion*, 1881, *Silenue* 1884, *Tiresias* 1886, and *Poems* 1887, but it was as a sculptor that Woolner was best known. His early life in London was a constant struggle for recognition, and so like many others he decided to try his fortune at the newly discovered Australian gold fields. He sailed for Melbourne 24 July 1852, being seen off by the Rosettis, Holman Hunt and Madox Brown, the latter of whom is said to have been inspired by the event to paint his well-known *The Last of England*. Like many others Woolner was disappointed in Australia and returned home in 1854 to find a great change in the position of English art and artists, very largely brought about by Ruskin and the pre-Raphaelites. Many of the friends whom he had left poor and struggling were now celebrities and Woolner soon joined their ranks. His reputation was made by his medalion portraits of Tennyson, Thomas Carlyle and Robert Browning exhibited in 1857, and the history of the remainder of his life is little else than a chronicle of his successes. Everywhere arose his statues, from 'Sir Stamford Raffles' in Singapore and 'Lord Lawrence' in Calcutta to the colossal 'Moses' outside the assize courts in Manchester, while 'The Housemaid' —long considered one of his most beautiful productions—was completed but a few weeks before his death 7 October 1892.

W. R. WRIGHT

Waller Rodwell Wright was, according to Davy, born at Bury St. Edmunds, of which borough he was for some years Recorder on his return to England from the Ionian Islands in 1804. He had been British Consul General to the Republic of the Seven Islands (Ionian Islands) 1800–4, and published his reminiscences as *Horae Ionicae: a Poem descriptive of the Ionian Islands*, 8vo, London, 1809, of which Byron wrote in his *English Bards*:

> Blest is the man who dare approach the bower
> Where dwelt the Muses in their natal hour . . .
> Wright, 'twas they happy lot at once to view
> Those shores of Glory, and to sing them too.

Wright was later president of the Court of Appeals at Malta, where he died in 1824.

JAMES YATES

Nothing definite is known of James Yates, save that he describes himself as a 'Serving man' in his only known work. Some of his verses seem to be dedicated to Suffolk gentry, for which reason he is usually supposed to have been a native of that county. His poems are distinguished more by their religious and moral tone than for any great literary merit and his main claim to fame is as the author of a volume of exceeding rarity, *The Castell of Courtesie*, 4to, London, John Wolfe, 1582.

APPENDIX
OF SOME OTHER SUFFOLK POETS

BAKER, Thomas, thatcher of Wickham Market, is said to have published *A Poem for the Winter Season*, 4to, Ipswich, 1759, but I have been unable to find a copy.

BARKER, Edward, 1621–65, *b.* at Bedfield, Suffolk, educ. Thetford Grammar School and Caius Col., Cambs., B.A. 1640, rector of Eye. Said to have written *A Buckler against the fear of Death by E.B.*, 8vo, Cambs., 1640, though more likely by Edward Benlowes.

BEALE, Mary, 1632–97, portrait painter and pupil of Sir Peter Lely, said to have been born in Suffolk: d. of Rev. J. Cradock: *m.* Charles Beale: wrote some of the psalms in S. Woodford's *Paraphrase upon the Psalms of David*, 4to, London, 1667.

BEVILL, Elizabeth Iliff, author of *Ipswich and Miscellaneous Poems*, 12mo, Ipswich, 1836. *b.* Ipswich, keeping a boarding school at Bury St. Edmunds, 1848.

BLACK, John, 1753–1813, curate of Butley, 1789–1813. Headmaster Woodbridge School, 1800–06. *Poems*, 8vo, Ipswich, 1799, *Conjunction of Jupiter and Venus*, 4to, Ipswich, 1801, and under pseudonym of 'Sappho Search' *A poetical review of Miss Hannah More's 'Strictures on Female Education'*, 8vo, London, 1800.

BLOODWORTH, Emma. *Thoughts suggested by a Few Bright Names*, 32mo, Sudbury, n.d. (but 1844).

BOND, William. *Verses sacred to . . . the Duchess of Grafton*, Bury St. Edmunds, 1727, possibly of the family of Sir Thomas Bond.

BONHOTE, Elizabeth, 1744–1818, d. of James Mapes of Bungay, and wife of Daniel Bonhote, a solicitor of that town and, according to Davy, a natural son of Sir Joshua Vanneck, first Bart. *Feeling . . . a desultory Poem*, 8vo, Edinburgh, 1810.

BOYCE, Thomas, 1731–93, s. of John Boyce of Norwich. Educ. Scarning Grammar School and Caius Col., Cambs., B.A. 1754, rector of Worlingham, Suffolk, 1780–93. *Harold*, 4to, London, 1786.

BRANWHITE, Peregrine, 1745–95, s. of Rowland Branwhite of Lavenham: said to have published *Thoughts on the death of Mr. Woodmason's children*, 1782, *Elegy on the Death of Mrs. Hickman*, 4to, Bury St. Edmunds, 1790, *Astronomy*, 4to, Sudbury, 1791. I cannot find a copy of any of these though the two first were reprinted in the *Gentleman's Magazine*.

BRUNDISH, John Jelliland, d. 1786. s. of John Brundish of Bury St. Edmunds. Educ. Bury School and Caius Col., Cambs., senior wrangler, senior classical medallist and first Smith's prizeman, 1773, *Elegy on a Family Tomb*, 4pp, Cambs., 1783.

BURRELL, Christopher, educ. Trinity Col., Cambs. B.A. 1619/20, rector of Great Wratting, 1623–60. Author of an elegy in *Suffolk's Tears*, 4to, London, 1653.

CAPELL, Edward, 1713–81, s. of Gamaliel Capell of Troston Hall, Suffolk. Educ. Bury School and Catherine Hall,

[249]

Cambs. Edited works of Shakespeare. A few of his sonnets printed by his nephew and heir, Capel Lofft, in *Laura*, 8vo, London, 1814.

CHEVALLIER, Charles Henry, 1824–85, s. of Rev. John Chevallier of Aspall, discoverer of 'Chevallier' barley: educ. Trinity Col., Oxford. B.A. 1846. rector of Aspall, 1849–85. Author of a number of moral tales in verse, undated but published in the 1860's in 16mo. *Village Ballads, Village Scenes in Verse, Village Scenes in Verse, Series 2, A Drunkard's End,* and *John Porter, the poacher.*

CLARKE, A. Davy records *Original Poems*, 12mo, Eye, n.d. (but mid nineteenth century) by 'A. Clarke of Eye': I have been unable to trace a copy of this work or the author.

CLARKE, Stephen Reynolds, according to Clarke's *History of Ipswich*, was born at Ipswich and educated at the Grammar School in that town. *Ode on the Death of Nelson*, 4to, Ipswich, N.D., *The Kiss*, 8vo, London, 1811. Of the first I can find no copy.

COCKBURN, Catherine, b. 1670 d. of David Trotter a naval commander: m. 1708 Patrick Cockburn c. of Nayland in Suffolk and had a child baptized there in 1712: died Long Horsley, Northumberland 1749. Published a number of plays and philosophical writings: some of her poems in *Gentleman's Magazine* 1737 and in *Poems by Eminent Ladies* 1755.

COLE, William, 1759–1812, s. of Rev. Denny Cole of Sudbury and Wickham Market, educ. Eton and King's Col., Cambs., curate of Theberton. *To the Feeling Heart*, 8vo, London, 1789, *A Loyal Congratulation to His Majesty*, 8vo, London, 1789, *A Tear of Regret for Lt. Col. Shadwell*, 4to, London, 1799.

COLLINS, Charles, 1800–66, stepson of George Wilson of Yoxford: educ. Rugby and St. John's Col., Cambs. B.A. 1822. *Juvenile Blossoms*, 12mo, London, 1823, *Green Leaves*, 16mo, London, 1844, *Camala*, 16mo, London, n.d., *Death on the Pale Horse*, 16mo, London, N.D.

COOK, F., b. 4 Dec. 1779: of Capel St. Andrew; author of a number of pamphlets in verse published by Pite of Woodbridge: *Historical Verses* 1843, *Verses on Four Birthdays*, 1844, *Samson*, 1844, *Hope*, 1844, *Mary Magdalene*, 1845, *Birthday Verses*, 1847, *Great Miracles*, 1847, *Harvest*, 1849, *On the Sparrow*, n.d., *Jonah*, n.d.

COWELL, Elizabeth, 1812–99, d. of Rev. John Charlesworth, rector of Flowton, m. 1845 Edward Byles Cowell, professor of Sanskrit at Cambridge. Published anonymously *Historic Reveries by A Suffolk Villager*, 12mo, Sudbury, 1839, most of the poems in which were republished in her acknowledged *Leaves of Memory*, 8vo, London, 1892.

DAY, Henry Thomas, 1799–1861. Educ. Clare Col., Cambs. Ll.B. 1836, rector of Mendlesham, 1834–61. *Algarsife and other Poems*, 16mo, London, 1848, and according to Venn *An Ode on the Liberation of Abd-el-Kader*, but of this latter I can find no other trace.

DENNANT, John, 1767–1851, b. at Framsden, educ. non-conformist college at Hoxton, congregational minister at Halesworth, 1786–1840. *A Poem . . . or a Satire on Vanity, Dogmatism and Malice*, Halesworth, 1808.

DIBDIN, Thomas Frognall, 1776–1847. Bibliographer and founder of the Roxburghe Club. Educ. St. John's Col., Oxford. B.A. 1801. rector of Exning,

[250]

1823-47, though living mainly in London. *Poems*, 1797, and *Bibliography, a Poem*, 1812.

EDGE, William John, b. 1813, d. 1871, s. of Rev. William Edge, rector of Nedging: Educ. Emmanuel Col., Cambs. B.A. 1834, rector of Waldringfield, 1838-48. *The Vision of Peace*, 8vo, London, 1847.

EXTON, Richard Brudenell, 1780-1863, rector of Athelington, 1822, vicar of Cretingham, 1827, J.P. Suffolk. *A Monody on the death of the Earl of Clarendon*, 8vo, London, 1837, *The Castle of Indolence*, 12mo, Ipswich, 1836 (Anon), *An Essay on ... the Sense of Feeling*, 8vo, London, 1851, and *A Discourse in Blank Verse delivered at the Parish Church of Framlingham*, Woodbridge, 1838.

FINCH, Sarah Watson, d. of John Finch of Cambridge ('Esquire' in D.N.B. but 'Ironmonger' in *Ipswich Journal*, 13 March 1802), m. 1802 Capel Lofft of Troston Hall, in whose anthology *Laura*, 5 vols., 8vo, London, 1814, appear some of his wife's sonnets.

FORD, David Everard, 1797-1875, b. Long Melford, later became a congregational minister serving at Lymington (1821-41), and Manchester (1841-58). *Hymns*, 12mo, London, 1844.

GARNONS, John, b. circa 1592, fellow of Emmanuel Col., Cambs., 1616, rector of Glemsford 1624, author of an elegy on the death of Edward Lewkenor, in Timothy Oldmayne's *Life's Brevities*, 4to, London, 1636.

GIRDLESTONE, John Lang, 1763-1825. Educ. Scarning under Robert Potter and Caius Col., Cambs. B.A. 1785, headmaster Fauconberge School at Beccles, 1791-1813, *All the Odes of Pindar Translated*, 4to, Norwich, 1810.

GLANFIELD, John, of Martlesham Hall, s. of John Glanfield (d. 1807) and Elizabeth Skeet, m. 1796 Jane Butcher of Darsham. *A Selection of Poems*, 32pp. Great Yarmouth, n.d. (but circa 1850).

GOOCH, Rebecca, b. at Denton, d. of Pashley, m. in 1820 T. Gooch, printer of Southwold, by whom was published her *Original Poems*, 12mo, 1821, 2nd Ed. (8vo. London) dated 'Brandeston Nov. 1828'.

GOOD, John Mason, 1764-1827. Educ. Guys Hosp., surgeon at Sudbury 1784-92. *Maria, an Elegiac Ode*, 4to, London, 1785, *Song of Songs*, 8vo, London, 1803, *The Triumph of Britain*, 8vo, London, 1803, *The Nature of Things, from Lucretius*, 2 vols, 4to, London, 1805-7.

HALL, James, a native of Clackmannan. Educ. St. Andrews, curate of Bawdsey, 1814, perpet. curate of Stoke-by-Clare, 1815. According to Davy, author of *Cottage Poems*, of which I can find no trace.

HERBERT, Daniel, b. 1751, d, 1833, a resident of Sudbury, of his *Hymns and Poems* I have only seen 2nd Ed., 8vo, London, 1813.

HERVEY, John, 1696-1743, s. of John, first Earl of Bristol of Ickworth. Educ. Westminster and Clare Hall, Cambs. B.A. 1715. *Verses addressed to the Imitator of Horace*, folio, 1731, is usually ascribed to the joint authorship of Lady Mary Wortley Montagu and Hervey in reply to Pope's *Imitation of the First Satire of the First Book of Horace*, some of Hervey's poetry in *The Laurel*, 12mo, London, 1825.

HOWES, Francis, 1766-1846. Educ. Trinity Col., Cambs. B.A. 1798, rector of Wickham Skeith, 1809. *Miscellaneous Poetical Translations*, 8vo, London, 1860, *The Satires of A. Persius Flaccus, translated*, 8vo, London, 1809.

HOWORTH, William, 1805–75, *b.* Ipswich. Educ. Caius Col., Cambs. B.A. 1827, rector of Whitton, 1835–75. *The Redeemer, A Poem*, 8vo, London, 1840, in which is a copy of a review of the author's poem *The Cry of the Poor*, but of this I can find no other trace.

JENKYN, William, 1613–85, *b.* Sudbury, s. of William Jenkyn, vicar of All Saints. Educ. St. John's Col., Cambs. B.A. 1632, rector of Christ Church, Newgate, 1642, ejected 1662 though a Royalist, arrested 1684 and *d.* in Newgate: some of his verse prefixed to Samuel Clarke's *Marrow of Ecclesiastical History*, 4to, London, 1654.

JERMYN, Louisa, d. of James Jermyn of Southwold, m. 1851 Rowland Jermyn, a Lieutenant in H.E.I.C.'s Naval Service, *d.* Pimlico, 1858. Edited *Poetry for Youth*, 8vo, London, 1851, publishing in that anthology some of her own verse.

JOHNSON, Thomas, *b.* 1675(?), *d.* 1750 Educ. Eton and King's Col., Cambs. B.A. 1688. Usher at Ipswich Grammar School, 1688–91, master at Eton, 1705–15, imprisoned for debt and died in poverty. Edited works of Sophocles and is said to have translated into English verse the *Illiad of Homer*, but of this I can find no trace.

LEIGH, William, curate of Denston 1626, rector of Groton 1628–69, presented to the latter by John Winthrop, later Governor of New England: an English elegy in Edmund Calamy's *The Saints Transfiguration*, 4to, Cambridge, 1655, and a latin elegy in Samuel Jacombe's *Moses his death*, 4to, London, 1657.

LETCHWORTH, Thomas, 1739–84, *b.* Woodbridge, s. of Robert Letchworth, a quaker. *Miscellaneous Reflections . . . a Poem by T.L.*, 4to, London, 1765.

Mornings Meditation . . . a Poem by T.L., 4to, London, 1765.

LOFFT, Capel, the younger, 1808–73, s. of Capel Lofft of Troston Hall. Educ. Eton and King's Col., Cambs. *Ernest*, 8vo, 1839 (anon), *d.* at his property Millmead, Virginia, 1873.

LUSHINGTON, John Impit, 'of good family and descent, but poor', for sometime in the E. Suffolk Police, in the Commissariat Dept. of the Army in the Crimea, and from 1860–68 lived at Theberton as Clerk to Chief Constable, later master of the workhouse at Braintree and an auctioneer in Norwich where he died 1881, aged 51. *A Suffolk Larges by Quill*, 24pp, London, 1865.

MALKIN, Benjamin Heath, 1769–1842. Educ. Harrow and Trinity Col., Cambridge. B.A. 1792. Headmaster of the Grammar School at Bury St. Edmunds, 1809–28, *Almahide and Hamet*, 8vo, London, 1804: friend of William Blake by whom there is a frontispiece in Malkin's prose *A Father's Memoir of his Child*, 8vo, London, 1806.

MASON, John, *b.* 1582, s. of Richard Mason, priest of Cavendish. Educ. Bury St. Edmunds and Caius Col., Cambs., graduating B.A. as of Catherine Hall, 1601. *The Turk, A Worthie Tragedie*, 4to, London, 1610, reprinted in 4to in 1632 as *The Excellent Tragedy of Mulleasses the Turke*.

MOORE, James Lovell, 'incumbent of Denham' is said by Davy to have published *The Colombiad, A Poem*, 8vo, 1798, but I have been unable to find a copy.

MOTHERSOLE, William, *d.* of consumption in Bury St. Edmunds 1829, having been publicly baptized there June 1825: memoir in his posthumous *Poems written*

[252]

in aid of the *Society for Circulating the Scripture amongst British Seamen*, 48pp, Dalston, n.d. but circa 1830.

MURDOCK, Patrick, b. Dumfries. Educ. Edinburgh University: rector of Kettlebaston 1749–60 and Gt. Thurlow, 1760 till his death there in 1774: wrote sixty-eighth stanza in Canto i of Thomson's *Castle of Indolence*, and is himself described by that poet in the sixty-ninth.

PLOWMAN, William 1768–1820, a tanner of Bungay; having been caught poaching on the land of Sir Charles Blois, Bt., of Yoxford, published in revenge *Concise remarks on Game Mania . . . by Flagellus*, 8vo, London, n.d. The B.M. copy was destroyed in the blitz, I know of no other.

PORTER, Elizabeth, d. of Robert Porter, farmer, of Henham and South Cove. *The Harvest and other Poems, by E.P.*, 8vo, Saxmundham, 1848.

QUAYLE, Thomas, of Barton Mills, J.P. and Captain West Suffolk Militia, b. 1759, d. 1844: said to have published a translation into English verse of the *Goorgics of Virgil*, but of this I can find no trace.

RAYNER, William, 1742–1800. Educ. St. Paul's and Caius Col., Cambridge, B.A. 1765. curate of Worlingworth where he published his *Miscellanies in Prose and Verse*, 4to, Ipswich, 1767.

REEVE, Susan, d. of Daniel and Elizabeth Bonhote of Bungay, m. first, Samuel Jeaffreson, R.N., second, Richard Reeve, M.D., of Norwich, and third, Rev. George Glover, Archdeacon of Sudbury, and died *sine prole*, 1847. *The Flowers at Court*, 8vo, 1809.

RIBBANS, Rebecca, 1795–1821, d. of William East, postmaster at Lavenham, wife of Frederic Ribbans, schoolmaster of that village, who edited her posthumous *Lavenham Church*, 8vo, Ipswich, 1822, and *Effusions of Genius*, 8vo, Ipswich, 1829.

ROW, Thomas, 1786–1864, baptist minister, lived at Hadleigh travelling and preaching throughout E. Anglia: 1838–64, minister at Little Grandsden, Cambs. *Concise Spiritual Poems*, 12mo, London, 1817, *Original and Evangelical Hymns*, 12mo, London, 1822.

ROWE, Henry, 1750–1819. Educ. Eton and Brasenose Col., Oxford, rector of Ringshall. *Poems*, 2 vols., 8vo, London, 1796, *The Montem*, 4to, London, 1808, *Fables in Verse*, 8vo, London, 1810.

SCARLETT, Robert, the author of *Poems*, 8vo, Woodbridge, 1841, was 'of Woodbridge. His parents are now living at Friston near Saxmundham' (Davy MSS).

SCOTT, Thomas, 1705–75, minister at Lowestoft, 1733, succeeded Samuel Say at the St. Nicholas Street Chapel in Ipswich, leaving 1774, to die in Norfolk. *The Book of Job in English Verse*, 8vo, 1771, *Lyric Poems*, 8vo, 1773: many of his hymns appear in contemporary collections.

SERVICE, David, b. Dumbartonshire, d. Yarmouth Workhouse 1828, aet. 52. For a time a cobbler at Beccles. *Elegy on the Death of Mr. Swanton*, 8vo, Yarmouth, 1802, *The Caledonian Herd Boy*, 12mo, Yarmouth, 1802, *Crispian*, 8vo, Yarmouth, 1804. *The Wild Harp's Murmurs*, 12mo, Yarmouth, 1806. The *East Anglian Magazine*, April 1814, has a review of *The Village Cobbler*, by D. Service, of which I can find no copy or other trace.

SPENCE, Sarah, author of *Poems*, 8vo, Bury St. Edmunds, 1795: Davy says 'Of this person I have no account'.

STEELE, Mrs. *Pathetic and Religious Poems by Mrs. Steele* was first published in 8vo by L. Brightly of Saxmundham in 1834. There are in the British Museum 4th (Romford 1836) and 5th Editions (London 1837), *Early Days and Riper Years*, 16mo, London, 1850, *Hymns and Verses*, 12mo, London, n.d. (but 1855). Coppinger mentions *Fireside Musings*, 12mo, Bury St. Edmunds, 1857—of which I have been unable to find a copy—as being by Elizabeth Anne Steele of Bury St. Edmunds.

STEWART, Charles Edward, 1751–1819, s. of Giles Stewart of Long Melford. Educ. Long Melford Grammar School and St. John's Coll., Cambs., migrated to Magdalen Coll., Oxford, 1772, rector of Rede 1807–19. As 'A Suffolk Freeholder' published various political tracts in prose and some in verse as 'C.E.S.', *Charles's Small Clothes by C.E.S.*, 4to, 1808, *The Political Works in Verse of C.E.S.*, 8vo, London, 1816, and acknowledged *Collection of Trifles in Verse*, 4to, Sudbury, 1797, *Last Trifles in Verse*, 4to, Sudbury, 1811.

STRONG, William, 1788–1866, of Thorpe Hall, Peterborough, Chaplain in Ordinary to William IV and Queen Victoria, s. of Rev. William Strong (d. 1842) of Thorpe Hall. His grandson, Brig. Gen. W. Strong of Thorpe Hall, tells me that according to family tradition, he was curate of Woodbridge 1819–21: he published three sermons in Woodbridge in those years and later *Frithioffs Saga*, 8vo, London, 1833.

SYMONDS, William, b. Bury St. Edmunds 1782, d. at sea 1856, surveyor to the Navy 1832–47, designed over 200 ships, including Royal Yacht *Victoria & Albert*: Vice-Admiral 1847. *Holiday Trips*, 12mo, London, 1847.

TAYLER, Charles Benjamin, 1797–1875. Educ. Guildford and Trinity Coll., Cambs. B.A. 1819, curate of Hadleigh 1821–26, rector of Otley 1846–75. Published a number of anti-Roman Catholic tracts and pamphlets, and *May you like it by A Country Curate*, 2 vols., 12mo, London, 1823, and *Sacred Records in Verse*, 16mo, London, 1872.

TAYLOR, Jefferys, s. of Isaac Taylor of Lavenham and Ongar, b. Lavenham 1792, d. 1853. Author of many books for the young of which *Aesop*, 12mo, 1821, and *Tales and Dialogues*, 12mo, London, 1822, were in verse.

URQUHART, D. H., of Hobland Hall, Bradwell, d. there 1829, according to Davy MSS, published *The Odes of Anacreon, translated from the Greek*, 8vo, London, 1787, but I can find no other trace.

WALKER, John, 1754–1867, s. of William Walker of Oxford, Superior Bedell of Divinity. Educ. Magdalen Col., Oxford. B.A. 1775. In 1774 is said to have published a poem *Mirth*, of which I can find no trace, rector of Bawdsey and Stoke Holy Cross near Norwich, his posthumous *Poems*, 8vo, Norwich, 1809, were edited by J. F. Walker.

WARREN, Robert, s. of Erasmus Warren, R. of Worlington, Suffolk, b. there 1680: ed. Bury St Edmunds and Christ's Col., Cambs.: B.A. 1700–1, M.A. 1704, D.D. 1716: R. of Charlton, Kent, 1704–36. V. of Hampstead 1734 until his death 1 June 1740. Is probably the R. Warren who was the author of *The Tablet of Cebes* 4to 1698, *Miscellany Poems* 4to 1700, in which latter is an advertisement for *A Poem on Christmas Day* of which I can find no other trace.

WHITE, Henry, 1594–1661, s. of John White of Ipswich. Educ. Ipswich School and Caius Col., Cambs. B.A. 1614/15, rector of Rougham 1636–61. Author of an eulogy to the author prefixed to Zachary Catlin's translation of Ovid's *De Tristibus*, 8vo, London, 1639.

WHITE, Richard. *An Essay on Religion*, 4to, Ipswich, 1741, is by the Rev. Richard White. I cannot identify the author, but a Richard White (1694–1747) of Magdalene Col., Cambs., was rector of Stutton, 1728–47 and another (1725–80), educ. Ipswich School and Emmanuel Col., Cambs., rector Thrandeston 1759.

WILKINS, George, *b*. Norwich 1785: ed. Bury St. Edmunds and Caius Col. Cambridge. B.A. 1807: Curate at Hadleigh 1808–15: to Gretna Green with Rector's dau. 1816: Archdeacon Nottingham 1822: *d*. 1865. *Paraphrase of fifteenth chapter of St. Paul's 1st Epistle to the Ephesians, 4to, Ipswich 1816.*

INDEX OF SUFFOLK PLACE NAMES

Aldeburgh, 161, 183, 204, 216
Alderton, 190, 233
Alpheton, 231
Athelington, 250
Ballingdon,
—, Printing at, 203
Barsham, 235
Barton Mills, 253
Bawdsey, 251, 254
Beccles, 220, 251, 253
—, Printing at, 201
— School, 222, 251
Bedfield, 186, 215, 249
Belstead, 237
Benacre, 195
Benhall, 216
Bentley, 168
Bildeston, 222
Boulge, 189
Boxted, 244
Bradfield, 184, 214
Bradwell, 254
Bramford, 189
Brandeston, 177, 251
Brantham, 240
Bredfield, 189
Bungay, 146, 154, 172, 233, 249, 252, 253
—, Printing at, 155, 217
— School, 172, 183
Bures, 186

Bury St. Edmunds, 155, 165, 184, 191, 196, 198, 202, 212, 214, 221, 223, 228, 230, 231, 234, 241, 246, 249, 252, 253, 254
—, Printing at, 187, 202, 226, 228, 249, 253
— School, 155, 180, 182, 189, 214, 223, 230, 234, 241, 249, 252, 254, 255
Butley, 249
Campsea Ash, 225
Capel St. Andrew, 250
Cavendish, 174, 252
Charsfield, 190
Chelmondiston, 206
Clare, Printing at, 208
Combes, 192
Creeting, 155
Cretingham, 250
Darsham, 251
Debenham, 195, 209
Denham, 252
Drinkstone, 155
Dunwich, 164, 235
Earl Soham, 175, 177
Earl Stonham, 164
East Bergholt, 176
— School, 220
Easton, 175
Edwardstone, 203
Exning, 250
Eye, 150, 163, 170, 249
—, Printing at, 250

[256]

Eyke, 233
Flowton, 177, 250
Fornham, 184
Foxhall, 220
Framlingham, 164, 177, 183, 194, 227, 236
—, Printing at, 194
Framsden, 250
Freston, 223
Friston, 253
Gazeley, 220
Glemsford, 251
Gt. Glemham, 183, 184
Gt. Thurlow, 252
Gt. Wratting, 249
Groton, 252
Gunton, 167
Hadleigh, 154, 162, 164, 168, 187, 205, 227, 246, 253, 254, 255
—, Printing at, 164
— School, 162, 205
Halesworth, 88, 138, 208, 224, 250
—, Printing at, 164, 188, 207, 208, 209, 250
— School, 168
Hartest, 244
Hasketon, 241
Haverhill, 175, 242, 243
Hawstead, 199
Henham, 253
Higham, 168
Holton, 173
Honnington, 164, 165
Horringer or Horningsheath, 207, 225
Ickworth, 251
Ilketshall St. Lawrence, 233
Ilketshall St. Margarets, 190
Ipswich, xvi, 99, 116, 153, 159, 163, 173, 177, 178, 179, 180, 181, 182, 187, 191, 193, 194, 197, 201, 202, 203, 210, 212, 218, 221, 223, 226, 229, 231, 232, 233, 237, 238, 240, 242, 243, 245, 249, 250, 251, 252, 253, 254, 255

Ipswich, Printing at, 153, 160, 163, 173, 175, 176, 177, 179, 180, 182, 197, 198, 202, 206, 217, 221, 224, 229, 237, 245, 249, 250, 251, 253, 254
— School, 197, 252, 254
Ixworth, 171, 211, 225
— School, 165
Keddington, 185
Kentwell, 197
Kesgrave, 153
Kessingland, 223
Kettlebaston, 252
Kettleburgh, 204
Kirton, 223
Lackford, 234
Lakenheath, 226
Lavenham, 237, 249, 253, 254
— School 253
Leiston, 231
Letheringham, 204
Lidgate, 212
Little Ashfield, 239
Little Bealings, 220
Little Glemham, 183
Little Thurlow, 186
Long Melford, 178, 188, 251, 253
—, Printing at, 178,
— School, 253
Lowestoft, 218, 223, 226, 253
Martlesham, 251
Mendham, 217
Mendlesham, 185, 250
Mildenhall, 219, 243
Middleton, 194
Mutford, 188
Nayland, 230, 250
Nedging, 250
Needham Market School, 164
Newmarket, 188, 210
—, Printing at, 210
Orwell, 54, 96, 108, 116
Otley, 254
Oulton, 168
Pakenham, 232

[257]

Palgrave, 157
Palgrave School, 157, 217
Parham, 183, 184
Ramsholt, 176
Rattlesden, 209
Rede, 254
Rendham, 184
Rendlesham, 206
Reydon, 217, 234
Ringshall, 253
Risby, 187
Rougham, 254
Rushmere, 99, 153, 229
Saxmundham, 183
—, Printing at, 253
Ship meadow, 235
Shottisham, 233
Slaughden, 164
Somerleyton, 188
South Cove, 156, 253
Southolt, 158
Southwold, 235, 251, 252
—, Printing at, 251
Sproughton, 173
Stanton, 232
Stoke Ash, 220, 236
Stoke by Clare, 167, 251
Stonham Aspal, 163, 250
— School, 163
Stowmarket, 209, 244
— School, 183, 243
Stradbroke, 175
Stradishall, 241
Stratford St. Andrew, 216
Stuston, 170
Stutton, 254
Sudbury, 187, 193, 203, 215, 224, 225, 226, 250, 251, 253
—, Printing at, 153, 179, 193, 224, 225, 249, 250, 254
Sutton, 227, 233
Sweffling, 184

Swilland, 193
Tattingstone, 162, 173
Theberton, 250, 252
Thorrington, 209
Thorndon, 156, 200
Thrandeston, 254
Thurlow, 230, 240
Thwaite, 243, 244
Thurston, 173
Troston, 213, 249, 251, 252
Ubbeston, 181
Waldringfield, 250
Wattisham, 222
Waveney, 129
Wenhaston, 209
Westley, 202
Westleton, 194
Weston, 216
Wetherden, 229
Whatfield, 177
Wherstead, 189
Whitton, 191
Wickhambrook, 183
Wickham Market, 249, 250
Wickham Skeith, 169, 251
Wilby, 24, 172, 190, 187
Woodbridge, 112, 160, 169, 175, 183, 188, 189, 190, 209, 211, 241, 252, 253, 254
—, Printing at, 161, 175, 176, 188, 191, 192, 204, 211, 216, 225, 250, 251, 253, 254
— School, 188, 190, 249, 254
Woolpit, 177
Worlingham, 249
Worlington, 170, 254
Worlingworth, 157, 158, 253
Wortham, 180
Wrentham, 158, 191
Yoxford, 158, 159, 164, 173, 194, 207, 240, 250, 252

INDEX OF AUTHORS

Ablitt, Nat	1784–1855	99, 153
Acton, Eliza	1799–1859	114, 153
Alabaster, William	1567–1604	20, 154
Ashby, Samuel	1761–1833	74, 154
Bacon, Nicholas	1509–1579	12, 155
Baker, Thomas	c. 1759	249
Bale, John	1495–1563	9
Barbauld, (Mrs) Anna Laetitia Aikin	1743–1825	55, 156
Barker, Edward	1621–1665	249
Barlee, E.	1799–1853	115, 157
Barlee, Thomas Dalling	1796–	108, 158
Barmby, Goodwyn	1820–1881	128, 158
Barton, Bernard	1784–1849	100, 112, 160, 174, 176, 189, 191, 193, 211
Beale, Mary	1632–1697	249
Beaumont, Joseph	1615–1699	34, 162
Bennett, John	1781–1855	94, 163
Betham, Matilda	1776–1852	93, 163
Bevill, Elizabeth Iliff	c. 1836	249
Bird, James	1788–1839	101, 161, 164, 191
Black, John	1753–1813	249
Bloodworth, Emma	c. 1844	249
Bloomfield, George	1757–1831	68, 164, 165
Bloomfield, Nathaniel	1759–	70, 164, 165
Bloomfield, Robert	1766–1823	76, 104, 164, 165, 187
Blundeville, Thomas	Fl. 1561	19, 167
Bokenham, Osbern	1393–1447	8, 167
Bond, William	c. 1627	249
Bonhote, Elizabeth	1744–1818	249
Borrow, George	1803–1881	119, 167
Boyce, Thomas	1731–1793	249
Bradstreet, Robert	1764–1836	75, 168
Brand, Fitz-John	1746–1808	57, 168, 169

[259]

Brand, Hannah	1760–1821	72, 169
Branwhite, Peregrine	1745–1795	249
Broome, William	1689–1745	43, 170
Brundish, John Jelliland	–1786	249
Bucke, Charles	1781–1846	95, 170
Burges, James Bland	1752–1824	59, 171
Burnett, Richard	1772–	90, 172
Burrell, Christopher	c. 1653	249
Calver, Edward	1598	38, 172
Candler, Ann	1740–1814	53, 173
Capell, Edward	1713–1781	249
Carr, James	c. 1859	144, 173
Catlin, Zachary	c. 1585(?)	27, 173
Cavendish, George	1500–1561	9, 174
Chambers, James	1748–1827	58, 174
Chevalier, Charles Henry	1824–1885	250
Clarke, A.	–	250
Clarke, James	1798–1861	112, 175
Clarke, Stephen Reynolds	c. 1811	250
Clarke, William Branwhite	1798–1878	112, 161, 176, 191
Clubbe, William	1745–1814	56, 77, 177
Cobbold, Dorothy	1770–1857	87, 177
Cobbold, Edward	1798–1860	113, 178
Cobbold, Elizabeth	1766–1825	78, 173, 178, 180
Cobbold, Richard	1797–1877	109, 180
Cockburn, Catherine	1670–1749	250
Cockle, Mary	1772–1836	91, 181
Cole, William	1759–1812	250
Cole, William	1769–1835	84, 181
Collins, Charles	1800–1866	250
Cook, F.	1779–	
Coote, Edmund	c. 1600	29, 182
Coppinger, Mathew	–1695	41, 182
Cordingley, John	c. 1827	134, 182
Cowell, Elizabeth	1812–1899	250
Crabbe, George	1754–1832	63, 183, 189, 239
Crossman, Samuel	1624–1684	35, 184
Dallas, Robert Charles	1754–1824	62, 184
Darby, Charles	1635(?)–1709	37, 185
Day, Henry	1827–1893	134, 185
Day, Henry Thomas	1799–1861	250
Day, John	1566–1627	20, 186

Deare, James	1770–1824	87, 186
Deer, James	c. 1864	145, 187
Dennant, John	1767–1851	250
Dibdin, Thomas Frognall	1776–1847	250
Drake, Nathan	1766–1836	79, 187
Duck, Arthur	1680–	41, 187
Edge, William John	1813–1871	251
Exton, Richard Brudenell	1780–1863	251
Feist, Charles		131, 188
Felltham, Owen	1602–1688	31, 188
Fenn, John	c. 1670	88, 188
Finch, Sarah Watson	c. 1814	251
Fitzgerald, Edward	1809–1883	123, 161, 189
Fletcher, Giles	1588–1623	28, 189
Fletcher, Joseph	1577–1637	24, 190
Fletcher, William	1794–1852	104, 161, 176, 190
Flowerdew, Alice	1759–1830	70, 191
Ford, David Everard	1797–1875	251
Fox, William Johnson	1786–1864	100, 191
Freeman, Philip	1818–1875	128, 192
Fulcher, George William	1795–1855	106, 193
Garnons, John	c. 1692	251
Gaye, Selina	1814–1881	142, 193
Glanfield, John	c. 1850	251
Girdlestone, John Lang	1763–1825	251
Girling, Harriet	c. 1800	118, 194
Gissing, T. W.	c. 1850	142, 194
Godwin, William	1756–1836	67, 195
Gooch, Elizabeth	1758–	69, 195
Gooch, Rebecca	c. 1820	251
Good, John Mason	1764–1827	187, 251
Goodall, Charles	1671–1689	40, 196
Gower, John	1327–1408	5, 197
Green, Thomas	1769–1825	85, 197
Grice, Charles Valentine Lee	1773–1858	92, 198
Hall, James		251
Hall, Joseph	1574–1656	23, 199
Halloran, Lawrence	1766–1831	80, 200
Hannah, John	1802–1854	118, 201
Harcourt, Thomas	1618–1679	34, 201

Harding, Samuel	1618(?)–	35, 202
Harrall, Thomas	c. 1820	129, 202
Harrison, Susanna	1752–1784	61, 202
Hart, Mary Kerr	1792(?)–	102, 203
Hart, Samuel	c. 1840	138, 204
Hawes, Stephen	–1523	10, 204
Hawkins, William	1602–(?)1637	32, 162, 205
Henley, John	1692–1756	45, 205
Henley, Samuel	1740–1815	55, 206
Herbert, Daniel	1751–1833	251
Hervey, John	1696–1743	251
Howes, Francis	1766–1846	252
Howorth, William	1805–1875	252
Hughes, George	–1830	126, 207
Hughman, John	1770–1846(?)	89, 208
Hughman, Robert		140, 207
Hurn, William	1754–1829	66, 209
Ingelow, Jean	1820–1897	129, 210
Isaacson, W. P.	c. 1840	139, 210
Jenkyn, William	1613–1685	252
Jermyn, Louisa	–1858	252
Johnson, Thomas	1675(?)–1750	252
Knight, Ann	c. 1829	135, 211
Lamb, John	1789–1850	101, 211
Langston, John	1639–1704	39, 211
Leigh, William	–1699(?)	252
Letchworth, Thomas	1739–1784	252
Lidgate, John	1370–1451(?)	6, 212
Lofft, Capel (the elder)	1751–1824	59, 187, 213, 252
Lofft, Capel (the younger)	1808–1873	213, 252
Lushington, John Impit	1830–1881	252
Lye, Thomas	1621–1684	35, 214
Madan, Spencer	1758–1836	69, 214
Malkin, Benjamin Heath	1769–1842	252
Marriot, Sir James	1730–1803	48, 214
Marston, Charles Dallas	1824–1876	131, 215
Mason, John	1582–	252
Mitford, John	1781–1859	95, 216
Moodie, Susannah	1803–1885	120, 217
Moon, Peter	c. 1548	15, 217

Moore, James Lovell	c. 1798	252
Mothersole, William	–1829	253
Mott, Thomas	1761–1788	74, 217
Moufet, Thomas	1553–1604	15, 218
Murdock, Patrick	–1774	253
Nash, Thomas	1567–1601	21, 218
North, Henry	1609–1671	39, 219
Nuce, Thomas	1540(?)–1617	14, 220
Nursey, Perry	1799–1867	115, 220
Pack, Richardson	1682–1728	41, 220
Paget, William	c. 1741	54, 221
Pearson, Esther	1817–1833	127, 222
Plowman, William	1768–1820	253
Porter, Elizabeth	c. 1848	253
Potter, Robert	1721–1809	46, 222, 251
Quayle, Thomas	1759–1844	253
Randall, John	1666–1722	39, 223
Rayner, William	1742–1800	253
Reeve, Clara	1729–1807	47, 223
Reeve, Susan	–1847	253
Revell, Sarah	c. 1829	136, 224
Ribbans, Rebecca	1795–1821	253
Richards, George	1768–1837	82, 224
Roche, Hamilton	1780(?)	93, 225
Rogers, Thomas	1555–1616	18, 225
Rolfe, Ann	c. 1840	139, 225
Rolph, Richard	1801–	118, 226
Row, Thomas	1786–1864	253
Rowe, Henry	1750–1819	253
Say, Samuel	1675–1743	40, 226
Scarlett, Robert	c. 1841	253
Scott, Thomas	1705–1775	253
Service, David	c. 1775–1828	253
Sewell, Mary	1797–1884	110, 227
Shaw, Cuthbert	1739–1771	52, 228
Shepherd, Richard	1732–1809	51, 228
Shewell, John Talwin	1782–1869	96, 229
Slater, Samuel	1627(?)–1704	36, 230
Soane, Henry Francis Robert	1768–1803	83, 230
Smith, William	1730–1819	49, 230
Smythies, Humphrey	1724–1806	46, 231

Spence, **Sarah**	*c.* 1795	253
Spilling, James	1824–1897	130, 231
Spring, William	1613–1654	33, 232
Squirrell, Mary Elizabeth	1838–	137, 233
Stebbing, Henry	1799–1883	117, 233
Steele, Mrs	*c.* 1834	254
Stephens, Thomas	–1647(d)	214, 234
Stewart, Charles Edward	1751–1819	254
Strickland, Agnes	1796–1874	108, 234
Strong, William	1788–1866	254
Suckling, John	1608–1642	32, 235
Surrey, Earl of (Henry Howard)	1517–1546	11, 236
Symonds, William	1782–1856	254
Tampen, John		102, 237
Tayler, Charles Benjamin	1797–1875	254
Taylor, Jane and Anne	1782–1866 1783–1824	96, 237
Taylor, Jefferys	1792–1853	254
Thew, William	1794–	103, 238
Thurlow, Edward	1731–1806	49, 239
Turnley, Joseph	*c.* 1850	143, 240
Tusser, Thomas	1534(?)–1580	13, 217, 240
Tymme, Thomas	1560–1620	19, 241
Urquhart, D. H.	–1829	254
Valpy, Richard	1754–1836	67, 241
Wade, Thomas	1805–1875	122, 241
Walker, John	1754–1867	254
Ward, Samuel	1577–1640	25, 242
Warren, Robert	1680–1740	254
Webb, John	1767(?)–	81, 243
Whistlecraft, Orlando	1810–1893	125, 243
White, Henry	1594–1661	225
White, James	1803–1862	121, 244
White, Richard	*c.* 1741	254
Whytehead, Robert	*c.* 1836	137, 245
Wilkins, George	1785–1865	254
Wodderspoon, John	1807–1862	123, 245
Woolner, Thomas	1825–1892	132, 246
Wright, Walter Rodwell	–1824	125, 246
Yates, James	*c.* 1582	26, 247